FIND A GOOD JOB IN PITTSBURGH

The Hillman Foundation has generously underwritten the costs of producing this book. Job Advisory Service of the Center for Professional Development, Chatham College, gratefully acknowledges this support.

Original edition design and illustration, Joseph Daniel Fiedler

Printed in Pittsburgh, PA
        Geyer Printing Company, Inc.

ISBN 0-9612254-0-8

FIND A GOOD JOB IN PITTSBURGH

The Tri-State's only local employment guide

First edition by:
BETTY CONNELLY / CAROL F. HERSHEY

Second edition by:
BETTY CONNELLY

CONTENTS

PART THREE
A CRASH COURSE IN
JOB MARKET SAVVY

PART FOUR
WHATEVER IT TAKES

PART FIVE
COMMUNICATIONS: PITTSBURGH STYLE

PART ONE
THE PITTSBURGH JOB OUTLOOK

1
ARE THERE ANY JOBS IN PITTSBURGH?

The Pittsburgh region has attracted international notice and has figured in documentaries as a how-to model for surviving the demise of a major industry. The attention is well deserved. In the 1980s we lost over 100,000 jobs, primarily in steel and manufacturing, but before the decade ended we created almost as many different new jobs. The transition from an industrial to an information and service economy has been nothing short of remarkable. Estimates of the jobs created here during 1989 (latest year available) range from 14,000 to 28,000. Even if we take the lower estimate, that's 38.3 new jobs *each day!*

This is encouraging news for job hunters who define a *livable city* as one where they can find work. So the answer to the question: "Are there any jobs in Pittsburgh?" is a definite **YES**. As a practical fact, however, the jobs are not evenly distributed across all fields and the way people get those jobs has changed.

What's the Pittsburgh Job Market Like?

Finding a good job here has changed for the better, in one sense, because since 1983 when the first edition of this book was published, there have been more jobs available. Yet the drop in our unemployment rate, from 15.7% then to under 6% in 1988, has not created a "bed of roses" for job hunters. There remains an abundance of local talent. We may also be witnessing a real shift in how people find work. Even if the reasons behind it cannot be pinpointed, what it is actually like to hunt for a job in Pittsburgh today seems to be the following:

For the out-of-towner who is job hunting here: Competition for jobs is serious. You may be asked to have a degree in your field here, even though in other towns they may only ask for experience. In many fields, you'll face as qualified a group of competing applicants as anywhere else in the country. Employers are selective because they *can* be. Make sure you have a good presentation (written and verbal). Take the time to find out what the salary level here is for your skills. Don't expect to mail out resumes and get responses. Do bank on a degree of willingness to lend a hand to a newcomer who needs to learn about the market, but don't expect to be handed a job.

For experienced managers and administrators: Being out of a job is not the stigma it used to be. When you're looking for options, the job market seems to be even more of a "hidden" job market than it has been in the past. Many "networks" have dissolved. Insider information—jobs the industry knows about before they become public knowledge—is skimpier than it once was. This means you may have to expose yourself more, have more direct contact and conversations, in order to get consideration.

For recent college graduates, those re-entering the job market and those with less than five years experience: The downsizing of corporations means, generally, fewer entry level and management training spots for which to compete. Gear up for a serious job hunt. Smaller firms are the answer, but they are not as easy to search out. Often they don't have formal training programs or advancement routes, so you'll have to be able to identify *for them* where you fit and why you are a good long term prospect. Make this part of your preparation.

For steelworkers and large scale manufacturing production workers: There are few job openings in major steel but your chances, if you want to stick with specialty steel, are as good here if not better than in other parts of the country. Employment lines for skilled production workers are long, however. Jobs are as likely to be non-union as union and wages correspond. Retrain or look to other jobs that may offer lower pay in the first or second steps but that ultimately can offer equal pay or satisfaction.

4

For minimum wage workers: The market is finally turning in your favor. There is a smaller pool of willing and available workers for an increasing number of positions. Shortages are beginning to be felt in the suburbs and by firms not accessible by public transportation. In spite of employer resistance, there will be pressure to raise wages, although improvements in hours and work conditions are likely to come first. Expect that wage increases will not occur uniformly; that employers will reach out to non-traditional groups like retirees for workers and that there will be more opportunities for the unskilled, for minorities and for school dropouts to enter a labor force that has been closed to them for some time. Minimum wage and entry jobs are only dead-end jobs if you make no plans to utilize your experience in them to improve your job marketability, either by using the job as the first step up the ladder in that field or as a way of financing the training you need for employment in another field.

For upper management: Expect to take on multi-disciplinary responsibilities. Downsizing in larger companies and flat organizational pyramids in small and mid-sized companies mean fewer management specialists. Be prepared to educate smaller firms about the practicality of hiring you. Foreign firms may see local managers as "buffers." Since everyone seems to want to "stay in town, at least for a while," expect it to take some flexibility and patience to get most of what you want.

For support personnel: The word from those who have compared is that Pittsburgh's secretaries and paralegals are some of the best there are around. Although a "good secretary" can always find a job, salaries are slow to increase in spite of a need. You may shortchange yourself if you take the first job offer or only apply at a few places. Create your own future with a broad job hunt that includes places where you can satisfy your needs for increases in pay and chances to develop your skills and advance in your specialty.

For career changers: If you realize you must shift to a new industry or field, don't expect that your letter saying you feel you can easily make the switch will trigger a flood of replies. Direct conversation is almost always the way it works. Despite all the competition in every field, the increased pace of change works in your favor. Firms feel a need to create their own edge and often will look outside their traditional hiring ranks to get it. So it is in one-to-one communication with those responsible for change that you have the best chance of being offered a job tailored for you.

These are impressions about Pittsburgh's job market from those who've been there. But whether one uses statistical tools or down-to-earth viewpoints to conclude that there are always jobs open, the key is knowing how to find them and how to present oneself in such a way that the job is offered. PART ONE of this book will look at the Pittsburgh job market to help you find where those jobs are. In PARTS TWO through FIVE the focus will be on how to get the job offered to you.

PART ONE first presents the Pittsburgh job market in an overall way. These concrete facts are especially helpful if you are a newcomer or if this kind of information did not seem personally significant to you before you started job hunting. After that the focus is on where the jobs are in ten of the most popular career fields in Pittsburgh.

A Corporate Town

One of the area's strengths is its corporate community, a key to where many employment opportunities lie. Pittsburgh is home to 55 "big ones"—public and private firms with annual gross revenues or fiscal sales over $100 million. They employ more than 45,000 local people. Their specialties are steel, electrical equipment, oil, aluminum, glass, coal, chemicals and plastics. In 1988, *Fortune* magazine again ranked Pittsburgh third largest headquarters city in the country because it is home to 14 of the largest industrial firms in the nation. Measured in terms of control of invested capital, Pittsburgh is the fifth largest business center in the United States, although it is 17th in terms of metropolitan population (about 2 million) and 35th in terms of actual city population. Hometown bias aside, Pittsburgh is more than a regional center, it is a center of power.

Big companies like Westinghouse, PPG Industries, Alcoa, USAir, H.J.Heinz and Bayer USA (parent company of Mobay) have helped transform the area employment scene from blue collar to white. Nationally the government classifies 52% of the workforce as white collar. Locally we have an above average proportion of white collar workers, 56%, and of these there are as many professional and technical workers as there are clerical workers.

These corporations have a multi-billion dollar impact on the community in payrolls, purchases, taxes, dividends, employee benefit spending and charitable contributions. They have been the initial financial backing for office towers in the downtown area and employ many of the 140,000 who work there.

The city's concentration of corporate headquarters generates business support jobs ranging from architects, attorneys and office equipment suppliers to public relations firms, printers and messenger services. Executives' pension and profit sharing money finds its way into the dozen or more venture capital funds that back start-ups of local advanced technology firms. Most of the headquarters that have research and development facilities have located them in nearby communities. This contributes a "leading edge" quality to the area.

Given the headquarters and regional offices already established here, it is not surprising that 222 foreign owned firms have located in the area. For about half (107) this is also their U.S. headquarters. While most of these companies are small, together they provide some 55,000 jobs in the region. Their operations may involve sales, service, distribution, warehousing or manufacturing.

The corporate presence, despite downsizing and merger trends, has been a major source of stability for the area.

The community and its corporate citizens have a relationship of mutual support for the quality of life. This indirectly contributed to the factors that converged to earn Pittsburgh the Places Rated Almanac's *Most Livable City* award in 1985. Pittsburgh's upscale lifestyle includes the availability of the arts, recreation, education, health care, good air/rail/road transportation and superior income levels along with the advantages of a relatively low cost of living, especially for housing, a shorter commute time than other major cities and a mild climate.

Pittsburgh's Biggest Employers

One out of every three working Pittsburghers gets a paycheck from one of our 50 largest employers. These employers include not only the Fortune 500 companies just mentioned, but labor intensive places like schools, hospitals, department stores, banks and supermarkets. The accompanying chart shows the current 50 largest employers of local people. A number of companies that were on the list in this book's first edition are not there today, yet the percentage of people employed in large firms (over 1,500 workers) remains almost the same.

Who Employs the Most Pittsburghers

Rank	Company	Number of Employees Locally 1988	1982
1.	Westinghouse Electric Corp.	21,000	27,000
2.	Federal Government	17,900	17,197
3.	State Government	14,300	14,611
4.	University of Pittsburgh	8,500	6,000
5.	USAir	8,100	5,300
6.	Allegheny County	7,763	8,215
7.	USX Corp.	6,625	34,000
8.	Mellon Bank Corp. (tie)	6,000	6,700
8.	Giant Eagle Supermarkets (tie)	6,000	4,400
10.	The May Co. (Kaufmann's)	5,592*	3,700
11.	City of Pittsburgh	5,300	5,500
12.	Pittsburgh Board of Education	5,164	6,000
13.	Bell of Pennsylvania	4,550	8,018**
14.	Allegheny Ludlum Steel Corp.	4,500	3,700
15.	Schneider Group	4,450	NA
16.	McDonald's Corp.	4,420*	1,600
17.	Duquesne Light Co.	4,300	4,959
18.	J.C. Penney Co. (includes Thrift Drug)	4,118*	3,000
19.	Sears Roebuck & Co.	4,002*	4,950
20.	Allegheny General Hospital (tie)	4,000*	3,100
20.	PPG Industries (tie)	4,000	5,000
22.	PNC Financial Corp.	3,600	3,152
23.	Carnegie Mellon University	3,235*	1,875
24.	Eat 'n Park Restaurants	3,100*	2,808
25.	Hills Department Stores	3,058*	2,024
26.	Presbyterian-University Hospital	3,004*	1,902
27.	The K-Mart Corp. (tie)	3,000*	NR
27.	Joseph Horne Co. (tie)	3,000*	2,183
29.	Mercy Hospital	2,933*	2,500
30.	St. Francis Medical Center	2,927*	2,969
31.	Alcoa	2,600	2,900
32.	West Penn Hospital	2,566	2,550
33.	AT&T	2,500	8,018**
34.	Forbes Health System	2,485	1,200
35.	United Parcel Service	2,412	NR
36.	South Hills Health System	2,380	1,388
37.	LTV Steel Corp.	2,254	NA
38.	Children's Hospital of Pittsburgh	2,200*	NR
39.	Union National Corp.	2,190*	1,730
40.	Rockwell International	2,000*	2,300
41.	Blue Cross of Western Pennsylvania	1,986	1,590
42.	Consolidated Natural Gas (tie)	1,900	1,750
42.	Equimark (tie)	1,900	1,827
44.	The Pittsburgh Press	1,806	1,900
45.	Montefiore Hospital (tie)	1,800*	1,800
45.	St. Clair Hospital (tie)	1,800*	NR
47.	Mine Safety Appliances Co.	1,780	1,685
48.	Medical Center of Beaver County	1,772*	NR
49.	Buick-Olds-Cadillac Group	1,750	1,638
50.	H.J. Heinz Co.	1,716	2,460

Note: *includes part time employees; **Bell and AT&T were one firm in 1982; *NR* indicates data not rated in 1982; *NA* indicates data not available.

Companies on 1982 list, not on 1988 list: Jones & Laughlin Steel, Armco, Babcock & Wilcox, Volkswagen USA, Elliott Co., Dravo Corp., Kroger Supermarkets, Wheeling-Pittsburgh Steel, McGraw-Edison, G.C. Murphy, American Standard, Gimbels, Gulf Oil Corp.

Small Is Beautiful, Too

Two-thirds of local jobs (about 600,000) are at firms with *less* than 1,500 workers. This fact is more important than it might seem. The job seeker who limits his or her efforts only to the largest businesses has unwittingly eliminated the bulk of the job opportunities.

It is in smaller firms that the real story of job growth is found, for they are responsible for creating 80% of all new jobs in Pennsylvania. Smaller companies continue to grow partly because the economy is increasingly dominated by the provision of advanced services, many of which are most efficiently performed in a decentralized fashion. A software engineering firm, for instance, is huge if it employs 80 computer engineers. Further, large companies are contracting with outside sources (smaller firms) for services traditionally performed in-house. This includes virtually every department from security and health to data processing and engineering.

Though called "small," the category includes every firm with less than 1,500 employees. Thus not all are one-man shops nor are they all small in volume. Of the 53,600 small businesses in Southwestern Pennsylvania, 13,600 have sales over $1 million. "Small" does not necessarily mean new, either. A research study showed that the greatest creators of jobs locally were small businesses that were established for ten or more years.

There is so much diversity under the title "small business" that a job hunter cannot characterize any working condition, benefit, payscale or employer-employee relation as typical. This is indeed one of the attractions, as you can find whatever working conditions or environment best suits you. In addition, smaller companies offer a proportionately higher ratio of entry level positions (to their total number of jobs) than do their larger counterparts—a real plus for first-time job hunters.

Small businesses are a less visible part of the job market. Often it is not easy to locate them, hence a job search is best thought of as an information search. How do you find them? Each description of the ten job fields in Chapter Two includes a listing of books and charts where you can find names of more Pittsburgh employers in that particular field. But don't stop there; to concretely develop your job market, carry out the steps in Chapter Six.

A Healthy Mix

A dominant employment trend in the United States has been the decline in the number of people who are employed in the manufacturing of goods and the rise in the importance of jobs in non-manufacturing industries. This shift has been characteristic of Pittsburgh as well. Even though we are considered an industrial center, our top three industries, as you can see from the chart, are not connected with heavy (durable goods) manufacturing. This has proven to be not only a healthy mix but a lifesaving one. As manufacturing employment declined across the nation by 11%, it fell four times as much in Pittsburgh.

Where Pittsburghers Work

Industry	Subtotal	Total
Services		273,100
Health Services	96,131	
Business Services	54,074	
Education (non-public)	27,856	
Social Service	14,747	
Personal Service	12,563	
Amusement & Recreation	10,924	
Membership Organizations	10,105	
Legal Services	7,920	
Other	38,234	
Retail Trade		160,200
Government		106,600
Durable Goods Manufacturing		89,800
Primary Metals (includes steel)	25,400	
Machinery	15,600	
Fabricated Metal Products	11,900	
Electrical Machinery	11,300	
Other	25,600	
Finance, Insurance & Real Estate		53,200
Wholesale Trade		51,100
Transportation & Public Utilities		43,400
Contract Construction		36,900
Nondurable Goods Industries (includes Chemicals, Printing and Food Products)		35,500

Source: **William J. Ceriani, Dept. of Labor & Industry, and** *Pittsburgh Labor Market Letter,* **Vol. XLII, no. 1, March 1988, Nonagricultural Wage & Salary Employment for Pittsburgh Primary Metropolitan Statistical Area (which includes Allegheny, Fayette, Westmoreland and Washington counties only).**

It is no secret that we are no longer "Steel Town." The jobs that have been newly created did not develop because 100,000 steel-related jobs were lost, but in spite of that. One need only witness the steady growth of financial services, business services, educational, health and retail services to see that Pittsburgh has done well in maintaining its economic balance.

Most of the new jobs are in the service industries. Negative statements about "service" jobs as the dead-end of minimum wage jobs can be misleading. There are at least two different uses of the term "service" in employment statistics. First of all, the Department of Labor makes a distinction between all manufacturing industries and all nonmanufacturing industries. This is often called the division between the goods-producing and the service industries. Here, "service" refers to banks, hospitals, colleges—every field written about in this book *except* manufacturing. This is the basis for statistics that say that 80% of all jobs will be located in the service sectors.

A second use of the term "service" comes when statisticians classify what people do. In this usage, workers are classified as doing, for example, professional, managerial, fabricating or service work. In this kind of classification, service work means home and building cleaning, food serving, security and protection work and personal servicing like haircutting. These jobs, by and large, *are* at the lower end of the wage scale; however, they represent only 17% of the jobs in Pittsburgh, not the 80% that looms using the other definition.

Pittsburgh is an adaptive city where its economic survival is concerned and the mix of its industries reflects that.

What We've Learned

Economic conditions in the four-county Pittsburgh area were better than the national average until the onset of the 1980 recession. From that time on, the area was buffeted by plant closings, company departures and job losses. Much of the job loss occurred in what had been the region's traditional source of strength—steel and large corporate headquarters. The modest but steady creation of jobs could not offset the losses until well into the second half of the decade. Pittsburghers, typically reluctant to transfer, did leave the area (our population will be lower in the next census, but probably higher in the one after that). Jobs are spread out differently across the area now and we have a generation of steelworking careers that have been closed. The generally positive tone of the numbers masks a disparity in conditions in the counties in the region and even in Allegheny County there are pockets of very high unemployment. The legions of laid off steel workers and many black neighborhoods are, as yet, virtually untouched by the growing prosperity.

Blue collar workers face the cruelest job market, but they are not alone. About 20% of the dislocated workers are in management, clerical or other white collar jobs. For instance, in 1982 the former U.S. Steel Corporation employed over 30,000 management workers. At this writing the company, now USX, has less than 9,000 even though it acquired its Marathon Oil and Texas Oil and Gas subsidiaries in the meantime. When this white collar dislocation is added to the general corporate trend to shrink middle management, the result has been a steady pool of talent in the local job market.

All this is of little practical use for the job hunter today, except for the following: because it has been an employers' market, employers, without much effort, could expect to be continually approached by any number of applicants qualified to fill their needs whenever they occurred. How long this will last, or can last, is only a guess. What is not a guess, but a genuine insight for job hunters today, is that, having been "spoiled" by this abundance of talent, employers will be reluctant to use any extra effort to find employees until they are forced to, even though the pool is shrinking. This is only human nature, but the alert job hunter who takes advantage of this and makes the effort to put himself or herself in front of potential employers may have the best competitive edge that's been seen in years.

We've learned other things from the 1980s; in fact, we may have a headstart on the rest of the country in absorbing some hard realities concerning employment. One is that the 30-year career in one job is no longer to be expected. Another is that "lay off" no longer implies "call back." Years ago the only acceptable pattern was to go from one job to a better job; today, even good people get fired.

Yet another lesson is that even if you have a good job, you are a potential job hunter. Being essential to your department is no protection when the whole department may be gone tomorrow if it does not fit into the immediate plans of the outfit who bought your firm yesterday.

Survival Tactics

You may not be able to prevent these happenings, but you can protect yourself as much as possible. If you want a survival route through the increased changes that are expected to affect employment during your work life, you will do well to follow these tactics of career development:

See yourself as the user of skills and abilities rather than the holder of a specific job title. If you work as a telephone lineman, for instance, don't limit yourself to that job title when it comes to thinking about what you can do. See yourself in terms of your skills; namely, as someone who works indoors and outdoors, using your whole body as well as your hands to work, who is able to learn electrical and electronic procedures and carry out technical operations needing attention to small physical details in situations where constant caution prevents life-threatening or expensive accidents. If you see yourself this way then you can visualize yourself working in any number of different jobs where one or more of these skills are needed. Future job possibilities could include installing transformers on solar energy systems, wiring instrument panels in synthetic enzyme plants—and who knows what else. A changed attitude about what you "do" can give you flexibility to move with the changes in the workplace. Chapter Four of this book deals with skills and interests and can serve as a starting point for developing this attitude.

Operate from your strengths. This is one of your best protections. If you are better at helping people than at selling, move away from the sales counter and find your way to the technical support or service departments of the company. That way you will be doing your best work at your highest capacity and you may well be the "cream of the crop" when it comes to advancement.

Seek work in a field that you value, enjoy or find challenging. This seeming idealism is very realistic in the long run, for you will find satisfaction and like your work regardless of supply and demand factors. If you hate the stock market, don't go into it only because it promises good money today. Tomorrow may be a very different story. This truism of career development has never made more sense.

Keep flexible and up-to-date on developments in your field. This will protect you from being caught unaware by change—either technological or managerial. Lend a wary eye to statistics. Don't plan a career based only on what you read in a prediction about good jobs for the future. Those predictions can be changed in a flash but you can't necessarily do that.

What About the Future?

Overall the picture is positive. Gradual improvement in the local economic scene is predicted. In creating new jobs, Pittsburgh has outpaced other Rust Belt cities like Buffalo and Cleveland. Although our net growth (jobs created minus jobs lost) is slightly below the growth rate of the nation as a whole, forecasters expect that we will catch up soon. A smaller labor force suggests that those once excluded from all employment will have better opportunities in entry level and service jobs. Those with skills and education, including women, minorities and youths who always have the hardest time getting good jobs, will have a chance at career advancement.

No one knows how long the health care boom can continue, although it appears to be shifting to non-hospital based care. The next infusion of economic vitality may well be the one-half billion dollar airport Midfield Terminal construction project and the development surrounding it.

Looking at other industries, the upturn in manufacturing jobs in 1988 suggests that we've seen the bottom and that manufacturing is moving from a depressed state to a level condition. In the steel industry, the signs are good: operating costs are down and labor productivity is up, but job opportunities continue to be limited. In this region, specialty steel, chemicals, electronic equipment, non-electrical machinery, instruments and rubber are likely to receive the biggest boost if the U.S. dollar is steady or declines in value. Forecasters feel that the production of highly technical machinery and systems along with engineered materials are realistic future industries for the area.

Using production automation to become globally competitive means factories no longer generate thousands and thousands of jobs and those that remain require increasingly more skill. "It doesn't take very many people for actual hands-on assembly of any manufactured goods anymore," said Audrey Freedman, a labor economist at the Conference Board in New York, a business-research organization. "It does take more people to design them, test them and arrange for acquisition of required production materials and financing."

While the manufacturing sector remains a significant part of the regional economy, it is still somewhat specialized. It has less variety than the manufacturing sector in other cities of similar size, like St. Louis, Cleveland or Houston. There are some encouraging signs of diversity. Firms that joined Pittsburgh's list of publicly held companies recently include Calgon Carbon, a chemicals manufacturer, New Brighton-based Tuscarora Plastics, and II-VI, Inc., a precision instrumentation firm. Established firms diversify, too. The biggest private employer, Westinghouse Electric Corporation, has been expanding its product mix for more than twenty years and today is involved in credit, broadcasting and public power systems, as well as traditional industrial products.

The city's service industries, especially business services and financially oriented ones are projected to have gradual expansion. Retail trade and education look stable. While high technology is the overworked rescuer of many a community, our technically oriented companies and research labs already have their own niche here and, as they grow, they point the way to the next recognizable transformation of the area's economy.

The Pennsylvania Department of Labor projects there will be more openings for clerical, sales, service, professional and technical workers. While projections are only "probable directions," the Pittsburgh area's largest number of new jobs from 1985 to 1995 should be in the following industries:

Projections

Job Gains by Volume	Employment Gain 1985 to 1995
1. Business Services	15,970
2. Health Services (private)	13,950
3. Eating & Drinking Places	10,180
4. Educational Services (private)	3,640
5. Food Stores	3,240
6. General Merchandise Stores	2,730
7. Social Services	2,660
8. Banking	2,600
9. Wholesale Trade	2,370
10. Miscellaneous Services	2,210
11. Special Trade Contractors	2,040
12. Local Government	1,970
13. Legal Services	1,450
14. Miscellaneous Retail	1,380
15. General Building Construction	1,320

Source: "Projected Employment Changes for Selected Industries from 1985 to 1995," *Pittsburgh Primary Metropolitan Statistical Area, Industry Trends and Outlook.* PA Department of Labor and Industry (includes Allegheny, Fayette, Westmoreland and Washington counties only).

Some other fields are fast growing, although they employ comparatively smaller numbers of workers and so are not on the list. These include Transportation Services (30% growth), Holding and Investment Offices (18%), Security and Commodity Brokers (17%), Building

Materials and Garden Supplies (16%), Insurance Agents and Brokers (14%) and Credit Agencies (13%).

There are growing fields and shrinking fields, but even in a stagnant field there is movement of people from spot to spot and retirements and promotions. Each movement is an opportunity for someone. You can't talk personally to each of Pittsburgh's employers, nor do you need to. What you need to do, when facing a job market as large and complex as Pittsburgh's, is to become very knowledgeable about one or two segments. Looking closely at the segments of Pittsburgh's job market is the task to which we now turn.

2

A JOB HUNTER'S VIEW OF 10 PITTSBURGH JOB MARKETS

In the brief surveys in this chapter, you'll find detailed information about ten of the most popular career fields in town. The ten areas represent over two-thirds of all local jobs and include **Finance, Health, Human Services, Education, Culture and Leisure, Government, Wholesale and Retail Trade, Research, Advanced Technology and Manufacturing** and **Professional Services** (Law, Engineering and Accounting). This is information that can get a newcomer to the area or to the job market started quickly.

Each survey has a practical orientation. Categories overlap, as they do in real life, and there is no claim to be comprehensive. However, each section: (1) introduces you to fundamental facts about a particular market including the number of jobs in the area. (2) Reports trends, current job shortages and impressions about the field. (3) Gives you a start on finding possible Pittsburgh employers. The first time an employer in a field is mentioned, the name is put into *italics* to remind you that you are reading this data with a very concrete objective. Each survey ends with a **Resource** section telling you where you can find directories that name the local employers in one field or find publications that list the largest ones in a specialty. Often these directories have details, like addresses, names and statistics, that are helpful.

Having some employers' names is one place to start. You also need to know what you can offer to those employers; PART TWO of this book will help you do so. With both these elements in place, you'll be in position to work on your actual employment targets, the focus of PART THREE.

A note on those directories: local libraries and college libraries may have some of them. A few can be purchased through regular bookstores. But the greatest number of job hunt related materials are found either at Carnegie Library of Pittsburgh's main location or its Business Branch. This library system is available to everyone and it's free, too. The main library is located on the Schenley Plaza side of the Carnegie Institute which is at 4400 Forbes Avenue in the Oakland section of town. The Carnegie Library Business Branch is on the lower level of the One Mellon Bank Center building, 500 Grant Street, downtown Pittsburgh. Call 622-3131 for the hours they are open.

FINANCE

Pittsburgh's financial community, composed of banking, insuring, investing, credit lending and real estate firms, has been a job generator for the past decade. To the present 53,600 jobs in this field, 25,000 are projected to be added by the end of the century. Many of the new jobs will be in mortgage or insurance companies, investment firms and in growing financial specialties such as international finance, estate and corporate planning, tax management and leasing services.

Banks

Banks employ the majority of Pittsburgh's financial workers. Banking, however, is no longer the stable, professional employment spot it once seemed to be. Deregulation brought competition with non-banking firms. Changes in state regulations resulted in acquisitions and mergers. Loan losses squeezed profits for some. This meant job losses in some firms in an overall growth field.

Mellon Bank, the epitome of corporate structure yesterday, reflects many of the current changes transforming banking. Modified by deregulation, expanded by acquisition, pressured to maintain profitability and gripped by the necessity to downsize, Mellon in 1988 lowered its local employment rolls back to 1981 levels of 6,000 and lowered total employment from 19,500 to 16,500.

Mellon Banking Corp., still the area's largest bank holding company in several respects, was surpassed in 1988 by *PNC Financial* as the state's largest banking organization in terms of total assets. Pittsburgh headquartered PNC Financial Corporation has 4,000 local employees, most working for its *Pittsburgh National Bank* operating unit. It is currently the 13th largest banking organization in the country. Like Mellon, it owns and operates several other firms. PNC's include *Provident National Bank, the Central Bancorporation, Citizens Fidelity Corp.,* the *First Bank and Trust Co., Hershey Bank, Marine Bank, Northeastern Bank and PNC National Bank of New Jersey.*

If Mellon and PNB hold the top two spots, the "merger of equals" between Pittsburgh based Union National Corp. and Titusville headquartered Pennbancorp to form *Integra Financial Group* places that resulting entity firmly in third place locally. *Equimark* and *Dollar Bank* follow in the rankings.

Banks are adding new services and seriously marketing to small businesses, as well as large. Cash management products for businesses, such as account reconciliation, sweeps, remote disbursement and lockboxes, along with other merchant banking services like leasing and corporate finance, are competitive items and banks have been hiring people for operating and marketing these services.

Large banks utilize their computer capacity to sell financial processing services to smaller banks. Mellon, a leader in this, counts 450 other banks in 39 states as customers for these correspondent banking services. Jobs involved in such bank-to-bank services have grown. Mellon's *Field Services Division,* for instance, employs 200 involved in repairing and servicing computer terminals, automatic teller machines, safes and vaults owned by the bank and its customers.

Together the ten largest local banks have over 600 branches spread throughout the extended metropolitan area. *Equibank* (subsidiary of Equimark), for example, has 57 branches in Western Pennsylvania and 17 in Philadelphia, along with some 47 offsite automatic teller machines in Western Pennsylvania. Banks are expected to close some old branches while opening new offices in growth communities.

Large banks are not the only ones interested in community banking. Small banks (those with less than $110 million in assets) appear to be thriving in Pennsylvania although mergers, acquisitions and increased competition are the norm. New banks are being chartered within the state, benefiting, perhaps, from the loss of depositor loyalty that can result when local banks merge.

Savings and Loans locally are also subject to merger and acquisition trends. Some are doing much better than others. Erie and Beaver counties' *Colony Savings Bank,* for instance, moved its headquarters to Pittsburgh where it now is the sixth largest thrift institution and opened two additional branches for the North Hills.

Trends

While the Pittsburgh financial climate has decelerated over the past few years, financial companies are expected to continue hiring managers to oversee the computerization of operations. Marketing skills are in demand. About half of all new and replacement hiring is in the area of clerical work: tellers, clerks, secretaries, shift workers and computer operators. There is a global trend toward the elimination of single function clerical jobs in the financial industry. As smaller banks find it economical to purchase or computerize functions, expect some job losses. Locally, larger banks that have grown and marketed their services report no big decline in clerical employment.

Large financial institutions operate like most other corporations in terms of their annual recruitment of college graduates for management training programs. Financial professionals are usually sought from applicants with previous banking experience. The same is not true necessarily for personnel who work in client relations, marketing and computerization. For staff areas like human resources and auditing, a banking background is common but not essential. When initiating new financial services like selling stocks or financial planning, banks here have been willing to go outside the banking industry to hire experienced persons who can get their new ventures off to a running start.

Banking may seem to have stopped leading the growth pack in Pittsburgh, but, as one bank administrator said; "There certainly is opportunity in banking in Pittsburgh. You need your degree and you have to be in the right place and make the right contacts. Professional associations like our chapter of Women in Banking are also a help."

Investments and Securities

Pittsburgh is not to be compared to a Chicago or New York Stock Exchange, but it has a representative showing of national brokerage houses and investment firms that are well established. In their three Pittsburgh branches, for instance, *Merrill Lynch* has 67 brokers. *Parker/Hunter* has four branches. *Shearson Lehman Hutton, Paine Webber, Prudential Bache, Dean Witter Reynolds* and *Kidder Peabody* are all represented, along with local firms like *Financial Estate Planning, Legg Mason Masten,* and *Hefren-Tillotson.* In addition to serving individuals and marketing to major companies, investment firms are moving into small pension fund management. *Federated Investors* is a hometown mutual fund management firm that has earned a national reputation for excellence. Though purchased by Aetna Life and Casualty Co. in 1982, it remains Pittsburgh headquartered, managing $44.5 billion with 750 employees.

Financial Planning

Just barely starting in terms of its potential, financial planning is a field that seems to promise job opportunity. Independent financial planners, some with certification, are long familiar. Today, the independents share the field with a variety of financial concerns: banks, brokerage firms, "Big 8" accounting firms, and insurance companies. The result is job opportunities with those firms, as well as with firms like *Allegheny Investments* that specialize in financial planning.

Insurance

Insurance firms and many of their agents today are licensed to sell securities and advise about other investments. Insurance is often marketed to individuals as one element of a total financial plan. The present training programs at life insurance companies like *Prudential, New York Life* and *Equitable Life* reflect these changes. Business insurers and employee benefit consultants have shown steady growth. *Gateway Financial Group* (92 employees), *Pen-Wel* (75), *MMC&P* (70) and *Babb* (85), all local firms, along with *William M Mercer/Meidinger/Hansen, Inc.,* are the top five employee benefit consulting firms here, ranked by number of employees. *Chubb,* a local property casualty insurance company is ranked by *Fortune* magazine as the 39th largest diversified financial organization in the country.

Credit

Credit lending firms may focus on consumer lending or commercial loans. Both are active parts of the local financial marketplace. Both types are experiencing the trend toward expanding the number of services they offer to their customers. *Gateway Financial Group* is an example of a commercial lending firm that expanded its financial services to include equity loans, insurance, benefit programs, investments and merchant banking. *Westinghouse Credit Corporation,* whose business over the past ten years has grown at a 20% clip, is the nation's 14th largest finance company in terms of total capital. It operates in many respects like finance companies such as *Household, Beneficial* and *Atlantic,* but it serves only big companies. Commercial real estate is Westinghouse Credit's largest service area, followed by leasing and corporate finance.

Collection agencies, like *Dun & Bradstreet, The Credit Bureau, Equifax PMI* and *United Mercantile Co.,* can be commercially oriented or retail-oriented, just as lending firms are. Good collection agents are always needed and professionals in commercial credit can find rewarding niches. Credit agencies other than banks are expected to employ 7,300 by 1995.

Venture Capital

Venture capital firms, hardly in evidence a few years ago, now actively seek new—especially high technology—businesses in which to invest. In 1980 there were four venture capital firms operating in Pittsburgh.

Now there are 17, with 14 of these headquartered here. Among them are the *CEO Venture Fund* (I and II), the *Pittsburgh Seed Fund* and *Hillman Ventures* (one of the largest funds in the U.S. with major investments outside this area). Banks, such as *PNC,* also have formed venture capital funds.

Real Estate

Real estate marketing, both residential and commercial, follows the health of the economy. Things have been improving since 1984. Moderate residential housing costs, which bring Pittsburgh favorable ratings in cost of living indexes, keep real estate commissions from being as lucrative as they are in booming metropolitan areas. Locally, Fox Chapel housing sales show the highest average price. Jobs in real estate result more from turnover than from sheer growth; by 1995 such jobs will have expanded slightly to 9,000. In real estate, as in insurance sales, the "80/20 rule" applies: 80% of the real estate usually ends up being sold by 20% of the people doing the selling. Employment possibilities are mostly commission-based, and there are few formal requirements for entry jobs. The biggest firms offer advanced marketing as well as training. Some hold free seminars to describe the work and answer questions. If you are interested in this field, become familiar not only with job want ads but the real estate pages and TV shows of homes-for-sale. Larger firms include *Coldwell Banker, Howard Hanna, Northwood Realty* and *Merrill Lynch Realty.*

Commercial real estate has focused on tenants for the downtown office building openings and for the numerous industrial parks under development. Just in the Allegheny Valley area, for example, one can count the North Moreland Industrial Park, MAC Industrial Park in Ford City, Highlands Industrial Park, the University of Pittsburgh's U-PARC, Schreiber Industrial District and an RIDC proposed development off Little Deer Creek Road in Harmar Township. The anticipated prime commercial areas resulting from the location of the to-be-completed Midfield Terminal at Greater Pittsburgh Airport will take time to develop. Meanwhile, "It's a decent living, as usual," said one commercial real estate broker.

The finance field, increasingly, is one where companies provide customized services and broad expertise—"high value-added service" as it is called. This field needs professionals with skills that include the ability to plan and allocate work, to communicate and interact in complex settings and to think strategically and comprehensively. The time of straightforward growth, however, is mostly over. The alert worker in the finance field does best to see himself or herself not in terms of a present title ("banker" or "insurance sales") but as a user of specific skills (for instance, "I can do financial planning for estate management"). In the long run, it is these skills that will prove to be marketable and less the type of financial institution in which they were learned. Such an attitude positions a person to find opportunities for success wherever they arise in different financial settings, whether that be in a bank trust department, an insurance brokerage firm, a merchant banking firm or as an independent financial planner.

Where to Find More Pittsburgh Employers in Finance

BOOK OF BUSINESS LISTS, Pittsburgh Business Times, 1988.
- "Bank and Bank Holding Companies" (21 largest Pittsburgh area), p. 33
- "Credit Unions" (20 largest Pittsburgh area), p. 58
- "Employee Benefit Consulting Firms" (25 largest Pittsburgh area), p. 29
- "Life Insurance Agencies" (25 largest Pittsburgh area), p. 111

Find this at Carnegie Library, Oakland, in the PA Room and at the downtown Business Branch. Also at newsstands and bookstores.

CORPORATIONS REVIEW, annual publication. Names of directors and divisional officers of 105 Western Pennsylvania companies. Carnegie Library, PA Room and Business Branch. Also purchasable through Oliver Realty.

MOODY'S BANK AND FINANCE MANUAL, Dun & Bradstreet, NY. Three times a year, comprehensive. Carnegie Library, Business Branch.

PENNSYLVANIA BANKS WITH INTERNATIONAL DEPARTMENTS AND BRANCHES, Department of Commerce, Harrisburg. Free publication. 4 pages.

RAND McNALLY INTERNATIONAL BANKERS DIRECTORY. 4,000 banks in alphabetical order. Carnegie Library, Oakland, Reference Room.

SHOWCASE, quarterly supplement to the Pittsburgh Business Times, focus on commercial real estate. Carnegie Library, Oakland, Periodical Room.

HEALTH

Experts see health care as the field with the best long term career opportunities in Pittsburgh, an opinion based on the city's established medical centers and its aging population. Overall, the short term is positive, too. Health services is our third largest employment field with 96,000 people employed in 1988. This is a larger number than was ever projected for the field a few years ago. Estimates are that it will grow 38% to 133,000 by the year 2000. That's 3,000 additional jobs each year. But the growth is neither straightforward nor simple. In fact, if you work in some hospitals, you may well wonder where the growth is.

Hospital Health Care

About 45% of the health care jobs are within a hospital setting. The 50 local hospitals employ more than half the 4,000 doctors, 19,000 registered nurses and 13,000 health technicians. Over a billion construction dollars have been put into local hospitals during the 1980s for equipment and space. This sometimes—but not always—means more employees. *McKeesport Hospital* added the equivalent of 125 employees when it opened its new facilities. *St. Francis Hospital's* new psychiatric building with computers, shorter corridors, video monitors and automated doors, allowed employees to be more efficient, reducing the number needed.

Pittsburgh's medical centers provide care not only for local residents; but about 78% of the patients at the *University of Pittsburgh's Medical and Health Care Division* are from outside the region, an economically healthy sign. The PMR (Partnership for Medical Renaissance) is a coalition of *Presbyterian University Hospital, Eye and Ear Hospital,* and the University of Pittsburgh's Medical and Health Care Division, which includes the *School of Medicine, Western Psychiatric Institute and Clinic, Falk Clinic,* the *Pittsburgh Cancer Institute,* the *Joint Radiation and Oncology Center* and *Mathilda Heiss Health Center,* as well as the university's five schools of health sciences. This group, PMR, has begun a renovation project centered in Oakland that will take several years and $280 million to complete. *Allegheny General Hospital,* on the North Side, has grown steadily into a major health system. It recently jumped in size largely by acquiring the *Medical College of Pennsylvania* in Philadelphia. It also has a neuropsychiatric facility on the site of the former West Allegheny Hospital in North Fayette.

General Trends

A trend expected to continue is that some smaller hospitals will be pressured to close or become feeders for larger ones. Larger hospitals are becoming diversified health care providers. The *Forbes Health System,* for example, with 2,485 total personnel, consists of three acute care hospitals, one hospice, one center for gerontology and an award winning system for after-discharge monitoring. The *South Hills Health System* (2,025) includes one hospital, a skilled nursing facility, an emergency and family medical center, a home care agency, a counseling center and a personal care residence. The *Southwest Health System* (1,400) consists of four conventional care centers: *Westmoreland Home Health, South West Therapy Services* and two hospitals.

The trend resulting in the merging and combining of health care organizations can mean that some management and department assistant jobs are eliminated to reduce duplication. Direct care jobs are less affected. While direct caregivers are essential employees, some hospitals are exploring different ways of using their traditional three-tiers of service: registered nurses, licensed practical nurses and nursing assistants. Some hospitals are using fewer RNs but positioning them as managers of a larger number of LPNs; another approach has been to utilize fewer LPNs and more NAs. So far, no approach has proven superior.

Challenged to behave like businesses, hospitals are employing traditional business strategies—marketing, advertising, purchasing outside consultant services, new business development and diversification. Increasingly, they are marketing their specialties: medical genetics, head injury rehabilitation, laser surgery, pain clinics, etc. They can be expected to evaluate closely non-money generating departments and those that are farther removed from direct service, such as communications departments, accounting, planning and assistant administration spots. As in business, these workers have to justify their contribution to the bottom line and should educate their superiors as to how they generate money.

Expect more changes in hospitals over the next decade since there are too many acute care, medical-surgical beds in the region, but few hospital administrators would agree any of the excess is in their hospitals. Part of the reason for the excess is the dramatic shift to outpatient care. Nearly half of all operations in this area are done on outpatients, compared to 17% done in 1981, according to the Hospital Council. Because they are in an information-intensive industry, expect hospitals to make dramatic changes in the way information is used to diagnose and treat

26

patients. There is overall growth in hospital employment; however, compared to non-hospital health care, hospitals are expected to register lower growth in jobs over the near term as they streamline and cope with their more competitive marketplace. Still, sheer job turnover will mean many openings.

Non-Hospital Health Care

As the burden of patient care becomes less hospital-dependent, it creates all sorts of medically related jobs — in health maintenance organizations, private nursing placement, ambulatory care centers and home medical equipment rental firms. There are people with health care experience in fitness centers, insurance companies and law firms. Expect to see more independent rehabilitation centers, drug and alcohol clinics, psychiatric facilities and mobile medical testing and treatment centers. For doctors and dentists it will be increasingly important to locate where there is convenient access and to have convenient hours for patients.

One of the areas of greatest growth in non-hospital based care is personal care homes, where residents do not require 24-hour medical attention. *D. Dotter Inc.* is one of Pittsburgh's oldest firms specializing in personal care and has 160 beds in seven homes located in four counties. There are about 630 personal care homes in the 23 counties of Western Pennsylvania; in Allegheny county there are 172 such homes with 3,321 beds. Demand has encouraged many to get into the business. Corporations are coming in alongside sole proprietors and church-supported groups. Doctors are forming partnerships and joint ventures, while nursing homes and hospitals both are expanding to add personal care facilities. Health care professionals are needed to run them. To date there are few state requirements for care providers; but supervisors of personal care homes should know psychology, proper nutrition, first-aid and be able to spot side-effects to medication.

The Pittsburgh market for HMOs (Health Maintenance Organizations) seems to be particularly tough to crack. There are, currently, eight HMOs licensed in Southwestern Pennsylvania, but fewer than that number are expected to survive over the next four years.

Specific Job Trends

The 30% national decline in enrollment in nursing programs since 1983 has not affected Pittsburgh as much as other parts of the country. Although poor working hours, conditions and low salaries used to be the norm for nurses, more hospitals are designing attractive conditions. Entry level salaries for an RN average about $22,000 here and the local cap on salaries (once $29,000) is off. For instance *Shadyside Hospital* has a clinical career ladder that starts nurses at $23,000 and gives them the potential to earn $42,000 annually if they meet performance, education and experience levels. In a two step clinical ladder at *Presbyterian Hospital,* RNs' salaries range from $24,000 to $35,000. Hospitals with better pay packages, understandably, have fewer shortages of applicants. Some inducements are available in Pittsburgh, primarily shift length selection and shift differential pay; but there are few of the glamorous perquisites offered in some cities to keep experienced nurses at patients' bedsides rather than see them move into administration or private industry.

With the application of the DRG (diagnostic related groups) system to health care, the role of case manager has expanded qualitatively and quantitatively. This job, formerly called utilization review, involves finding the most cost effective methods for providing quality care for patients and planning discharge routes that insurers will pay for. Case managers must be capable of suggesting tests, conducting investigations, being diplomatic, coordinating a variety of health services, and being knowledgeable about local health resources. In some hospitals, ARTs (accredited records technicians) and MRTs (medical record technicians) are used. RNs, especially with certification, are desired by health insurers. There is, as yet, no training program in Pittsburgh for this field. Nurses who are in this relatively new field say it is primarily on-the-job training and can be a stepping stone into hospital management. The state of Pennsylvania also desires case managers for psychiatric units. A similar position in insurance companies reviews services for catastrophic illnesses.

In addition to case managers, critical care nursing specialists are in demand. Home care by private duty nurses is a growing field in light of shortened hospital stays. Other fields in short supply for hospitals are physical therapists and occupational therapists because many have chosen to work for the growing number of rehabilitation centers. Pharmacists, too, now have options to work for franchised drug stores, mail-order prescription houses or in pharmaceutical sales. Respiratory therapists and nurse anesthetists are also positions that take a little longer to fill. RNs looking for temporary work through agencies can find positions in long term settings like nursing homes and personal care homes and in small hospitals. Contracts with temporary service companies are not common in large, city hospitals yet. In 1988 there was still a need for medical record coders and ultrasound technologists.

Enrollment in medical laboratory training has dropped 25% since 1983, but this has not created shortages in Pittsburgh. Some medical lab positions will be streamlined as medical equipment that can do five times as many tests as current equipment becomes cost effective. New technology, in fact, can upset the present balance and put some technicians out of work. Persons considering training, especially shorter term certificate programs would do well to check with local hospitals about their anticipated needs in those areas before making tuition commitments.

In the psychiatric field, patient care assistant jobs (sometimes called psych techs) have been an entry into the system for degreed persons who plan to move up the administrative ladder. Non-degreed nursing assistants often find decent money in patient care positions but will have no upward career path without additional training.

Hospital administrators and executives, mimicking a national trend, are undergoing a job shakeout resulting from increased pressures to produce financially. Increased competition calls for marketing and political skills. Nationally, hospital administrators are leaving the field at an alarming rate; locally they are staying in their positions for shorter periods of time and promotion from within is not always likely. Those with the best track record are in demand.

Where to Find More Pittsburgh Employers in Health

ALLEGHENY COUNTY MEDICAL SOCIETY, official directory. Lists doctors' offices and specialties and by zip codes. Find this at Carnegie Library, Oakland, in the PA Room.

AMERICAN HOSPITAL ASSOCIATION, GUIDE TO THE HEALTH CARE FIELD. 1985 edition. Carnegie Library, PA Room, has a xeroxed list of hospitals in Pennsylvania.

BOOK OF BUSINESS LISTS, Pittsburgh Business Times, 1988.
- "Co-ed Health and Fitness Clubs" (25 largest Pittsburgh area), p. 109
- "Health Maintenance Organizations" (Pittsburgh area), p. 85
- "Hospitals" (25 largest Pittsburgh area), p. 73
- "Nursing Homes" (25 largest Allegheny County), p. 41

Find this at Carnegie Library, PA Room, and the downtown Business Branch. Also at newsstands and bookstores.

DUNN'S GUIDE TO HEALTH CARE COMPANIES. Carnegie Library, downtown Business Branch.

HEALTH SERVICES DIRECTORY, Gale Research Co. 34 categories such as sports medicine, genetics, etc., includes clinics, treatment centers and related service agencies. Carnegie Library, PA Room (index only), and Reference Room.

LONG TERM CARE FACILITY DIRECTORY. Western Pennsylvania counties, 1985 edition, type of service, address, number of beds. Carnegie Library, PA Room.

PENNSYLVANIA MEDICAL DIRECTORY 1985, Department of Commerce, Harrisburg. Free publication, 40 pages. Manufacturers and schools in the industry interested in international sales and service.

PROFILE OF PENNSYLVANIA HOSPITALS, Pennsylvania Department of Health, 1985. Lists types of service, number of beds. Covers general, drug & alcohol and psychiatric areas. Carnegie Library, PA Room.

RESEARCH CENTERS DIRECTORY, Gale Research Co. 1982 edition. A guide to university related and non-profit research established on a permanent basis. Includes life sciences. Supplemented between editions by *NEW RESEARCH CENTERS.* Carnegie Library, Oakland, Reference Room.

WHERE TO TURN, Guide to Health, Welfare and Community Services in Allegheny County. Published by HELPLINE. Updated frequently. Carnegie Library, PA Room.

HUMAN SERVICES

Despite federal budget cuts to virtually every human service sector of the economy, this employment field in Pittsburgh has not shrunk as might be expected. More people are receiving service and agencies seem to be holding their own through a combination of government and private funding. With an estimated 14,000 social service workers today, not counting government employees, and a 2% growth in jobs each year, expect most job openings here to be from turnover rather than from expansion. But there is plenty of turnover. Expect, too, increased alliances between the medical and the human service industries over the next few years.

Human services are provided through a truly diverse group of organizations. There are sectarian and non-sectarian, public and private social service agencies, hospitals, residential facilities, government departments and specialized agencies.

Pay Scales

The human service field does not rely on lucrative salaries but attracts those who want a job with social meaning or who value working with specific populations. Some human service jobs have room for creativity or have flexibility or less regimented accountability. While crossover from the non-profit sector to the private sector is more common, the job attractions of the human services have been responsible in some cases for the reverse happening.

A recently completed (1988) wage survey of *United Way* agencies in the area showed that entry level wages are low; middle levels have too great a variety to be fairly averaged out and higher levels are competitive with industry for comparable responsibilities. Wage scales are lower than, for instance, Boston's because of a generally lower cost of living plus the presence of many applicants. "Degree inflation," the phenomenon of asking for a degree that is not an absolute job requirement simply because it makes screening applicants easier, has also been noted. In non-profit agencies, benefits are not always available; firms without them may trade flexibility in duties or hours. In social service agencies there is usually a flatter organizational pyramid than in most corporations, that means fewer layers of management between workers and top management.

One 1985 survey showed a B.S. degree caseworker locally would average $15,000 at entry level and an M.S.W. caseworker with eight or more years experience could expect $22,000. A residential services worker might enter as a trainee for $8,000 but could advance eventually without a degree to $17,000. Management positions, such as catchment area senior supervisor or foster care coordinator averaged somewhere around $27,500. Project a 3% yearly salary increase to bring these figures roughly up to date.

Civil service employees have clearly defined pay levels. Social service workers find employment with the state funded *Public Welfare* and *Unemployment Compensation* offices and the *State Correctional Institutions;* and in federal positions such as the *Social Security Administration.* Numerous programs are operated through Allegheny County, such as those under the office of *Children and Youth Services* and the *Area Agency on Aging.* The county *Mental Health and Mental Retardation* and *Drug and Alcohol* programs have a network system of offices. *Action Housing* also utilizes a talented pool of human service professionals.

Family and Children's Service, like other agencies its size, needs support staff like payroll clerks, drivers and rehabilitation aides, along with professional caseworkers, play therapists, weekend supervisors for residential homes and consultation and education specialists. Child Life workers (usually with a B.A. degree) find employment there and at agencies like *Western Psychiatric, Louise Child Care Centers* and *Pittsburgh Rehabilitation Institute. Catholic Charities* delivers a variety of nonsectarian programs to the community. The *Association of Retarded Citizens,* another private, non-profit agency, has a staff of 300 high school and college graduates serving children and adults.

Trends

One trend expected to continue is the reallocation of resources to increase service to the elderly. *Vintage,* one agency providing day services to the elderly, for example, uses ten full time and an equal number of part time workers to provide health, counseling, social and recreational programs. Only the availability of funds stems the demand for workers in this field.

At skilled and intermediate nursing homes, the presence of an on-site social worker not only benefits those who live there but also helps market the quality of the nursing home. Private consultants providing speech, occupational and physical therapy are also hired. Home health care concerns employ social workers, respiratory technicians and speech and physical therapy specialists. Researchers, both social and statistical, can be found in human service agencies such as United Way and the *Health and Welfare Planning Association.*

Case management in the community is a newly growing field. Similar to hospital case management but more often using social workers, case management deals with the general welfare of the elderly and the planning of appropriate utilization of homecare, skilled nursing and other services to best meet housing and health needs.

Physical and vocational rehabilitation services are one of the fastest growing segments of the medical-human services industry. Some are associated with hospitals; others, like *Keystone Rehabilitation Systems,* which expects to have a staff of 800 by 1990, are for-profit independents. *Harmarville Rehabilitation, D.T. Watson* and *Gateway Rehabilitation* employ combinations of medical and human service workers.

Because of the need to continuously find funding sources, individuals with fund raising skills are valued. Even publicly funded agencies seek matching or supplemental money for special programs. Fund raising skills typically include writing grant proposals, soliciting donations and expanding membership rolls. Development work includes foundation solicitation, capital fund raising, individual donor campaigns and planned and corporate giving. The work carries a sales and marketing orientation and has proved to be particularly attractive to women. Even though Pittsburgh human service agencies depend more on the local United Way than other northeastern cities do, fund raising departments continue to grow.

The human service field also includes service agencies that are traditionally volunteer but operate with the support of a paid staff, such as the *Salvation Army,* the *YWCAs* and *YMCAs, Boy Scouts* and *Camp Fire Council.* There are health issue groups like the *Pittsburgh Blind Association, Planned Parenthood, Whale's Tale, Cancer Guidance Institute* and consumer issue groups like *GASP.*

If you seek a skilled technical position in this field, it is comparatively easy to measure whether the job requirements match your qualifications. But what about job hunting for the management positions which seem to require generalists? Says one highly placed professional with a good overview of the field, "Good people find jobs here in three months." When pressed to elaborate, he added, "By good, I mean someone with an employment or education background that is good, who has polish, who has a strategic mindset. I mean, someone who's able to mount a respectable job search: contact the right people, have a sharp resume, make the follow-up calls necessary and see the people they get referred to...There's a lot of good people here and a lot of moving around; but no one takes care of people who can't move themselves through an effective job hunt." In sum, you must be good *and* job hunt well.

Where to Find More Pittsburgh Employers in Human Service

BLUE PAGES section of the telephone directory. A mind-expanding array of human service agencies.

BOOK OF BUSINESS LISTS, Pittsburgh Business Times, 1988.
- "Charitable Trusts and Foundations" (25 largest Pittsburgh area), p. 61
- "Co-ed Health and Fitness clubs" (25 largest Pittsburgh area), p. 109
- "Day Care Centers" (25 largest area licensed), p. 59
- "Nursing Homes" (25 largest Allegheny County), p. 41

Find this at Carnegie Library, Oakland, in the PA Room, and at the downtown Business Branch. Also at newsstands and bookstores.

CHILDREN'S SERVICES DIRECTORY. Programs for children who have special needs and a listing of nursery schools primarily in Allegheny County. Carnegie Library, PA Room.

COMPENDIUM OF MENTAL HEALTH SERVICES FOR CHILDREN AND YOUTH, Pennsylvania Office of Mental Health, 1983. Out-of-date but contains a lot of information. Carnegie Library, PA Room.

CRIME VICTIM'S AID, ed. Robert Grayson, 1983. A regional directory of services for victims of crimes. Covers NY, NJ and PA. Could be out-of-date. Carnegie Library, PA Room.

DIRECTORY OF HOUSING FACILITIES FOR OLDER PENNSYLVANIANS, Pennsylvania Department of Aging, 1986. Lists independent housing facilities, number of units, services available. Carnegie Library, PA Room.

DIRECTORY OF PENNSYLVANIA FOUNDATIONS, 3rd edition. The Free Library of Philadelphia, PA, 1986. Carnegie Library, PA Room.

FIND OUT! HUMAN RESOURCE DIRECTORY FOR WASHINGTON AND GREENE COUNTIES. 1986. Carnegie Library, PA Room.

FOUNDATION CENTER COLLECTION. This is a regional repository and contains books and materials related to the philanthropic field and current editions of *THE FOUNDATION DIRECTORY,* a national directory. Find this at the University of Pittsburgh's Hillman Library.

HEALTH SERVICES DIRECTORY, Gale Research Co. 34 categories such as genetic counseling, includes clinics, treatment centers and related service agencies. Carnegie Library, PA Room (index only) and Reference Room.

LONG TERM CARE FACILITY DIRECTORY. Western Pennsylvania counties, 1985 edition. Type of service, address, number of beds. Carnegie Library, PA Room.

NATIONAL DIRECTORY OF CHILDREN AND YOUTH SERVICES 1988-89. Social, health and juvenile justice services, by county, with names. Xeroxed copy of the Pennsylvania section of this directory. Carnegie Library, PA Room.

PENNSYLVANIA DRUG & ALCOHOL FACILITIES/SERVICES DIRECTORY, Pennsylvania Department of Health, 1983. Most likely out-of-date for names. Carnegie Library, PA Room.

PENNSYLVANIA RESEARCH INVENTORY PROJECT. An inventory of research units in the state. Old (1983), but lists over a thousand centers in technical and academic research fields like social science. Carnegie Library, PA Room.

PROFILE OF PENNSYLVANIA HOSPITALS, Pennsylvania Department of Health, 1985. Lists types of services, number of beds, includes general, drug and alcohol and psychiatric services. Carnegie Library, PA Room.

RESEARCH CENTERS DIRECTORY, Gale Research Co. 1982 edition. A guide to university and non-profit research established on a permanent basis. Includes life sciences, social sciences, humanities and religion. Supplemented between editions by *NEW RESEARCH CENTERS.* Carnegie Library, Oakland, Reference Room.

SIXTY AND OVER? GOOD! YOU QUALIFY. Lists area volunteer opportunities and the agencies who use volunteers (useful for salaried volunteer directors). Carnegie Library, PA Room.

WHERE TO TURN, Guide to Health, Welfare and Community Services in Allegheny County. Published by HELPLINE, updated frequently. The most comprehensive local sourcebook for human service professionals. Carnegie Library, PA Room.

EDUCATION

It has been claimed that the most valuable export from Pittsburgh today is our production of engineering degrees. Education, undoubtedly, is a big business here, one of the larger industries once you add the number of employees in higher education to the over 36,000 people employed in elementary and secondary schools. As the next decade unfolds, though, growth will be modest and most jobs will take place through replacement. Successful job hunters will be dedicated, qualified and willing to apply to more than one employer.

Higher Education

Within an hour or two of the Golden Triangle there are 31 institutions of higher education and close to 100,000 full time students enrolled in 4-year colleges. Nine schools, including the 2-year *Community College of Allegheny County*, are within actual city boundaries: *Carlow College, Carnegie Mellon University, Chatham College, CCAC, Duquesne University, Pittsburgh Theological Seminary, Point Park College, Robert Morris College* and the *University of Pittsburgh*. Collectively, they employ 3,800 full time faculty and 2,400 part time faculty. The University of Pittsburgh with 8,500 total employees is the largest single employer within the city limits.

Despite a stable workforce, there are estimated to be 550 job openings yearly for college faculty, with 140 of these representing new jobs. Locally salary scales for tenured positions vary considerably from $32,000—$63,000 for full professors and from $17,000—$33,000 for instructors. Non-tenure track salaries lag behind their counterparts.

Faculty are only part of the total staffing picture. At local colleges and universities there are from two to four times as many staff as there are faculty. In higher education people are needed to provide the entire range of legal, financial, clerical, administrative and personnel services that any corporation requires. They also need employees to meet the housing, health, counseling and social activity needs of their students 24 hours a day, as well as advertising, recruiting offices and alumni services. Emphasis on fund raising has expanded the development departments of almost every college. Larger schools have several offices or divisions within the development department. The same is true of the business departments.

Librarians and permanent library staff are found in all universities, although librarians have job opportunities in community libraries such

Selected Colleges and Universities

Within City of Pittsburgh	Undergraduate Enrollment full/part time	Faculty full/part time
Carlow College	478/427	45/70
Carnegie Mellon University	4,133/157	510/138
Chatham College	435/207	51/23
Community College of Allegheny County (Allegheny Campus only)	6,670/11,305	151/1,228
Duquesne University	3,799/459	313/203
Pittsburgh Theological Seminary	238/63	20/19
Point Park College	1,056/1,615	76/99
Robert Morris College	2,987/2,097	131/87
University of Pittsburgh (Pittsburgh campus only)	13,048/5,560	2,540/643
Within Tri-State Region (10 largest, within 2 hours, not listed above)		
Allegheny College	1,844/47	154/29
California University of PA	4,420/900	279/47
Clarion University of PA	4,816/583	320/22
Edinboro University of PA	4,990/783	318/18
Grove City College	2,114/28	106/15
Indiana University of PA	11,030/1,161	682/89
Slippery Rock University	5,453/499	364/6
Westminster College	1,259/16	97/22
West Virginia University	11,736/1,064	1,180/36
Youngstown State University	9,407/4,114	450/395

Note: does not include graduate enrollment. Data gathered from public information and university sources; should not be used for rankings.

as *Mount Lebanon Public Library* and *Carnegie Library of Pittsburgh.* Other positions are in private libraries belonging to research centers, legal firms and large corporations.

A shrinking population of college-age students in the next decade means there will be no free-wheeling growth and perhaps difficulties for smaller colleges tied solely to this market. Graduate programs have grown in number and variety. M.B.A. programs can be found in a variety of formats; the University of Pittsburgh, for instance, is combining health and an M.B.A. in a joint degree program.

Adult and continuing education programs expect growth during the next decade. Larger institutions are meeting the adult market with executive programs and certificate programs. Smaller colleges are marketing specialties, like Point Park's insurance review programs, Robert Morris' preparation for professional exams (CPA, CMA, SEDS) and *Wheeling Jesuit College's* LADO, an intensive English program for foreign nationals.

Branch campuses also provide jobs. *Pennsylvania State University* has 2-year, 1,000 student branch campuses in each of Allegheny, Fayette, Beaver and Westmoreland counties. Associate degree programs are also available. The Community College of Allegheny County with 16,000 students and four campuses has grown into one of the largest community college systems in the nation. Because of their public service purpose, community colleges provide more social service-oriented job opportunities than most 4-year institutions. *Butler County* (2,000 enrollment), *Beaver County* (2,000) and *Westmoreland County* (3,000) community colleges provide associate degrees and some unique technical training programs. Non-credit education or continuing education programs usually hire instructors on a per-course contract basis.

Rounding out the post-secondary school picture are the 70 private vocational schools, most of whom specialize in technical training. The *Art Institute of Pittsburgh, Boyd School, School of Computer Technology, Duff's Business Institute, Pittsburgh Institute of Aeronautics and ICM School of Business* all have 800 or more students each year.

The biggest schools and in-city schools are the most visible to job hunters, but faculty schedules can at times accommodate a longer commuting distance than other jobs.

Elementary and Secondary Education

Jobs involved with elementary and secondary education have declined over the past 30 years, reflecting a decline in the area youth population. The biggest public school system is the *City of Pittsburgh* with 5,000 employees, over half of whom are teachers. Allegheny County has 42 school districts. Those with more than 300 teachers include *Penn Hills, North Allegheny, Woodland Hills, McKeesport Area, Mt. Lebanon, Shaler Area, Gateway* and *North Hills.* Conditions vary considerably; in some school districts money is a tight commodity and there has been substantial cutting of positions. Those with expanding populations and tax bases, such as the northern districts and *Quaker Valley* to the west, are in a more comfortable position.

Teacher Salaries, 1988-89 School Year
Selected Districts

Public School District	Starting Salary	Maximum Salary	Steps
Allegheny Valley	$19,000	$39,000*	22
Bethel Park	21,000	44,964	17
Carlynton	20,450	42,950*	15
Chartiers Valley	19,432	46,470	20
Fox Chapel	20,353	44,000	20
Gateway	23,500	42,540	18
Keystone Oaks	23,000	46,751	15
Mt. Lebanon	24,814	48,840	19
North Allegheny	24,905	45,125*	18
North Hills	NA	46,249*	16
Penn Hills	16,527	43,462	15
Pittsburgh	22,000	44,600*	10
Plum	23,500	42,350	21
South Park	21,380	40,245*	15
South Fayette	19,850	40,555	16
Upper St. Clair	22,905	50,385	19
West Allegheny	22,350	41,020	21
West Jefferson	17,240	45,240*	18
West Mifflin	18,075	44,569	16

Notes: **Starting salaries are for B.A.s.**
   Maximum salaries are for Ph.D.s, except where noted by an *, then maximums are for master's degree plus additional credits.
   "Steps" indicate the number of years it takes to reach top salary.
Source: **American Federation of Teachers, Pittsburgh.**

Salaries for teachers have been outpacing the gains of average U.S. workers in recent years. The current contract of city teachers places them among the best paid in urban districts nationwide. By 1992, the contract will push starting salaries over their current level to $28,000 and provide teachers with nine years' experience and a master's degree an annual wage of $50,990. The chart gives starting and maximum salaries for the 1988-89 school year for selected districts. Ninety-two percent of the Pittsburgh School District's teachers are at top scale. Salaries that permit schools to hire the best people assure there will be no local teacher shortage.

The greater Pittsburgh area has a relatively large Catholic population and a long established *parochial school system* supported by the diocese. It has become smaller (by 63%) since 1963 but still educates 39,000 students in a six-county area. Lay teachers labor for rewards other than money since their salary scales are only about half that of others.

Non-teachers employed by school districts include auditors, design drafters, media electronics technicians, computer programmers, psychologists and transportation field agents. Each *Intermediate Unit* in the area is another employer of those who offer special services to school districts. Schools also hire paraprofessionals as assistant teachers and security aides as well as the usual complement of clerical support staff.

Even in the relatively stable educational job market, there is movement. An estimate of average job openings for elementary and secondary teachers in the area is 730 a year with over 200 due to growth, the rest to retirements and general turnover. Pittsburgh city schools see about 280 openings a year. At this time there are needs for foreign language, high level math, science and library science teachers. The shortage of industrial arts teachers of a few years ago has been met. Special education teachers find a tight job market in Pittsburgh but are in short supply in the rest of the nation. Dual certification is desirable and minority candidates are increasingly recruited. The Pittsburgh School District, third largest in the state, has more administrative opportunities than smaller districts.

Opportunities to teach in non-traditional settings are increasing. For example, *Sylvan Learning Centers,* non-existent a few years ago, offer instruction in basic skills to elementary and high school students and use close to 50 teachers on a part-time basis. After-school and pre-school programs anticipate an inevitable expansion but such programs have yet to arrive at salary scales that do not overprice services but still attract people with educational and developmental expertise. In addition to volunteers, there will be some opportunities here for non-degreed persons, for older professionals and those who want special flexibility, as well as for younger professionals who see these jobs as their first steps up the ladder in this new career field.

Where to Find More Pittsburgh Employers in Education

AMERICAN LIBRARY ASSOCIATION DIRECTORY. National listing of private, specialized libraries owned by businesses and industries, their holdings and patron privileges. Find this at Carnegie Library, Oakland, in the PA Room.

BOOK OF BUSINESS LISTS, Pittsburgh Business Times, 1988.
- "Colleges and Universities" (25 largest Pittsburgh area, 4-year), p. 63
- "Day Care Centers" (25 largest area licensed), p. 59
- "Private Career Schools" (25 largest Pittsburgh area), p. 35

Find this at Carnegie Library, PA Room, and at the downtown Business Branch. Also at newsstands and bookstores.

BUSINESS RESOURCES DIRECTORY, Pittsburgh Council on Higher Education, 1986. Lists addresses, phone and head of each library belonging to its ten member educational institutions. Carnegie Library, PA Room.

CHILDREN'S SERVICES DIRECTORY. Programs for children who have special needs and a listing of nursery schools primarily in Allegheny County. Carnegie Library, PA Room.

CHOICES: A GUIDE TO PENNSYLVANIA'S COLLEGES AND UNIVERSITIES, 1985. Carnegie Library, PA Room.

CHRONICLE OF HIGHER EDUCATION. Weekly newspaper. Good statistics on salaries; also faculty and administrative job listings. At most college libraries. $50 annual subscription.

DIRECTORY OF LICENSED PRIVATE BUSINESS SCHOOLS AND APPROVED PROGRAMS. Free publication, Pennsylvania Department of Education, 1985. Also lists the programs they teach. Carnegie Library, PA Room.

DIRECTORY OF LICENSED PRIVATE CORRESPONDENCE SCHOOLS. Free publication, Pennsylvania Department of Education, 1985-86. Carnegie Library, PA Room.

DIRECTORY OF LICENSED PRIVATE TRADE SCHOOLS. Free publication, Pennsylvania Department of Education, Harrisburg.

DIRECTORY OF PENNSYLVANIA LIBRARIES. Free publication, Pennsylvania Department of Education, 1986. Includes some special libraries. Carnegie Library, PA Room.

DIRECTORY OF PENNSYLVANIA ASSOCIATION OF PRIVATE SCHOOL ADMINISTRATORS, 1983. Find this inside an older booklet, the *DIRECTORY OF PRIVATE SCHOOLS, TRADE SCHOOLS, CORRESPONDENCE SCHOOLS AND COMMUNITY COLLEGES.* Outdated, so check for accuracy of names. Carnegie Library, PA Room.

DIRECTORY OF SELECTED PERSONNEL AT INSTITUTIONS OF HIGHER EDUCATION IN PENNSYLVANIA. Free publication, Pennsylvania Department of Education, Harrisburg, 1987.

DIRECTORY OF SPECIAL LIBRARIES IN PITTSBURGH AND VICINITY, Special Libraries Association, Pittsburgh Chapter, 1986. Excellent for special libraries; lists staff, phone numbers, specialties and size of collection; from the Alcoa Laboratories Information Center to the St. Francis Hospital School of Nursing Library. Carnegie Library, PA Room.

41

HANDBOOK OF PRIVATE SCHOOLS, 1984. National; emphasis is on "leading" schools. Carnegie Library, PA Room.

HIGHER EDUCATION FACULTY AND STAFF. Free publication, Pennsylvania Department of Education, Harrisburg, 1985-86.

OFFICIAL DIRECTORY-CATHOLIC SCHOOLS, DIOCESE OF PITTS-BURGH, 1986-87. Includes phone numbers and addresses. Find this in an older booklet titled *ALLEGHENY COUNTY AND PITTSBURGH SCHOOLS.* Carnegie Library, PA Room.

PENNSYLVANIA COMMONWEALTH AND FEDERAL DEPOSITORY DIRECTORY, 1986. Listed alphabetically by municipality. Carnegie Library, PA Room.

PENNSYLVANIA EDUCATION ATLAS. Free publication, Pennsylvania Department of Education, 1985. Identifies and locates all school districts, intermediate units and area vocational technical schools in the state. Carnegie Library, PA Room.

PENNSYLVANIA EDUCATION DIRECTORY, Applied Arts Publisher, 1985-86. Public School Districts. Carnegie Library, PA Room.

PENNSYLVANIA RESEARCH INVENTORY PROJECT, Center for the Study of Higher Education. An inventory of research units in the state. Old (1983) but lists over a thousand research centers, both technical and academic (law, social science and health). Carnegie Library, PA Room.

PITTSBURGH PUBLIC SCHOOLS, MEMBERSHIP REPORT, 1986. Statistics on students enrolled at all 79 schools. Carnegie Library, PA Room.

PUBLIC SCHOOL PROFESSIONAL PERSONNEL. Free publication, Pennsylvania Department of Education, Harrisburg, 1985-86.

'QED'S SCHOOL GUIDE, 1987-88. For Pennsylvania: addresses, enrollments, some names of administrators, public and private schools. Carnegie Library, PA Room.

CULTURE AND LEISURE

The cultural amenities of Pittsburgh helped it win America's *Most Livable City* award. These same factors make it attractive for new firms to locate here and hard for inhabitants to move away. Pittsburgh is said to rank third (behind New York and San Francisco) in total arts funding and reportedly is in first place in per-capita spending on the arts with $17.03 per person.

Definitely a plus when it comes to recruiting newcomers, culture and leisure are also the employment of choice for a growing number of Pittsburghers. Recreation and hospitality occupations are growing, too, and add to the ambiance of the area.

Hospitality

The five major hotels downtown each have about 400 employees. The *Pittsburgh Hilton, Vista International Hotel, Westin William Penn, Sheraton Station Square* and *Hyatt Pittsburgh* all offer the services expected

Jobs Typically Filled by Local Employees at a Large Hotel/Motel

FRONT OFFICE MANAGER	RESTAURANT MANAGER	SECURITY CHIEF
NIGHT MANAGER	ASST. RESTAURANT MANAGER	SECURITY GUARDS
CONCIERGES	BANQUET CAPTAIN	
FRONT DESK CLERKS	NIGHT CHEF	STOREROOM MANAGER
DESK SUPERVISORS	BANQUET CHEF	STOREKEEPER
RESERVATION CLERKS	GARDE a MANGER	
	TIMEKEEPER	
TELEPHONE CLERKS	SOUS CHEF	RECEIVING CLERKS
FILE CLERK	LINE COOK	
BELL CAPTAIN	BAKERS	EXECUTIVE SECRETARIES
BELL PERSON	COOKS HELPERS	
DOOR PERSON	POT WASHERS	HEALTH CLUB MANAGER
	WARE WASHERS	LIFEGUARDS
ROOM SERVICE MANAGER	PANTRY PERSONS	
ROOM SERVICE CAPTAINS	BARTENDERS	HOUSEKEEPER
ROOM SERVICE WAITER/	BAR PERSONS	FLOOR SUPERVISORS
WAITRESS	FOOD WAITER/WAITRESS	HOUSEPERSONS
CATERING DIRECTOR	COCKTAIL WAITER/WAITRESS	LINENROOM ATTENDANTS
CONVENTION		
COORDINATORS	FLOOR STEWARD	LAUNDRY ROOM SUPERVISOR
CATERING RECEPTIONIST		LAUNDRY ROOM ATTENDANTS
BANQUET MANAGER	BUS PERSONS	ROOM ATTENDANTS
EXECUTIVE STEWARD	CASHIERS	PUBLIC SPACE CLEANERS
BEVERAGE MANAGER	HOSTESS	
SET UP HOUSEPERSONS	EMPLOYEE CAFETERIA ATTDNT.	SYSTEMS MANAGER
		NIGHT AUDITOR
MAINTENANCE ENGINEERS		ACCOUNTS RECEIVABLE
LANDSCAPE WORKERS		CLERK

in a corporate headquarters city. Traditionally, hotels divide jobs into front desk and back desk ones, but these include a wide variety of skills. The list here is an example of the range of talents needed in a large hotel. Typically in the hospitality field, experience and track record count more than formal education both for entry positions and for promotion. Paying your dues by working up the job ladder is standard. For top management positions in national firms, transfers are a necessary part of the advancement ladder. Suburban motels, too, are a steady employment source. All told, hotels and other types of lodging places employ about 8,000 people in the area.

Recreation

Recreation and entertainment services employ about 9,700. Recreation is a broad field. Among many others it includes the jobs of boat salespersons, amusement park workers, fitness experts, tennis racket restringers, canoe paddle makers, snowmaking machine mechanics and vacation community managers. Possibilities in entertainment are there not only for those who do it but for those who make it possible: event managers, promoters, food providers, sound and lighting professionals, those who set up and take down stages and plan for traffic and security. Then, too, the city has three professional sports teams and closely followed collegiate and high school sports events that operate with support staffs.

Trends suggest an increase in participation sports and corresponding job opportunities in these areas. Whether the sport involves pleasure boats (the number of pleasure boat licenses issued in Allegheny County each year is among the highest for any county in the country), adult softball teams, bowling leagues, sculling the Allegheny River or mountain biking in one of the city's 104 parks, there are support services and job opportunities. These jobs are especially attractive to those who have a life-long interest in the activity or who work best in an informal setting, away from a desk. Working hours may be when others have their leisure time. Job security and advancement may be very much dependent on one's own initiative. Charting yourself a career advancement course from novice to skilled practitioner who earns a family-supporting living at the work can be a vital exercise. Success and satisfaction, however, are measured by more than money alone and it is hard to beat the feeling of some people in these fields who say "It is amazing that I get paid to do what I love."

Arts

Pittsburghers take their art in large groups, like the *Three Rivers Art Festival* and the *Wind Symphony* concerts, and in small ones, like the *Renaissance and Baroque Society* concerts and openings at South Side galleries; but mostly, they take art of all kinds. For example, just in the area of chamber music we have, on an ongoing basis, two new music ensembles, an early music series, a string quartet, six recital series, an outdoor summer series and two full-time woodwind quintets, in addition to the long time *Y Music Society* and *Pittsburgh Chamber Music Society*. There are, by one count, 39 galleries for arts and crafts both non-profit and commercial.

If you are an artist or performing artist, don't feel that job hunting doesn't apply to you. Indeed, precisely because most employment agencies and the state employment service rarely have appropriate job listings for you, you need to remain in charge of your own search, defining your job market profile (see Chapter Six) and researching your potential employers more than the average person. Seek your unique niche and operate from a flexible plan that includes your first and second preferences for using your talents and abilities.

Museums

There are over 60 museums and landmarks in the area. All-volunteer and combinations of volunteer and paid professional staff are the norm but each place has its own particular mix. The museum's past history and ambitions for the future are important for the job hunter to learn in deciding which places are part of his or her primary job market. The consolidation recently of Andrew Carnegie's *Museum of Art and Natural History* in Oakland with the *Buhl Planetarium* on the North Side has made the resulting *The Carnegie* an indisputable giant in the area.

Arts Administration

Arts administration is becoming increasingly professional with more and more people acquiring a formal background from recognized schools

45

of arts administration, such as Carnegie Mellon and Drexel. The traditional route is from a volunteer role to a paid one and many organizations have a mixed staff. Average salaries nationally for 1987 are $33,073 for full-time and $12,299 for part-time arts administrators. Salaries here are low but not appreciably lower than the national averages. Partly for this reason, there is noticeable turnover in arts administration jobs. But this also reflects the creative and adventurous spirit characteristic of the whole field, as well as self-designed career development routes as administrators move from smaller to larger organizations. Such inter-organization movement is common in Pittsburgh and people freely move from the *Civic Light Opera* to the *Pittsburgh Dance Council* or from the *Pittsburgh Filmmakers* to the *Pittsburgh Center for the Arts.*

Essential for those interested in employment in the arts is to spend some time learning about the arts community first hand—see today's productions and shows—whether or not you are a newcomer. Do not rely on yesterday's impressions about organization directors and philosophies. Get it fresh. The *Pittsburgh Trust for Cultural Resources* a public-private partnership formed in 1984 to oversee the development of a downtown cultural district, has been a factor in raising the profile of arts in the area. It is an exciting time; there is more cooperation and a sharing of resources along with increased visibility for smaller arts groups. The PTCR also acts as a clearinghouse and will share its information about jobs in the arts with interested applicants.

Where to Find More Pittsburgh Employers in Culture and Leisure

ALL MUSE LITERARY NETWORK NEWS, published three times a year by the American Poetry Center, 1204 Walnut St., Philadelphia, PA 19107. Good state-wide information. Free.

ARTSOURCEBOOK: A Directory of Minority Artists in Pennsylvania and Resource Guide for Pennsylvania's Arts Constituency, Pennsylvania Council on the Arts, Harrisburg, 1983. Old but lists sponsors and presenters interested in presenting minority arts performances and exhibitions. Find this at Carnegie Library, Oakland, in the PA Room.

BOOK OF BUSINESS LISTS, Pittsburgh Business Times, 1988.
- "Co-ed Health and Fitness Clubs" (25 largest Pittsburgh area), p. 109
- "Conventions" (25 largest Pittsburgh), p. 77
- "Hotels and Motor Inns" (25 largest Pittsburgh area), p. 45

- "Luncheon Clubs" (Pittsburgh), p. 74
- "Public Entertainment Facilities" (25 largest Pittsburgh area), p. 106
- "Travel Agencies" (25 largest Pittsburgh), p. 79

Find this at Carnegie Library, PA Room and at the downtown Business Branch. Also at newsstands and bookstores.

DIRECTORY OF SELECTED EDUCATIONAL AND CULTURAL ORGANIZATIONS IN PENNSYLVANIA, 1987-89, Education Information Services, Harrisburg. Not complete, but includes aquariums, art museums, ballet companies, historical museums, nature organizations and theater companies. Carnegie Library, PA Room.

DRAMATISTS SOURCEBOOK, 1985-86, M. Elizabeth Osborn, ed., Theatre Communications Group, NY. Opportunities for playwrights, translators, composers, lyricists and librettists. Carnegie Library, Oakland, Workplace Room.

FICTION WRITERS' MARKET, Writer's Digest Books, Cincinnati, OH, 1981. Old but frequently used at the library. Kept as a desk reference book at Carnegie Library, Oakland, Reference Room.

LITERARY MARKETPLACE, R.R. Bowker Co. National list of book publishers, associations, agents, agencies, radio and television. Available through bookstores.

MOTION PICTURE MARKETPLACE, 1976. An old directory of production, talent, services and equipment for the theatrical, television and film industries. National. The 71 separate categories, from advertising agencies to wardrobe, can give you ideas applicable today. Carnegie Library, Reference Room.

OFFICIAL MUSEUM DIRECTORY, American Association of Museums, 1982. Lists art museums and organizations by state; includes addresses, principle administrators, income figures. A good general resource but check that names are accurate. Carnegie Library, Reference Room.

PENNSYLVANIA PRODUCTION MANUAL, Pennsylvania Film Bureau, Dept. of Commerce, Harrisburg. Free. Lists services and companies who can assist filmmakers coming to the state; useful for film-related employment.

PITTSBURGH ARTS RESOURCES: A CULTURAL DIRECTORY, Pittsburgh Trust for Cultural Resources, 1988. Best local collection; includes music, theater, visual arts and craft organizations with short biography of the group, addresses, contact persons and phone numbers. Carnegie Library, PA Room, and through the PTCR.

POET'S MARKETPLACE, Joseph J. Kelly, Running Press Book Publishers, Philadelphia, 1984. Sourcebook of where to get your poem published (over 400 magazines) plus list of writers' and poets' associations. Through bookstores.

SCRIPTWRITER'S NEWS (newsletter), Writer's Publishing Co., 250 W. 57th St., NY, 10019. Includes national listing of writing awards, scripts wanted, summer programs and theaters. 20 issues per year, $36.

UPDATE, monthly newsletter of the PTCR, includes job listings, available to the arts community through PTCR, Benedum-Trees Building, Pittsburgh, PA, 15222; 471-6070.

WRITER'S MARKET, Writer's Digest Books. 4,500 places to sell every kind of writing. Through bookstores.

GOVERNMENT

Over 100,000 Pittsburgh area people are employed by local, state and federal government operations making it the region's second largest employment field. The chart on the next page shows how these jobs are distributed.

The *U.S. Postal Service* employs half of the 18,000 federal government workers in the area. Federally funded hospitals, like the *Veterans Administration Medical Center,* are also big employers. Many of the Pittsburghers employed by the state of *Pennsylvania* are in jobs that involve the administration of programs and the operating of regional offices. State hospitals here have downsized about one-third, now employing only 2,500. Employment with the state police and state-owned liquor stores has remained steady.

The majority of government workers (69,000) are employed at the local level. Teachers and school employees, by far, are the largest group working for local governments. They are followed in number by administrative and office workers and by those who handle municipal services. The city of *Pittsburgh* and *Allegheny County* are the two largest sources of local government jobs. The city of Pittsburgh (5,300 employees) provides a full range of municipal services. Major units include public safety, public works, parks and recreation, engineering and water. There are regional authorities for solid waste management, for public transportation *(Port Authority Transit)* and for *Three Rivers Stadium.* Allegheny County (7,763) has responsibilities for two airports, vital records, health, youth, housing and other government services in the area. There are hundreds of *borough* and *township* units. Each has its own municipal government and often police, fire, water and street departments.

Trends

Government employment is not the stable career it once seemed, although it has a larger share of long-term employees than many other fields. Job shifts occur not only because of changes in elected administrators but because of economic conditions and national trends. One trend that experts forecast is a shift in public spending with less going for education and more for services for the elderly. Another trend is contracting for services and using part-time workers. The *U.S. Postal Service,* for example, now hires part-time workers for $5 an hour during peak times.

Government Employment
Pittsburgh Primary Metropolitan Statistical Area

	Total	Allegheny County	Fayette County	Washington County	Westmoreland County
Federal Government, Total	18,643	16,350	520	726	1,047
Post Offices	9,066	7,253	391	530	892
Hospitals	3,646	3,646	0	0	0
Federal Courts	499	495	0	2	2
Public Finance & Taxation	794	770	0	21	3
National Security	1,723	1,561	55	66	41
Administration of Social, Environmental, Health, Veterans, Trans. & Economic Programs	2,593	2,334	43	107	109
Misc. Federal Government	322	291	31	0	0
State Government, Total	13,692	7,405	1,043	2,181	3,063
Liquor Stores	821	631	32	58	100
Hospitals & Nursing Homes	3,437	1,814	0	787	836
Colleges & Universities	1,137	206	137	648	146
Public Order & Safety	1,697	789	70	115	723
Administration of Programs	2,292	1,379	526	129	258
Misc. State Government (including Highway Construction)	4,308	2,586	278	444	1,000
Local Government, Total	69,234	49,866	3,413	5,915	10,040
Local Passenger Transit	2,837	2,837	0	0	0
Water, Sanitation, etc.	1,616	896	75	157	488
Elementary & Secondary Schools	34,997	22,831	2,396	3,840	5,930
Colleges & Universities	2,937	2,528	0	0	409
Executive & Legislative Offices	22,150	16,866	797	1,638	2,849
Administration of Programs	1,339	1,027	115	88	109
Misc. Local Government	3,358	2,881	30	192	255

Source: **William Ceriani, Department of Labor & Industry, May, 1988.**
Data current as of September, 1987.

Changes at the municipal level have been forced by economic conditions. Because of drastic declines in some area tax bases, workers in some municipalities have been laid off and services reorganized. Mergers of police departments, water authorities and school districts would seem to be in the wind, but there is no predictability for these kinds of changes. The picture is not one only of job shrinkage. Some high growth geographic areas, like *Cranberry Township,* will need to expand all their services. The same is true of areas affected by the airport expansion. Realistically, essential municipal services—those like police, ambulance, fire protection, sanitation and education—will still be carried out and people will be needed to do the work, but it may be done in a fashion different than in the past. There may be fewer tax collectors and administrative layers, there may also be more part-time work and contracting to outside sources for services. Government employees, especially at the municipal level, need to be alert to turn changes into opportunities for themselves.

Government has not been a "rapid growth" field. Projections are for increases of 2.2% each year in the Pittsburgh area. Enough people, though, are employed by government that this increase places the field on the area's list of largest job gains by sheer numbers between now and 1995. Every level of government has its own set of regulations for applying and competing for jobs. See Chapter Eight for the first steps you should take for information about federal, state, county and city positions. Be aware, too, that not every position falls under civil service. Consulting spots, contract work and single project positions are most often pursued as any other job.

Where to Find More Pittsburgh Employers in Government

BLUE PAGES section of the telephone directory lists many government offices.

BOOK OF BUSINESS LISTS, Pittsburgh Business Times, 1988.
  • "Municipalities" (25 largest Allegheny County), p. 50
  Find this at Carnegie Library, Oakland, the PA Room and at the downtown Business Branch. Also at newsstands and bookstores.

BUDGETS, of the state of Pennsylvania and of the city of Pittsburgh, can be useful in learning the hierarchy of their departments and amounts of money they have to spend. Carnegie Library, PA Room.

CIVIL SERVICE COMMISSION, P.O. Box 569, Harrisburg, PA. Free pamphlets:
"Decisions—Entry Level Jobs for College Graduates"
"Entry Level Exams for College Graduates"
"Facts About Pennsylvania State Civil Service"
"Information on Rapid Promotions Examinations"
"Jobs for High School Graduates"
"Jobs in Pennsylvania State Government"
"Jobs for Skilled Hands."

COMMONWEALTH TELEPHONE DIRECTORY, 1986. A listing and the numbers of all of the state of Pennsylvania's departments, bureaus and offices. Carnegie Library, PA Room.

COUNTY EXECUTIVE DIRECTORY, Carroll Publishing. Each state divided into counties with the names of commissioners, department heads and officers. Carnegie Library, Business Branch.

MOODY'S MUNICIPAL MANUAL, Dun & Bradstreet. Gives names of officers of municipal areas, school districts and water-sewer authorities who have issued bonds. Carnegie Library, Business Branch.

MUNICIPAL EXECUTIVE DIRECTORY, Carroll Publishing. Covers municipalities the same way the *COUNTY EXECUTIVE DIRECTORY* does. Carnegie Library, Business Branch.

MUNICIPAL YEARBOOK. Covers all counties and cities with a population over 2,500. Includes police and fire, finance officers, personnel officers. Carnegie Library, Business Branch.

TRADE—WHOLESALE AND RETAIL

Fully a quarter of the employed population works in the retail and wholesale trade industry in Pittsburgh and the number is expected to grow to 237,000 by 1995.

Wholesale Trade

Currently about 52,000 people work in wholesale trade, an umbrella term that includes industrial marketing, international trade, and professional sales, as well as wholesale distribution. Wholesale trade generally means sales to businesses rather than to individuals or the selling of components used in making finished products. For example, wholesalers sell the organic chemicals used in manufacturing a line of food products or distribute name brand watches to retail jewelry stores or sell equipment used in constructing power plants. Much of the computer industry is included under this classification, since the majority of computer equipment is sold to other businesses.

Although less visible than retail trade workers, wholesale sales personnel are among the highest paid of all sales workers, some with no upper limit on the amount of commission they can earn. The more successful frequently have specialized knowledge about their products and/or trade markets, as well as being real professionals at selling. It is primarily an insider's job market for the best spots. The "Sales" section of the Want Ads only begins to hint at the kinds of job opportunities available. It is possible to become a knowledgeable job hunter in this field and it requires good investigative research, especially talking to the right people.

In some fields, such as pharmaceutical sales, sales trainee positions for college graduates especially those who have had technical or scientific coursework are a standard entry route. Another entry route is from the production side. Engineering or operations personnel may move over to sales to add this experience to their career advancement or for the attractiveness of commission income.

Retail Trade

The 162,000 people in the retail trade industry work primarily in restaurants, department stores and grocery stores. The accompanying chart details this and the expected employment in each area by 1995.

Employment in Wholesale and Retail Trade by Type of Goods Sold

INDUSTRY	1985 estimated employment	1995 projected employment
WHOLESALE TRADE TOTAL	51,730	55,000
WHOLESALE TRADE-DURABLE GOODS	35,830	38,200
WHOLESALE TRADE-NONDURABLE GOODS	15,900	16,800
RETAIL TRADE TOTAL	162,410	182,000
BUILDING MATERIALS & GARDEN SUPPLIES	4,110	4,800
GENERAL MERCHANDISE STORES	28,970	31,700
Department Stores	26,670	29,000
Other Gen. Merchandise Stores	2,300	2,700
FOOD STORES	27,860	31,100
Grocery Stores	23,050	26,000
Other Food Stores	4,810	5,100
AUTOMOTIVE DEALERS & SERVICE STATIONS	16,360	17,200
APPAREL & ACCESSORY STORES	8,800	9,000
FURNITURE & HOME FURNISHINGS STORES	5,750	6,100
EATING & DRINKING PLACES	53,840	64,000
MISCELLANEOUS RETAIL	16,720	18,100

Source: Pittsburgh Primary Metropolitan Statistical Area, Industry Trends and Outlook for Nonagricultural Wage and Salary Workers, 1985 and Projected 1995. PA Department of Labor and Industry, Office of Employment Security.

Although retail trade projects the image of a sales person in a department store or fast food outlet, only one out of four workers is employed in this fashion. The remaining three-fourths are in management, purchasing, clerical, financial, shipping and transportation jobs in the retail industry.

Pittsburgh, like much of America, has been thoroughly malled. Many of the increased jobs in retailing have come from expansion in the suburbs. Locally there are six shopping centers with over a million square feet of space: *Century III Mall, Monroeville, Ross Park, Beaver Valley, South Hills Village* and *Westmoreland Mall*. Based on an estimate of one net new job for every new 500 square feet of retail space, you can figure on about 2,400 jobs in a shopping area like the Ross Park Mall. Century III Mall, our largest, has some 200 retail stores.

Kaufmann's department stores employ over 5,500 full and part time workers; *J.C. Penney Co.* (including *Thrift Drug*) has over 4,000, as does

Sears Roebuck. Larger stores often have in-house advertising, accounting, security and handling services; in smaller operations, these business services may be handled by managers or contracted out.

National department store chains are frequently mentioned candidates for Pittsburgh locations. National franchises, such as *Hechingers* and *Jos. A. Bank,* are already here. It is from these newcomers and others like them that job growth is expected and to a lesser extent from already established retailers.

Upscale retailing established itself in the central city with *One Fifth Avenue Building, One Oxford Centre, PPG Place* and *Saks Fifth Avenue.* The 20,000 local retail establishments include many smaller retail stores, found both in the malls and in neighborhood shopping areas. Neighborhood shopping districts that want to attract customers from a broader area are identifying their own niches. Marketing packages are currently topics of avid interest in the retail community. The shopping districts of *Shadyside,* the *Strip District* and *Squirrel Hill* are well defined. *South Side, East Liberty* and *Station Square* are three more city neighborhoods actively establishing their images. Individual retailers want to attract specific kinds of customers and they select employees who project compatible images.

Restaurants and bars are labor intensive and employ close to 54,000 here. Most jobs involve the preparation and serving of food; but managers, accountants and other auxiliary staff members are also needed. *Eat'n Park,* one of the area's largest chains, has over 3,000 employees. Jobs in retail trade may be the most widely distributed geographically of all employment opportunities.

Retail stores and restaurants frequently hire on a part-time basis. Because the number of openings is high and the pay relatively low, retail sales positions are characterized by high turnover. This is an opportunity for persons who want quick employment for whatever reason. Positions in management are full time and provide opportunities for advancement, but they are not as easy to obtain. There are also commission sales positions in some stores featuring higher priced items, again, there is more competition for these spots. In the larger retail environment, companies conduct their own management and executive training. Find out if fields that you are interested in interview and hire applicants specifically for a "management training track." The retail industry demands executives with the flexibility to respond quickly as consumer tastes change. Strong marketing, merchandising and planning skills are a must.

Trade industry jobs are tied to the general health and wealth of their sales areas. Growth and recession periods affect both wholesale and retail sales, but in highly specific ways. For instance, wholesale food products sold to hospitals and institutions are rather immune to economic swings. On the other end of the scale, retail costume jewelry sales follow the swings closely. Sales of plumbing valves bear a closer relation to the level of construction than to the unemployment rate. The best firms will stay ahead of changes, move into new markets and adapt to population shifts.

Where to Find More Pittsburgh Employers in Wholesale and Retail Trade

There are few lists of Pittsburgh area firms that use professional sales personnel. Instead, when hunting for potential employers in this line of work, the usual rule is "If it is bought, someone probably sold it." If you want to sell, figure out first what it is you want to sell then find out who makes it. If one of the previous or following sections includes what you want to sell, check out the *"Where to Find More Pittsburgh Employers"* list there. Products made in Pittsburgh need to be sold; products distributed from here need to be sold. Products and services headquartered elsewhere also need regional salespersons to cover the Western Pennsylvania territory. Service fields like health, education and finance, increasingly, use sales professionals.

BOOK OF BUSINESS LISTS, Pittsburgh Business Times, 1988.
- "Employers" (largest Beaver County), p. 49
- "Employers" (largest Cambria, Somerset Counties), p. 110
- "Employers" (largest Erie County), p. 110
- "Employers" (largest Washington County), p. 49
- "Privately Held Firms" (50 largest Pittsburgh area), p. 103 (1987 edition)
- "Restaurant Chains" (17 largest in Allegheny County), p. 67
- "Shopping Malls and Centers" (23 largest in area), p. 84

Find this at Carnegie Library, Oakland, in the PA Room, and at the downtown Business Branch. Also at newsstands and bookstores.

CLASSIFIED DIRECTORY OF PRODUCTS AND SERVICES, Smaller Manufacturers Council, Pittsburgh, 1984-85. Directory of their 2500+ local members and of their products and services. Carnegie Library, PA Room. Current edition is available for sale ($90) and for limited individual use at the office of the SMC.

DIRECTORY OF MANUFACTURERS' SALES AGENCIES 1986, MANA publisher, CA. Carnegie Library, Oakland, Workplace Room.

GREATER ALLEGHENY REGIONAL INDUSTRIAL BUYING GUIDE, annual, Thomas Regional Directory Co., NY. A regional edition (41 tri-state counties), by the publishers of *THOMAS' REGISTER,* the standard buyers reference guide. Tells who makes what but only lists those who pay to be included; has a manufacturing orientation rather than a service one. Carnegie Library, PA Room.

INDUSTRIAL DIRECTORY: MANUFACTURING FACILITIES IN ALLEGHENY COUNTY, Greater Pittsburgh Chamber of Commerce 1985-86 ed. Lists firms with 50 or more employees. Carnegie Library, PA Room.

MACRAE PENNSYLVANIA STATE INDUSTRIAL DIRECTORY, 1987, MacRae's Blue Book Inc., NY. County-by-county breakdown. Carnegie Library, PA Room.

MAJOR FIRMS IN THE PITTSBURGH METRO AREA, Greater Pittsburgh Chamber of Commerce, 1987. Brief descriptions of 187 area firms with names of principals. Carnegie Library, PA Room.

PENNSYLVANIA DIRECTORY OF MANUFACTURERS, 1987-88 ed. Commerce Register Inc. Lists industries, mostly manufacturing, with 6 or more employees, city-by-city breakdown. Carnegie Library, PA Room.

PENNSYLVANIA EXPORTERS DIRECTORY 1985. Free publication, Department of Commerce, Harrisburg.

PENNSYLVANIA IMPORTERS. Free publication, Department of Commerce, Harrisburg. Listing of importers and their product lines.

PENNSYLVANIA MANUFACTURERS REGISTER 1988, published by Manufacturers News, Inc. Incomplete but, for those included, contains a description of products and the types of computers they use. Carnegie Library, PA Room.

SOUTHWESTERN PENNSYLVANIA INTERNATIONAL BUSINESS DIRECTORY, Penn's Southwest Association, 1987. A guide to the region's international business services. Carnegie Library, PA Room.

THOMAS' REGISTER, Thomas Publishing, NY. 115,000 U.S. companies and office locations. Several parts: I Products & Services Volumes; II The Company Profiles Volumes; III Selected Catalogues; and IV Inbound Traffic Guide. Newest edition usually at Carnegie Library, downtown Business Branch.

WHO'S WHO IN BUSINESS IN THE MOST LIVABLE CITY IN AMERICA, 1986-87 membership directory of the Greater Pittsburgh Chamber of Commerce. Carnegie Library, PA Room.

RESEARCH

Research is an important field in Pittsburgh and Pittsburgh's research is important. It has been growing for the past 30 years and by one account, more than 25,000 scientists, engineers and supporting technical personnel are on local research and development payrolls. Pittsburgh may well be the third largest research center in the country, following only Boston and California. The $1.18 *billion* spent annually here by the over 170 laboratories—63 of them major by any standard—pump both money and opportunities into the economy.

There are several interdependent reasons for this field's local prominence. Traditionally, major corporations maintain research facilities near their headquarters and Pittsburgh's Fortune 500 corporate presence results in second-to-none industry related research here. Second is the growth of two strong research-oriented universities within blocks of each other. The bent of both Carnegie Mellon University and the University of Pittsburgh is toward high technology: computer science and engineering research especially for the one, medical and scientific research a strong suit for the other. Over time a link between academicians and salaried researchers has evolved. If research facilities grow strong enough they attract related research, spin off other types and provide a market that can support independent commercial labs. The synergism often leads to products for advanced technology firms. All these elements are present today: there is corporate research, institution supported research through universities, hospitals and government funded agencies and there are independent research labs.

Corporate Research

Westinghouse's Research and Development Center is a world class industrial research facility. The eight building, 150 acre campus-like center spends $120 million a year on salaries. Of the 1500 people there, about 600 are professionals (400 with Ph.D.s), 500 are technical support personnel and 400 are general support workers. These proportions between staff types probably also apply to other research establishments. Westinghouse's three major areas of research are *materials* (batteries, ceramics, composite technologies, laser metal working, dielectrics, polymer technologies), *solid state sciences* (microelectronics, crystal growth and superconductor materials, process design, sensor technologies, plasma, nuclear and radiation physics, optics) and *engineering* (voice and vision manufacturing systems, robotics, integrated systems, fiber optics and sensor systems, applied artificial intelligence, process engineering for chemical based manufacturing). At the research center, scientific professionals have dual paths for career advancement. In addition to the traditional rise through administrative ranks, there is a technical path for those who flourish by working within their scientific disciplines.

A separate but related Westinghouse research division is the *Corporate Productivity and Quality Center*. Started here in 1980 to demonstrate and develop systems to improve manufacturing technologies in Westinghouse plants, it is now expanding its focus to include white collar productivity. Westinghouse also operates the *Bettis Atomic Power Laboratory* for the Department of Energy. Because of their sheer number, former Westinghouse employees now populate many smaller firms while others have moved on to form their own research related companies.

Other corporate research includes *H.J. Heinz* which, as expected, has a food research lab. *Alcoa* operates several labs in the Allegheny Valley: the *Aluminum Research Laboratory* (100 employees), the 1,300 employee *Alcoa Technical Center* doing materials research and the newly added *Composites Manufacturing and Technology Center* (at Upper Burrell). Research is seen as a way to keep the 100 year-old company on a path of successful evolution. *PPG Industries'* research into glass, coatings and resins, and fiberglas occurs in its labs in Hampton, Springdale borough and Harmar township. Currently it plans to move its chemical division's 150 workers and lab to the Pittsburgh area. The expressed purpose is to let research and marketing employees work closer together and develop ties to Pittsburgh's academic community. *Mobay Corporation,* quietly growing into a major presence here since 1958, maintains administrative headquarters and extensive applications research facilities on its 300 acre site in Robinson Township. Its focus is on polymeric activities in the field of materials engineering and it maintains polycarbonate extrusion laboratories.

Most large manufacturers have research and development support. *Wheelabrator Technical Center* researches waste and energy processes. Alloy steel research takes place at *USX Labs*. *Allegheny Ludlum,* leading producer of specialty materials, expected to spend over $32 million in 1987 in R & D technologies. Its research facilities in Natrona Heights employ 400 people who work on process improvements and applications for stainless, electrical and high-temperature alloy steels.

Corporate research labs are often tied to the locations of their companies. For instance, when National Steel Corporation moved to its new Detroit-based headquarters, R & D moved, too. The corporate lab facility itself, in nearby West Virginia, was sold to *Weirton Steel Corpora-*

tion, the employee stock ownership plan that purchased National's steel operation in Weirton, WV. Likewise, Gulf Oil Corporation's research center, at its peak in the late 1970s when it employed 2,000 and operated on a budget in excess of $100 million, became an excess facility with the Chevron takeover. The University of Pittsburgh received title to the property, a 55 building complex with over 400 labs. The research park is being rented out now with hopes it will employ 2,500 by 1993. It offers expansion space to other corporate labs (like Alcoa and PPG), space for the university's research and provides unique incubator facilities for independent research and scientific firms. Among current operations there are an analytical lab, a chemical processing simulation pilot plant, an automotive testing firm, a commercial fungi farm *(Mycorrtech Inc.)* and a crystal-growing firm *(Mercury LPE).*

Although chemicals, energy, metals and composite materials are heavily represented in Pittsburgh, corporate research also involves optical instruments, medical equipment and biological research into pollution.

Institutional Research

Research supported by institutions like government agencies and foundations takes place for the most part in universities and hospitals. The growth of funded research has been considerable. In 1982, the *University of Pittsburgh* had about $61 million and *Carnegie Mellon University* $37 million in research money; in 1988 they received more than $100 million each. The emphasis, in addition to health, is on computer software development, artificial intelligence and the solid state sciences. There is also research in economics, psychology and the social sciences.

The University of Pittsburgh oversees considerable health related research exploring cancer, AIDS, affective disorders, hypertension and epidemiology issues in its graduate schools and in the *University Health System.*

Carnegie Mellon has focused on sophisticated software development and advanced engineering. The original *Mellon Institute* founded in the 1930s to perform mission-oriented research for industry is now a part of the university and has 170 employees. The Department of Defense, National Science Foundation, the Defense Advanced Research Project Agency and the Office of Naval Research all fund projects at the *Software Engineering Institute* (about 190 employees, 140 of whom are in technical support positions), the *Robotics Institute* (125 employees) and the *Supercomputer Center* (35 employees) operated jointly with the University of Pittsburgh.

Carnegie Mellon and the University of Pittsburgh are sharing operation of the *Pittsburgh Technology Center,* being established on the site of the razed J & L steel mill along Second Avenue. This development is a fitting symbol of the transformation in employment opportunities that has taken place.

Government research occurs at the *Bruceton Research Center* and includes the *Energy Technology Center* (Department of Energy), the smaller *Mine Safety and Health Research Center* (Department of Labor) and the *Bureau of Mines' Coal and Mining Research Center* (Department of the Interior).

Universities and institutions have centers of study and research that are too numerous to mention. Only some of this work catches the public's eye and most newspaper articles focus on the results of the research rather than the employment opportunities involved. For instance, the general public is hardly aware that the *Allegheny-Singer Research Institute,* a subsidiary of Allegheny Health Services, has 100 employees. Although most jobs go to specialists, no project operates with researchers alone. Needed are clerical and, increasingly, computer support staff, along with respective medical, paraprofessional and mechanical technical support personnel.

Independent Research

The very favorable atmosphere for research in Pittsburgh is evidenced by the presence and growth of commercial laboratories. The long-established *Pittsburgh Testing Lab* is the world's largest independent testing facility. *Graphic Arts Technical Foundation, Bituminous Coal Research, M.K. Research and Development Co.,* and *West Penn Testing Laboratories* are all private research facilities. *Anter Laboratories* (18 employees) makes scientific instruments for research firms; *Zivic-Miller Labs* does contract biological research; *Applied Test Systems* in Saxonburg has 61 employees. *Satec Systems* makes special testing machines for metals; *American Glass Research* is involved with glass testing equipment.

Except for the larger firms, research jobs are not always easy for the job hunter, especially a newcomer, to track down. Talking to people, asking for reports and becoming active in local associations are good ways to raise your awareness of what is going on in smaller companies, hospitals and universities.

Where to Find More Pittsburgh Employers in Research

BOOK OF BUSINESS LISTS, Pittsburgh Business Times, 1988.
- "Computer Software Firms" (25 largest Pittsburgh-based), p. 87
- "Corporations" (24 top Pittsburgh), p. 27
- "On-going Sponsored Research Projects at Universities" (25 largest area), p. 59
- "Public Companies" (50 largest Pittsburgh area), p. 99

Find this at Carnegie Library, Oakland, in the PA Room and at the downtown Business Branch. Also at newsstands and bookstores.

CORPORATIONS REVIEW, annual publication. Names of directors and descriptions of 105 Western Pennsylvania companies. Carnegie Library, PA Room and Business Branch. Purchasable through Oliver Realty.

PENNSYLVANIA RESEARCH INVENTORY PROJECT, Center for the Study of Higher Education. An inventory of research units in Pennsylvania. Old (1983), but lists over a thousand research centers in both technical fields and academic research. Carnegie Library, PA Room.

PITTSBURGH HIGH TECHNOLOGY COUNCIL MEMBERSHIP DIRECTORY, annual. Carnegie Library, PA Room and in the Workplace Room, Oakland.

RESEARCH CENTERS DIRECTORY, Gale Research Co., 1982 edition. Guide to university and non-profit research established on a permanent basis, includes agriculture, conservation, engineering and technology, mathematics, physical and earth sciences and non-technical fields. Supplemented between editions by *NEW RESEARCH CENTERS.* Carnegie Library, Oakland, Reference Room.

SOFTWARE WRITERS' MARKETPLACE, D. Joyce & J.E. Pickering, Running Press Book, Philadelphia, 1984. Lists companies who will buy your software program. Check that firms are still in existence. Carnegie Library, Oakland, the Workplace Room.

ADVANCED TECHNOLOGY AND MANUFACTURING

The line between advanced technology firms and many manufacturing firms is blurred today, for the manufacturing firms with the brightest prospects are those whose management have their feet firmly planted in the future and whose workers are retooled by the most modern technologies. To emphasize this reality for today's job hunter, advanced technology and manufacturing are combined in this section.

Manufacturing, once automatically counted on for high paying blue- and white-collar jobs, has been almost overly discounted in regard to its positive contribution to the local economy. Compared to the past, the manufacturing situation in the area is painfully obvious. The steel industry employs half the number it did ten years ago. Manufacturing was concentrated in the materials production field, a mature market undergoing a three decade decline that abruptly accelerated in the mid 1980s. Of the manufacturing remaining in the area, new equipment and updating of existing processes raised efficiency and meant survival for some, but by no means all, companies. While no return to the employment numbers of the past is ever expected, manufacturing jobs increased by several thousand during 1988, the first increase in many years.

If expectations remain realistic, advanced technology in Pittsburgh can be seen for what it is: a definite component of the present economy; an employment field that may double in size by the year 2000 and employ 15% of the work force; one that employs about 90,000 in 1,000 firms today. By one estimate, fully a quarter of the *new* jobs formed here since 1984 are technology-related ones.

What is an advanced technology firm? Generally it refers to firms that begin the commercial production of technological developments. By that standard, Westinghouse Air Brake was a high-tech firm when it was established in 1869 to make and sell the newly invented railroad car brake. Likewise, a local manufacturer of mass spectrometers could slip out of the high-tech category if it did not continually produce advanced products. Firms need not be small or new, either. Westinghouse Electric Corporation's 1,000 employee *Automation Division* in O'Hara township qualifies because of its emphasis on the commercial applications of new technology.

High-Tech Products from Pittsburgh

Percentage of Firms Selling Products in the Following Areas	%
Medical	31
Computer Hardware	28
Software	28
Industrial Automation	25
Process Control	25
Military	21
Aerospace	18
Electronic Components	17
Telecommunications	16
Energy	16
Nuclear	14
Advanced Materials	13
Environment	13
Robotics	13
Artificial Intelligence	6
Pharmaceuticals	4
Biotechnical	3

Note: **More than 72% of the companies surveyed generate sales in more than two product areas; over 42% have sales in four or more.**
Source: **Reed Smith, 1986 survey of 100 companies. Reported in the *Pittsburgh Post-Gazette,* December 9, 1986.**

What do these firms do? Computers are often—but not necessarily—used in making or are components of advanced technology products. Applications may involve synthetic enzyme manufacture, the use of lasers or radioisotopes, waste water treatment systems or energy conservation processes. There are advanced technology firms with more familiar products like display panels, gauges, testing equipment, automated conveyors, computerized milling machines, motors and automatic temperature and lighting controls. A study showed that most are involved in the production or service of more than one product (see the chart). About half are involved in manufacturing and half of that manufacturing involves electronic equipment or instruments. Computer software and industrial automation (which is part of the instrumentation field) are the most developed high technology fields locally; materials engineering could be called the high-tech of the heavy manufacturing field; and biotechnology holds untapped potential.

Computer Software

Silicon Valley is recognized as a source of computer hardware, but Pittsburgh is gaining recognition as a center for the development of software, especially in the areas of expert systems (which has origins in defense funded research) and engineering software (which builds on the area's industrial heritage).

Carnegie Group (160 employees) has developed artificial intelligence software to solve problems and do diagnostics for firms like Ford Motor Co. *Intelligent Technology* (90 local employees) was launched to develop "smart" software that allows computers to mimic human decision making, primarily for information management and investment portfolio management. One of the stars of the local software business, *Duquesne Systems,* with a 200-person Pittsburgh work force, develops system productivity software for IBM products and is due for a name change because of its merger with Morino Inc. *Actronics Inc.* (now back up to 23 employees) pioneers in the interactive video disc market with a series of software-video disc programs used for training by the American Heart Association. The product permits users to participate in a video simulation of cardiac training and emergency cardiac situations.

The market for engineering software is relatively new, whereas other software markets—such as accounting—are already dominated by industry giants. Of the 146 area software firms, 17 are marketing their wares to engineers and the potential exists for Pittsburgh to create a name for itself as a center for engineering software. Probably the oldest and largest is *Swanson Analysis Systems,* of Houston, PA, founded in 1970 with over 100 employees today. One of Swanson's products, ANSYS, enables engineers to build computer models of structures for design and analysis purposes. *Iconnex Corporation,* a North Side company frequently mentioned as a leading firm, introduced its first product in late 1987, "M.E. Workbench," a conceptual design tool that allows mechanical engineers to manipulate both rough drawings and calculations. Another firm is *Formtek* (70 employees) whose engineering document management system is a player in an emerging market that has great potential.

Computer related equipment is sold by *Black Box Corp.,* primarily a distributor through catalog sales of cables and data communications connectors. It expects a spurt in its 74 million in sales (1987) because it jumped the market in supplying flame-resistant computer cable that meets new industry codes.

Biotechnology

Western Pennsylvania is betting a lot of money over the next few years on the development of a commercial biotechnology and biomedical industry, as the University of Pittsburgh's *Biotechnology and Bioengineering Center* takes root at the Pittsburgh Technology Center. Certainly the intrinsic resources are here: medical labs and research, sophisticated health services that are consumers of such products, venture capital and industrial corporations (like *Bayer, Westinghouse* and *PPG*) with interests in the biomedical field.

Currently there are approximately 35 viable biomedical companies operating in the region, with most involved in the development of medical diagnostic equipment. One of the oldest is *Medrad,* begun in 1959 with 8 staffers and now employing 450 people. This company primarily designs and manufacturers disposable equipment for angiographic studies (visualization of blood vessels by means of a photo).

Biotechnology, considered broadly as chemicals, food production and pharmaceuticals, is expected to be a long term growth area because Pittsburgh is headquarters not only for *Heinz* but for *Mobay,* a chemical firm, and *Aristech,* a firm that became a Fortune 500 company the moment it was formed from the chemical assets of USX Corporation. *Mylan Laboratories,* a generic drug producer in nearby West Virginia, has been expanding its production since 1965. According to a study by the Advanced Technology Center, the city's strengths in biotechnology exist in the areas of medical imaging, specifically in nuclear magnetic resonance (NMR) technology and cancer therapy research. Local advantages include the existence of the *Pittsburgh Supercomputing Center* and the relatively large number of X-ray crystallographers who work in the area. We have considerable expertise in biomedical data management networks, molecular biology, biosensors, fluorescent markers and medical instrumentation.

Instrumentation

For years Pittsburgh manufacturers have produced instruments like gauges, regulators and industrial valves. *Fisher Scientific* is a hometown firm that has maintained a respected position in the field throughout a series of takeovers and mergers. *Mine Safety Appliances* (1,780 employees) makes not only safety equipment but process control instruments. *Contraves-Goerz* produces measuring instruments, industrial controls and optical machinery. Westinghouse Electric keeps on the forefront of changes with its *Engineering and Instrumentation Division*, currently a part of its Advanced Industrial Systems Group. *MegaScan Technologies,* based in Gibsonia, manufacturers high-resolution graphic computer systems used primarily by the electronic printing and publishing industry.

Not long ago, "robotics" was a buzz-word. Today, robotic machinery is seen as one component of automated process controls. In the words of one instrumentationist, "It's the whole plant now, not just one machine, that's being automated." This is CIM—computer-integrated manufacturing. It uses computers and related electronic devices such as sensors, robots and driverless vehicles to tie together the diverse operations in a typical manufacturing enterprise, including product design, purchasing, production and inventory management. These systems are the buzz-words of today. The manufacturing engineers who prove capable of managing this integration of what once were very separate disciplines are expected to compete with financiers, lawyers and marketers for the top positions in the corporate America of the 21st century.

Process controls, robotics, industrial automation, automated system *anythings*—are part of a complex continuum that involves engineering, software design and manufacturing. It seems natural for firms making these products to take root in Pittsburgh. *American Cimflex Corporation* is an example; this local advanced technology firm, which was called American Robots until 1986, anticipates growth for its new family of production management products, the spin-off of a two year military research project. Cimflex broadened its focus from robots to building computer automated systems that include robots for industrial manufacturing sites. Cimflex products can coordinate electronic production so that circuit boards may be designed within a computer and immediately moved through controllers and robots to the factory floor for quick production changes. When completed, its merger with Teknowledge Inc. will increase its artificial intelligence base and position it for future products.

Materials Engineering

The circumstances which made large-volume materials manufacturing the heart of Pittsburgh's economy are gone. But considerable knowledge and capital assets have grown up around materials manufacturing in the region and many of these assets are being redirected into "engineered materials." These advanced materials encompass everything from radical new developments—like magnetic bubble information storage media—to enhancement of existing materials based on new formulations, combinations or processing approaches. High performance aluminum alloys, reaction injection molded polymers, titanium shape-memory alloys, float-zone silicon and ceramic-matrix composites are examples of engineered materials being developed in the area. Specialty steels are examples of commodity-type materials that have been engineered for specific market niches.

Three primary strategic trends are evident: concentration on higher value-added products; forward integration (producing components that are finished or near-finished for their end-use customers) and increased flexibility and miniaturization in manufacturing. Manufacturing of these products relies more on specialized expertise and equipment than mass manpower. New materials ventures can be outgrowths of corporate research centers, such as the production of ultra-pure silicon electronic materials at *Westinghouse* and specialty ceramics at *PPG*; there is also an emerging core of entrepreneurial start-ups, like the *ALTA Group* and *II-IV Inc.*

Predictions are that Pittsburgh will continue as a center for materials and manufacturing expertise. Its strengths in research and development will translate into entrepreneurial activity. *Gatan, Suprex, Advanced Metallurgy, Dynamet* and *Solid State Measurements* are all examples of materials-related, entrepreneurial companies. While this does not translate into substantial manufacturing employment, these firms are representative of the smaller firms in which employment growth takes place.

Not every job in an advanced technology firm is a great one; a data entry operator or purchasing assistant may have no path for upward mobility. Nor is every firm a successful one, even if it is a part of a growth industry. In terms of where future jobs in advanced technology will be, one study showed that most of the growth is with firms that are over ten years old. Electrical engineers continue to have opportunities. Secretaries with word processing skills who can make office functions flow smoothly are in demand at salaries in the high teens and low twenties.

Executive recruiters feel that there are a number of local firms just past the start-up phase whose hiring is shifting from a technical, engineering orientation to adding marketing and customer service professionals. National job searches and mergers are ways upper level employees are added. Where do these firms find their other employees? One company recruiter said that, especially for clericals, technicals and entry level jobs, they rarely run want ads or use employment agencies. Much is done by word of mouth: current employees are asked who they know. "We look to local colleges, the Community College and one of the tech schools, too," he said. "Off the street, we'll see those who happen to come in when we need someone and those who keep their applications current." In short, you've got to find *them* and follow up until they have a job opening.

Manufacturing

Manufacturing in Pittsburgh once meant steel; today it appears to mean specialty steel, chemicals and a small light manufacturing segment.

Southwestern Pennsylvania, center of the nation's specialty steel industry today, is benefiting from current import quotas and tarriffs. *Allegheny Ludlum Steel,* the nation's largest specialty producer, *J & L Specialty Steel, Armco, Cyclops* and *Washington Steel* all have plants in the area. Armco Steel's Specialty Steel Division in Butler has hired 400 new employees since August 1986, and now employs 2,900. With plants in West Leechburg, Natrona and Brackenridge, Allegheny Ludlum employment reaches 4,500 hourly and salaried workers. One of the reasons for the company's success is its emphasis on advanced technologies.

H.J. Heinz Company has improved production while the number of production jobs has dropped slowly. The North Side-headquartered plant's use of sophisticated food processing equipment lets them pack 11,712 single-service ketchup pouches each minute of the day. The *Pittsburgh Brewing Company's* investment in equipment permits daily production of the equivalent of 2.75 million bottles of beer. *PPG* has local plants in Greensburg, East Deer, O'Hara and Ford City.

Manufacturing may be on the upswing but that doesn't mean more job security. Plants are still subject to closure, downsizing and decisions to invest new technologies in plants that are closer to market areas. While a flooded job market has been the norm for manufacturing workers, both in management and production, recruiters see some pickup in the call for those with specialty steel experience. Production jobs have a seemingly endless pool of applicants but many who used to be appropriate no longer fit, for these jobs are requiring increasing skills for entry positions.

Light manufacturing is developing a regional presence. Firms like *TRACO* and newly public operations like *Tuscarora Plastics* show that they are a successful part of the new economy.

Western Pennsylvania has long been home for chemical firms. Production facilities for most are located away from Pittsburgh but hundreds are employed in the operations of major companies headquartered here. *Mobay, Alcoa, PPG Industries, Calgon Corp., Calgon Carbon Corp.* and *Fisher Scientific* are active in the manufacture of chemicals; some concentrate on commodity, others on specialty chemicals. The future for Pittsburgh's chemical companies is said to lie in their ability to develop new products and create new applications for plastics, resins and other products. Quality control personnel are always needed and sales personnel with technical orientations are desirable.

There are smaller chemical related firms like *LabChem* that custom manufacture chemicals for laboratories and *Microseeps* a firm that uses geochemical technology to detect the underground presence of hazardous materials. *Pennrun Corporation* analyzes the components of hazardous physical and chemical substances. The growing field of hazardous waste consulting and disposal includes firms like *Ecology Equipment, Petroclean and WMMC,* as well as Westinghouse.

Where to Find More Pittsburgh Employers in Advanced Technology and Manufacturing

BOOK OF BUSINESS LISTS, Pittsburgh Business Times, 1988.
- "Computer Software Firms" (25 largest Pittsburgh-based), p. 87
- "Employers" (largest Beaver County), p. 47
- "Employers" (largest Cambria, Somerset Counties), p. 110
- "Employers" (largest Erie County), p. 110
- "Employers" (largest Washington County), p. 49
- "Interconnect Suppliers" (largest Pittsburgh area), p. 93

Find this at Carnegie Library, Oakland, in the PA Room, and at the downtown Business Branch. Also at newsstands and bookstores.

CLASSIFIED DIRECTORY OF PRODUCTS AND SERVICES, Smaller Manufacturers Council, Pittsburgh, 1984-85. Directory of its 2500+ local members and of their products and services. Carnegie Library, PA Room. Current edition is available for sale ($90) and for limited individual use at the office of the SMC.

CORPORATIONS REVIEW, annual publication. Names of directors and divisional officers and a short history of 105 large Western Pennsylvania companies. Carnegie Library, PA Room and Business Branch. Purchasable through Oliver Realty.

GREATER ALLEGHENY REGIONAL INDUSTRIAL BUYING GUIDE, Thomas Regional Directory Co., NY, annual. A regional edition (41 tri-state counties), by the publishers of the standard buyers' reference guide. Tells who makes what but only lists those who pay to be included; has a manufacturing orientation rather than a service one. Carnegie Library, PA Room.

INDUSTRIAL DIRECTORY: MANUFACTURING FACILITIES IN ALLEGHENY COUNTY, Greater Pittsburgh Chamber of Commerce, 1985-86 edition. Lists firms with 50 or more employees. Carnegie Library, PA Room.

MACRAE PENNSYLVANIA STATE INDUSTRIAL DIRECTORY, 1987, MacRae's Blue Book Inc., NY. County-by-county breakdown. Carnegie Library, PA Room.

MOODY'S CORPORATE MANUALS, especially the *INDUSTRIAL MANUAL* and the *OTC INDUSTRIAL MANUAL,* Dun & Bradstreet Corp., NY. Carnegie Library, Oakland, second floor Reference Room; newest editions will be found at the downtown Business Branch.

PENNSYLVANIA DIRECTORY OF MANUFACTURERS, Commerce Register Inc., 1987-88 edition. Lists industries, mostly manufacturing, with six or more employees, city-by-city breakdown. Carnegie Library, PA Room.

PENNSYLVANIA FOOD PROCESSING AND PACKAGING EQUIPMENT DIRECTORY, 1986. Free publication from Department of Commerce, Harrisburg.

PENNSYLVANIA MANUFACTURERS REGISTER 1988, published by Manufacturers News, Inc. Incomplete but, for those included, contains a description of products and the types of computers they use. Carnegie Library, PA Room.

PENNSYLVANIA MINING EQUIPMENT AND SERVICES DIRECTORY, 1986. Free publication from Department of Commerce, Harrisburg.

PENNSYLVANIA PETROLEUM AND PETROCHEMICAL DIRECTORY, 1986. Free publication from Department of Commerce, Harrisburg.

PITTSBURGH HIGH TECHNOLOGY COUNCIL MEMBERSHIP DIRECTORY. About 300 listings. 1985-86 edition at Carnegie Library, Oakland, Workplace Room; current edition in the PA Room.

THOMAS' REGISTER, Thomas Publishing, NY. 115,000 U.S. companies and office locations. Several parts: I Products & Services Volumes; II The Company Profiles Volumes; III Selected Catalogues; and IV Inbound Traffic Guide. Newest edition usually at Carnegie Library, downtown Business Branch.

PROFESSIONAL SERVICES
LAW—ENGINEERING—ACCOUNTING

Several factors contribute to the growth of professional service firms in Pittsburgh during this decade. First is the downsizing that shrunk corporate staffs and resulted in the contracting out of essential business services. Independent professional service providers and their firms benefited. Another is the increasing complexity of doing business. Medium-sized firms need legal advice for contracts, benefit consultants for pension plans and specially tailored computer programs. Small firms, too, must follow today's maze of tax and accounting regulations and are expected to go to market using up-to-date approaches.

Law

The over 4,000 lawyers in the area are joined every year by a new crop of law graduates: about 400 or so from the University of Pittsburgh and Duquesne University combined. Three-quarters of them usually end up staying in the region. Even with moderate growth in the field of law, it is understandable that the market is competitive. Yet law is still a potentially lucrative profession in Pittsburgh—especially for someone with top grades. In the words of one recruiter, "While there is a glut of law graduates with mediocre grades, there is no overflow of the *Law Review* students." The top five local firms want to talk to the top students, who also have good options with out-of-town firms. The recruiting committees of local law firms fill entry level associate positions at starting salaries that range from $32,000 at mid-sized firms to $50,000 at the largest. There is the other side of the salary coin, too: lawyers who never top $40,000 or ones who have trouble finding work. Starting salaries in solo practices are usually low. In a survey, to which about half of a recently graduated class replied, 60% (of those who replied) were employed by private law firms; corporate (11%) and government employment (9%) along with clerkships (15%) accounted for most of the rest.

The city has four firms with over 100 lawyers: *Reed Smith Shaw & McClay* (191), *Buchanan Ingersoll* (165), *Eckert Seamans Cherin & Mellott* (155) and *Kirkpatrick & Lockhart* (145). There are about 20 mid-sized firms with more than 20 partners. The growth of inexpensive legal clinics such as those made famous by *Hyatt Legal Services* (eight offices in the Pittsburgh area) is at the expense of independent neighborhood lawyers. Standard Hyatt staffing of an office includes three attorneys and three legal secretarial assistants who handle bookkeeping, clerical and customer contact responsibilities.

Personnel at law firms often total two or three times the number of law partners. The paralegal profession is predicted to be a fast growing field during the next ten years. There is no clear demarcation between the roles of legal assistants and paralegals in some firms, persons with and without college degrees are found in both, but more firms expect a college degree. Several local schools have paralegal programs. Without a law degree, there is a cap on professional advancement specifically within the legal industry, but the kinds of skills developed by paralegals, such as becoming knowledgeable about real estate, tax law, labor law or contract law, translate well into corporate settings. Paralegal skills are also marketable to banks, insurance agencies and the health care industry.

Engineering

Career opportunities in the engineering field have been influenced by both positive and negative factors. Nationally, electronics and autos have slumped; petroleum and aerospace engineering have been hard hit. The downsizing of corporate giants—which included production and professional staffs—means the recruiting of fewer entry graduates, including engineers. This has had an impact in Pittsburgh. So, too, has the lack of expenditures for capital equipment and the absence of steel mill construction, the two areas in which many engineering firms in Pittsburgh specialized. All this has meant lean times during the 1980s.

Positively, the change in the value of the dollar in 1987 made firms like *United Engineering* competitive internationally. Its landing a contract in 1988 to design a $60 million rolling mill for An Feng Steel Co. in Taiwan, means it will require up to 100 more engineers, draftspersons and other workers at its Fort Duquesne headquarters. *Combustion Engineering's* participation (with Occidental Petroleum) in the biggest joint U.S.-Soviet venture ever, to build massive industrial plants in the Soviet Union should also have a positive local effect, as should an increase in planned capital expenditures.

Consulting engineers, independent professional engineers who perform services for clients on a fee basis, are involved heavily in bridge and highway design as well as municipal and institutional building and environmental engineering. Large local firms include *Michael Baker Corporation*, with 167 registered engineers, *GAI Consultants* (62), *The Chester Engineers* (39), *Mosure & Syrakis Co.* (40) and *SAI Consulting Engineers* (27).

Since engineering is essentially a "service" offered to clients, persons interested in career growth within the industry are advised to acquire human relations skills. Computer-aided drafting and design technologies are dramatically changing cost and time relationships. The temporary and contract hiring of engineers and technicians that was seen during the mid-1980s is still a reality of the local job market, but the pool of talent available for temporary work is shrinking.

Accounting

Accountants, like engineers, typically make a comfortable living but don't often reach the very top of the pay scales, except for those who make senior partner in one of the "Big 8" accounting firms.

The largest job market for accountants (60%) is in businesses (of all types) that need specialized preparation and analysis of financial information, ranging from bookkeeping to advising on company growth and acquisition. National salary averages for accountants are $20,577–$59,519; for auditors, $21,128–$39,253; for public accountants, $19,657–$31,416. (This is 1985 data, so adjust for inflation.)

The second largest market for accountants is in the public accounting area. The largest national accounting firms hire the best students from the top schools. All of the "Big 8" are represented in Pittsburgh. Minimum credentialing is a B.A. in accounting or similar field. Persons who are not strictly accountants are also hired and it is not uncommon for an entry level position to be filled by a M.B.A. holder. MBAs usually work in management consulting services, taxes or auditing. *Arthur Anderson's* Pittsburgh office hires an average of a dozen MBAs a year with entry salaries between $25,000–$35,000. *Price Waterhouse,* the largest firm in town with 135 staff CPAs, hires a smaller number of MBAs, not all at entry level.

As a rule, expect there to be about two other staff jobs for each Certified Public Accountant in a firm. Along with MBAs, professional staff can include those with law degrees or expertise in audit and tax. Successful smaller public accounting firms try to staff their firms with combinations of professional skills that will meet the increasingly sophisticated needs of the small and medium businesses they serve.

A CPA now in a successful partnership with a tax lawyer began with one of the "Big 8" in town. She described the differences between working for a large and a small firm: "At a larger firm, the staff is more specialized. You usually don't handle as many components of a job as you would in a smaller firm. I started where I did for the experience and because I wanted to become a CPA." After a few years she moved to a medium size firm that had been started some years before by people who had left her original employer. "I began with the understanding that if I was 'good' I could be a partner in three years. I watched other 'good' people around me not get what they were promised. When my turn came and I got no promotion except for a raise, I stayed for another year but moved over to a department that worked with business startups and closings. No way would I want to do that all my life, but that department rounded out my general managerial experience." In her opinion, "Regardless of the size of the firm where you begin your career, you should remain flexible during your first six years if you wish to advance. If your job is not what you expected, be willing to make a change. If the position rounds out your background, it usually is worth a temporary stay."

Where to Find More Pittsburgh Employers in Professional Services

BOOK OF BUSINESS LISTS, Pittsburgh Business Times, 1988.
- "Architectural Firms" (25 largest Pittsburgh area), p. 71
- "Construction Contractors" (25 largest Pittsburgh area), p. 91
- "Consulting Engineer Firms" (23 largest in Pittsburgh area), p. 25
- "CPA Firms" (25 largest in Allegheny County), p. 89
- "Law Firms" (25 largest Pittsburgh-based), p. 43

Find this at Carnegie Library, Oakland, the PA Room, and at the downtown Business Branch. Also at newsstands and bookstores.

CONSULTANTS AND CONSULTING ORGANIZATIONS DIRECTORY, Gale Research Co. 7th edition. Full copy kept at Carnegie Library, Business Branch; copy of the Pennsylvania *index* kept in Oakland, PA Room.

EXPORT MANAGEMENT COMPANIES AND INTERNATIONAL CONSULTANTS, Department of Commerce, Harrisburg; free publication. A listing of Pennsylvania firms and their product lines.

LEGAL DIRECTORY, 1986-87, published by Pittsburgh National Bank. Lawyers and law firms in Western Pennsylvania. Carnegie Library, PA Room.

MARTINDALE—HUBBELL LAW DIRECTORY. Xeroxed list of lawyers in Pittsburgh. Carnegie Library, PA Room.

PENNSYLVANIA BAR ASSOCIATION, Lawyers Directory, 1986. Carnegie Library, PA Room.

PART TWO
HOW TO FIND A GOOD JOB IN PITTSBURGH

NINE STEPS IN THE SEARCH

There's a common saying that the best jobs go to the best job hunters. What that means, according to successful Pittsburgh job hunters, is *be prepared.* Finding a good job rarely happens by accident. You start your search with the know-how and skills that you have right now; you put in a lot of hard work and you learn as you go along.

There are no absolute rules for job hunting. Absolutely. However, we have some "rules of the road" to share with you. As we and the staff of Job Advisory Service watched and helped hundreds of Pittsburghers find good jobs,the following 9 steps appeared again and again. This book will take you through each one. If you prepare by using them, you, too, will be more likely to join the ranks of the happily employed.

1. Know What You Need and Want.

Be as clear as possible about what you want from your next job in terms of working conditions, opportunities for advancement and money rewards. Know the difference between what you *must* have and what you'd *like* to have.

2. Know What You Can Offer.

Be just as clear about what you have to offer an employer. Identify the special skills and personality traits that make you an asset to an employer. Separate the skills you like to use from the ones that are drudgery for you, but which you are good at doing.

3. Know Your Job Market.

Identify the full range of jobs for which you qualify. See how Pittsburgh area employers view those jobs and how they find their employees.

4. Adopt and Adapt.

Consider all your options, then choose the part of your market where you are a desirable candidate. Decide whether you could increase your real opportunities by seeking work in related fields or industries. Expand the number of your potential employers through research.

FOR A GOOD JOB

5. Customize a Job Hunt Plan and Follow It.

Schedule your job hunting time to fit your life situation and your market. Make your schedule flexible enough to take advantage of every opportunity but firm enough to get things done.

6. Acquire and Polish Job Hunting Skills.

Practice using referrals; talking to contacts in your field; interviewing; writing cover letters and thank you notes. Write your resume — more than one draft, if necessary. Capitalize on the skills that come naturally to you while you master the ones that are not as natural. Learn from your mistakes.

7. Contact All the People Who Can Help You Find Employment.

The job market is composed entirely of people. So inform key individuals of your availability and keep in touch with them during the span of your job hunt so you will be remembered when an opportunity arises.

8. Act on All the Methods That Look Promising.

Use agencies, want ads, direct applications, referrals — any and all combinations of these methods as long as they keep your job hunt going. A useful method is one that keeps resulting in good interviews or in situations where you are a serious candidate for the job. Spend the most time on the methods that bring you success. Follow up faithfully on each route you take.

9. Keep Your Perspective.

Job hunting is not the beginning and end of the world. Develop a strong support system. Keep the belief that you are worth hiring and can do a good job through all the ups and downs of your job hunt.

3

KNOWING WHAT YOU WANT

No matter what field you're in, when you job hunt your goal is the same: to secure the best job for you as quickly as possible. The way to start is by knowing what you want. This part seems simple: everyone wants a good job. The trick is to figure out just what that means for you.

What Is a Good Job?

When you are in a good job, you know it. You enjoy your work, you produce results and you receive appropriate compensation for what you contribute. Most career planning experts agree that these are the three essential ingredients. If any of these are missing, then you are still looking for a good job.

Perhaps your job is a stop-gap one—not really good, but it beats unemployment. Maybe there's nothing "wrong" with it, but it is only on the way to a job you really want. Perhaps your job *was* a good one which you've outgrown or perhaps some of the factors that originally made it good have changed, like the hours or your boss's personality. Even if you are unemployed or the economy is bad, if you take any other kind of a job, you will still be wanting a "good" job.

Since a good job is defined as one where you have your needs met and which you do well, it obviously will differ for each person. Your personal abilities, past experiences, ambitions and life situation all define your requirements. Consequently, you will not find a neatly published list

81

of *GOOD JOBS IN PITTSBURGH* in a newspaper column or in this book. A good job, though, will frequently be found as part of a career, that is, integrated with your life.

Good Jobs and Careers

In the past, the term career meant that you joined a big company in an entry level spot and moved up an invisible ladder, rung by rung. There are still careers of this type. The people who have them are called "fast trackers" today. But it is possible for everyone to have a career if it is seen in a broader way: as a job or sequence of jobs unified by interest and ability that provides more than monetary satisfaction.

Even the best job in the world can be "dumb" if you do it for no reason other than to eat. But you are not alone if you do your job simply to pay the rent. Richard Bolles, noted writer on career development, is frequently quoted as saying that "the world is filled with people trying to do what they most enjoy after 5:00 P.M." It doesn't have to be that way. A guiding principle of this book is that everyone has a right to seek a degree of satisfaction from his or her work and the only way to job hunt is to seek work which will give that to you.

A career can be a succession of similar jobs or jobs that contain a common theme. For example, a young football player from Blawnox followed a successful college gridiron career with several years in the pros. Then he spent time as an assistant coach and finally moved to a spot as sports information director for a professional basketball team. His career centered around his abiding interest in competitive sports.

Although your career may not have such an obvious theme, if your jobs have sprung out of your strongest interests and skills, a pattern will emerge. An older woman from the South Hills, looking back on her checkered work history, said.

> It might not look like it to an outsider, but there is a connecting thread throughout my work. I've always loved putting things together visually, so that they will send a message.

She worked first as a photographer, taking family portraits; then in a furniture store where the only part she really liked was helping people to coordinate furniture styles with their living styles. Finally she directed advertising layouts for a department store.

There were some trial jobs that did not fit into my real career, like selling office supplies, but they were brief, unsatisfying and I was relatively unsuccessful in them. I ended where I am because of my needs, but not all of them were for money. Because I knew what I did well and liked doing, I was pretty well able to measure what a job had to offer against my own criteria so I could spot an appropriate job for me when I saw one.

An ideal career consists of a series of good jobs, but every job—even a good job—involves some undesirable elements. When you look at the variety of tasks that make up a good job, there are some you like more than others. Some you do better—with more efficiency or more creativity—or with more measurable success—than other tasks. Career advancement means taking jobs that increase the number of elements which you do well and enjoy and cutting down on the number of tasks that you dislike or in which you produce only mediocre results. At each stage of your career, a good job will be an improvement over the one before it.

This concept of a career based on work satisfaction and successes rather than on criteria such as salary increases or job titles reflects two truths. One, you change. Two, the world changes. In a world that changes more rapidly every day, it is realistic to think of a good job in flexible terms. If there were only one perfect job for you, once you found the "perfect niche" you would have to hope against hope that the world, including you, would freeze in time and place.

Recognizing a Good Job

Although there exists no such thing as a "good job" list, you need not worry that you can never know what a good job for you will be. On the contrary, it is possible to spell out exactly what you want in your next job. The operating answer, of course, will always involve both you and the job market, but the first step is a realistic look at what **you** want.

What you want to do with your life is a fundamental starting point for self-directed work/life planning, but from the point of view of job hunting, you need only know what it takes to satisfy you on your next job. If you don't plan ahead at least that much, you may fall into a job trap, as did the young McKeesport woman who quit one seemingly good office job after another—until she realized that all of them made her feel "cooped-up."

What Do You Want in Your Next Job?

If your answer is a little vague, but describes some of the skills (like graphics or typing, etc.) you want to use, some of the work conditions that you desire and how much money you want, then you are moving in the right direction and this section can help you put it all together.

A satisfying job involves a realistic combination of your values, needs, interests and abilities. In short, it combines what you *like* to do, what you *need* to do and what you *can* do. These elements are embedded in your daily work when you have a satisfying job.

The checklist for job satisfaction below looks at five aspects of a job. First is the *CONTENT* of the work itself. That is the work that you actually do, be it typing or selling. Then there is the *WORK PROCESS* —how it's done. Satisfactions also derive from the *WORK ENVIRON-MENT,* the *DECISION-MAKING/REWARD STRUCTURE* and how the work *INTEGRATES WITH THE REST OF YOUR LIFE.*

If you draw up a list of all the items that you must have, you will have a description of what an ideal next job will give you.

Checklist For Job Satisfaction
What I Want in My Next Job

Indicate with a 1, 2, or 3 the importance you want each factor below to play in your work.

Level 1: I must have this

Level 2: I'd like this but can do without it if other conditions were met

Level 3: Of no importance or undesirable

WORK CONTENT

_____ Creative: like to invent new things, design new products or develop new ideas.

_____ Influence people to change their attitudes or opinions.

_____ Authority to plan work for others to do.

_____ Supervision: be directly responsible for the work done by others.

_____ Decision-making power regarding policies or courses of action.

_____ Challenge of some sort that is met by my work.

_____ A chance to compete or where there are clear win and lose outcomes.

_____ Moral fulfillment: my work contributes to a valuable set of standards.

_____ Artistic engagement in any of several art forms.

_____ Opportunity to learn how or why things work or to analyze problems.

_____ Stimulating, adventurous: work that involves intense excitement, frequent excitement or significant risk-taking.

WORK PROCESS

_____ Interesting initial job duties.
_____ An opportunity to learn new skills.
_____ Varied duties or changes in setting.
_____ Systematic: fixed routine or largely predictable duties.
_____ A chance to use my hands.
_____ Precision work, physical or mental.
_____ Physical challenge that I find rewarding.
_____ Adequate equipment (if needed for the job).
_____ Immediate or at least, observable results.
_____ Work at a high pace of activity.
_____ Work under pressure: either deadline pressure or situations where the quality of work is judged critically by boss, customers or public.

WORK ENVIRONMENT

_____ Pleasant physical surroundings.
_____ Spend time outdoors.
_____ Work alone: do projects by myself.
_____ Work as part of a team.
_____ Develop close relationships with co-workers.
_____ Extensive contact with the public.
_____ Immediate boss under whom I work well.

DECISION-MAKING/REWARD STRUCTURE

_____ Autonomy: allowed to work independently, no significant direction from others.
_____ Recognition for good work in some visible or public way.
_____ Involvement in the decision-making of the company.
_____ Opportunities for advancement within the company.
_____ Secure job within the company.
_____ Prestigious job or recognition in my field.
_____ Small organization.
_____ Large organization.
_____ Stable, predictable company.

INTEGRATION WITH THE REST OF MY LIFE

_____ Regular, reasonable hours.
_____ Freedom in scheduling work hours.
_____ Limited involvement (can forget about it when off the job).
_____ Absorbing: get most of my recognition or identity from my job.
_____ Short commuting distance.
_____ Little or no travel involved.
_____ Little or no relocation involved.
_____ Work for reputable company.
_____ Work for socially responsible company.
_____ High starting salary.
_____ Lots of financial rewards "down the road."
_____ Good fringe benefits.
_____ Other needs that I know are important to me. (List)

Work Content

The content of the work that we do is a major determinant of satisfaction and we are quick to notice when the content shifts. A Pittsburgh woman who did college recruiting for a large oil company dreaded the interim between recruiting sessions because she had to spend that time in the home office compiling statistics. She was happier when she moved to a spot where she interviewed on a daily basis and did not have to take concentrated doses of figure work.

People in different fields of work can find the same values satisfied in quite different activities. A home remodeler may value the challenge that is represented by completing a project within financial and structural limits. The challenge for a doctor may lie in diagnosing an illness. One way to tell if your work's content is fulfilling is that when you are engaged in it you feel good about yourself and time passes quickly.

Work Process

The process of the work—*how* you do what you do is another necessary component of your satisfaction. It involves such everyday but important details as how free-wheeling or fast paced the job is and how systematic or detailed it is. Sometimes the same type of work can be done differently from one company to another. In one firm the preparation of reports takes place in a very calm fashion. In another, every report is finished on a "rush-rush" basis even when there could be plenty of time.

Having adequate equipment to get the job done right may be important. One university biologist moved into the private sector because inadequate budgets for lab facilities kept ruining his satisfaction. Your current dissatisfactions can clarify requirements for your next job.

Environment

Whether a job is satisfying is also influenced by your work environment: both the physical surroundings and the human surroundings. One person is comfortable in a pared-down, hands-on work setting like a supermarket or garage. Another finds corporate plush a real plus. The McKeesport woman who quit one office job after another had a strong need to work in an outdoor setting or to work where moving from one room to another was part of the job. Likewise, if you are claustrophobic, you might work well in the mine office, but not in the mine. The geriatric health field may seem like a great employment prospect, but it isn't if the thought of being around the elderly makes you uncomfortable.

Another commonly accepted theory of personal preference is one that asks whether a person wants to work with *people,* to work with *data* (facts or ideas) or to work with *things.* Very few people have an exclusive preference. A mechanic who works with things, like repairing motors, may also like to work with people around her. She could be happy in a large repair shop with a friendly atmosphere. Another mechanic might work comfortably with people but leap at a job where he can spend hours alone with schematic data. A job that is satisfying usually has a mixture that feels right to us. There are no wrong choices here; there are only preferences.

"I Like to Work With People"

More than one hapless job applicant, when asked "What do you like to do?" has answered with the old cliche: "I like to work with people." Even as the words leave their mouths these job hunters know that they are uttering a most unoriginal statement. There is nothing wrong about liking to work with people. But such a statement is so vague as to be meaningless in a job interview.

A roofer who has his own business and a beautician in a big shop have customers, but they relate to them in different ways. A lab technician and a receptionist both work with people but one works with employees of the company and the other deals with the public.

Take a few minutes to reflect on *how* you would like to relate to people in your next job. Do you like to work with co-workers around you or with people who are not in the company's employ? If you like working with co-workers, do you want to work as part of a close team or to work with them only physically near? If you want a mix, what kind? Would you prefer part of one day a week working with people and the rest of the time working alone?

Do you want to supervise others or follow clear instructions yourself? Do you want to work with co-workers, bosses or subordinates? You might not always get your preference in your next job, but you will come closer by being aware of it.

If you want to deal with the public, is there an age or type of person you prefer? Do you want to deal briefly with people in one-time contacts, like a receptionist, or do you prefer dealing with a group of clients on a regular basis, like shopkeepers do? One person finds a job vacuous without intense relationships bonded with his or her fellows; another finds his effectiveness diminished whenever he strays beyond a businesslike level.

Further, in working with the public, just what is it that you want to *do* with them? Howard Figler, vocational choice specialist and author of *Path,* suggested some of the many ways you might work with the public. Do you want to:

Help people with personal problems?
Provide services to others?
Organize people's activities?
Instruct them in skills?
Influence their attitudes?
Negotiate or mediate between them?
Present them with difficult decisions?
Study the behavior of people in general?
Investigate individuals through indirect means?
Gather information directly from them?
Make decisions about people?

Spending a little time thinking about these questions can give you an insight into the best kinds of working situations for you.

Decison-Making/Reward Structure

You may have difficulty identifying an organization's reward structure before you are hired, but you can become aware of your own level of ambition and how you want your work to be measured and rewarded. Are you content as long as you're growing more competent in your work or do you want a say in how things are run? Are frequent small salary raises a satisfying way to mark your progress or is authority over other workers a better gauge? Do you see every job as a stepping stone to another position? Your expectations will make all the difference in your satisfaction.

Employers reward success in many different ways. In some firms you may earn a relatively low salary but have a respected opinion in the company's decision-making processes. In another, the boss or department head may take all the public credit for your work but reward you in your paycheck. Naturally, it is nice to find both, but if you had to choose, which employer's reward structure would satisfy you most?

Will You Live It Night and Day?

Today, the level of involvement in our work has been coming under increased scrutiny. There is less sex-segregation in jobs. There are fewer traditional families, more two-paycheck families and an expectation that the all-around quality of life is a valued asset. How much of your life should a job take up? How much can a company demand? How much can you expect/demand of your family? Involvement is not an easy question and it has no easy answer. There is some rethinking taking place in companies as managements adapt to social realities they cannot change.

Two points, though, seem clear. First, there will always be jobs that will swallow up most of your living time or creative energies. Campaigning for elective office, coaching a pro-football team and some management spots are consuming jobs. Other jobs, like tax accounting, have peak periods. Recognize these realities if you are contemplating a move into such a job. Second, different people want or like to be absorbed by their work in different degrees. In addition, the needs of an individual may change as his or her life circumstances shift. A young man who is a new father and a new home owner may find that a job which was becoming boring remains satisfactory for a while longer because other life interests are new avenues for satisfaction and creativity.

$, $, $, $, $,

Money is important not only because we need it to live but because we value ourselves and measure our success to an extent by our salaries. Whether or not this is as it should be, these elements make the question "How much money do you want?" into an emotional and confusing issue for many job hunters.

There are two questions here, really. One is personal. How much do you need to live on? The other involves the job market. What is this work worth in the market place? Try thinking about them in two separate steps. First, look at how much it costs you to maintain your current life style. Find the basic figure that includes your fixed expenses, long term debts, discretionary spending and your savings. Then, decide whether you:

1. Absolutely insist on living better than this, and right now. You would take whatever job offer has the highest salary.

2. Would like more money, but can make some trade-offs. You would accept another job at the same salary you now make, if it included advancement, security or other advantages.

3. Don't mind your style of living but could tighten up, if need be. (There *are* people in this boat!) You've truly had it with slaving at a job without any satisfactions except money.

Putting it on paper can turn a vague idea about your monetary needs into a concrete figure to use in negotiating a salary and comparing jobs. It can make it possible for you to *choose* among the various types of satisfaction a job might bring.

"How Much Do You Want?"

However, the figure you come up with is your money need. **This is your private concern.** You need never tell an employer the minimum number of dollars you can get by on, even if it sounds like you are being asked directly. When a boss or personnel person ask how much salary you need, the answer is that you want what the job is worth. *That* figure is based on the prevailing market for that kind of work *and* your own willingness to accept a particular salary level. You can take a job for less money if you see it as an interim job. In some cases, overtime, extensive travel or other factors will make an otherwise attractive salary seem too low to be worthwhile when you think of what you'd have to give up to earn your paycheck. (See Chapter Five for salary research methods.)

Special Note for Women. Many women limit their potential earnings by automatically heading for traditional female jobs. Like it or not, if a field is predominantly female, it pays on a lower scale. It always has. Unfair? Yes. Will it ever change? Probably. Lots of forces are swelling to affect pay equity and negotiating can help you personally. But pay differential based on sex is a fact right now and changes of this sort take place gradually. Be aware of the job market and make your decisions with your eyes open.

Compromises

Because there are few perfect jobs, compromises are inevitable. Some career fields, like directing church music and writing poetry, are traditionally not high paying fields. Some remunerations come in the form of status or the satisfaction of working in your interest area. In other jobs, like public relations, low income is the norm at entry level but once you have proven yourself, you may command larger rewards.

Trade offs occur every day. People who like to direct the growth of youngsters are faced with some tough choices—like the Pittsburgh area man who had to choose between teaching third grade in the Catholic school system in Baldwin or selling wholesale hardware supplies and then participating in Boy Scouts in the evenings. You could trade doing what you really like for a job that removes the worry about money or you could balance a less desirable work environment with the opportunity to learn new skills.

Not all compromises are monetary and not all are so vital. But once you have made clear to yourself what really counts for you, you can make trade offs freely. There is no objectively right choice, only subjectively better choices. Keep control of that choice for yourself as much as possible.

If you look back over the checklist for job satisfaction and write down the top two or three items that you *must* have in a job, you will have a goal you can probably reach with your next job.

After you have been in your new job for a while, try the exercise again. Measure what you wanted your job to give you and what it actually does give you. This is career management in daily operation: continually checking to see that you are going in the direction you choose.

Still Don't Know?

If your answer to the question "What is a good job for you?" is only a frustrated "I wish I knew," and if you suspect that you wouldn't recognize one if, as they say, it bit you on the leg—then you need more help than this book is designed to give. In this book career planning, vocational choice and aptitudes are only touched on as they relate to getting a job.

At the end of the next chapter, in the section titled *Pittsburgh Resources for Putting Your Act Together before Taking It on the Road,* you will find some organizations that can help you if you want vocational testing or counseling.

If you are freshly reentering the job market after a long absence, are thinking of completely switching careers or are an unfocused and inexperienced college graduate, it may be best to step out of the job hunt process for a little while until you have a better handle on what you want from and can offer to an employer. Perhaps when times were easier, folks who belong to the supermarket school of thought *(Show me what's out there in terms of jobs available, and I'll pick from them),* could afford to job hunt that way. Today the competition is too great to waste any opportunities.

4

THE MOST IMPORTANT THING A JOB HUNTER CAN KNOW

Knowing what you want from a job is a good first step, but to put yourself into the job market you must also know what you bring to a job.

On a recent visit to Pittsburgh, Tom Jackson, author of several national job hunting books, pointed out a critical element of the inner workings of the employment process. "You will not be given a job because you need a job, however much you need it," he said, "but **because an employer needs you.**" If you show that you can produce results that fit an employer's needs, you will be a desirable candidate. To show this, you must know the breadth and depth of your skills and communicate their relevance to the employer.

This section equips you to describe your skills and abilities through an approach based upon what you have done and how you have done it. This is not only a clear way to understand your skills, but a most concrete and proof-positive way to put yourself into the job market.

Marketable Skills

Your marketable job skills include anything that people will pay you to do. Anything! Some skills are specific and concrete...typing 80 words per minute, for instance, or repairing an IBM 3600 computer. Others are more general: organizing civic events or selecting secure investments. The list of potentially marketable skills is enormous.

Just the way that you naturally behave can be desirable to an employer. For instance, an even-tempered, understanding, good listener can be paid well by a company who needs customer complaint representatives. The ability to work effectively under deadline pressure is another characteristic that can set an individual above other qualified job hunters. Too frequently these skills—variously called personality traits, behavioral characteristics or adaptive skills—are forgotten assets, since they do not easily show up on a resume or application form. Learning how to convey them can give your candidacy a decided advantage.

Where to Find Your Skills

You will find your skills in your paid work, in your hobbies, in the skills you used in your student days, in your community involvement and in your family and social interactions. If you plan to look for a job similar to the one you now hold, then you will find most of your skills in a close analysis of your current job. If you want to broaden your search into other related fields because you hate the work you are doing or are in a dying industry; if you are a full-fledged career changer or do not have much successful work experience behind you, then you will need to analyze a broader area of your life, in proportion to the degree of change you seek.

Uncovering Success Skills

Experts are of the opinion that the skills and abilities which bring you personal feelings of success are the same skills that will bring you success on the job. So look at your past life and work, seeking the *high points,* the personal *achievements.*

A success, in the words of Richard Germann and Peter Arnold (authors of *Job and Career Building*) "is the positive outcome, or result, of a plan or an action—your plan, your action."

A success can be obvious to others, i.e., your election to the office of class president, or exceeding your sales quota by 40%. It might also be a private challenge you have met, like learning to be a competent, relaxed public speaker. Personal achievement may come from your ideas —a marketing plan adopted by your company, without any public recognition of your contribution, for instance.

Successes do not have to be of earth-shaking magnitude before they are worth noting. Most employers do not have earth-shaking problems to solve. In fact, more frequently they are looking for people who are successful at performing the garden variety tasks that keep their organizations going.

Finding Yours

There are any number of ways to uncover your success skills. Richard Bolles, dean of the success analysis approach to job hunting, outlines nine different methods that a person could use. The most informal way is merely to think about what you'd like to do and what you are "good at" doing. But you may leave out some of your best selling points that way.

Job Advisory Service, in working with over 10,000 job hunting Pittsburghers, often encountered people who had launched their job hunt campaigns and sailed into interviews only to realize that they were blowing their chances. In many cases, the job hunter did not really know his or her strongest job-related skills and this was reflected in vague resumes and poor interviews. By using a method that ties together an assessment of success skills with the preparation of writing a job-focused resume—like the personal data project below—you can prevent this from happening to you.

A Personal Data Project

Carrying out the exercise described here requires a few sheets of blank paper, some time and also a certain freedom from pressure. Do not feel that you must fill in the blanks by 3 P.M. of the day you start this project so that you can write a resume by 4 P.M. and set up a job interview by 5 P.M. This kind of work requires the best that you have to give it in terms of time and mental effort.

Do keep all the information in a folder or notebook and write it as suggested below. At least once in your employment history you should do a full-scale detailed analysis such as this. This is a good time to dig out all the necessary dates for graduations and jobs. Keep the pages on file so you will never have to search out these basic dates and facts about yourself again.

Don't worry about how well you write at this stage. The goal is to get all your ideas down on paper. Whether you write phrases, key words or sentence fragments doesn't matter.

Personal Data Project

SECTION 1: EDUCATIONAL BACKGROUND

1. EDUCATION AND TRAINING
List most recent education first. Work backwards, include high school dates. Attach any transcripts.

School	Years Attended	Concentration or Major	Grade Point Average
			Overall _____
			Major _____

2. COURSES WHICH WERE MOST CHALLENGING OR ENJOYABLE FOR YOU
List reason or accomplishment.

3. HONORS, SCHOLARSHIPS
Detail, even if you did not accept scholarships.

4. INTERNSHIPS, ASSISTANTSHIPS, FELLOWSHIPS
List responsibilities first, then accomplishments, even if identical.

Position	Responsibilities	Accomplishments

5. SUMMER AND PART-TIME WORK WHILE IN SCHOOL

Employer's Name & Location	Dates or Description of Span of Employment	
Job Title	Responsibilities	Accomplishments

6. PERCENTAGE OF EDUCATIONAL EXPENSES EARNED

7. EXTRACURRICULAR ACTIVITIES
Include teams and social, service or cultural organizations. Include activities or offices held.

8. ADDITIONAL TRAINING
Include conferences, company-sponsored training programs, workshops, correspondence courses, etc.

Course Title	Conducted by	Date	Achievement

Your Education

The closer your student years are to you and the less on-the-job experience you have, the more detail you need to provide in this section. The object is to provide not just a recording of your educational background, but one that emphasizes your successes. To do this, use a **three-step method** to describe each of your accomplishments. For each activity you list, ask yourself three questions:

1. What were the problems or challenges you faced in this course or job? What was it that needed to be done?
2. What did you do to solve each problem? How—step by step—did you do it?
3. What were the results of your actions?

The key is to be detailed and specific. Use numbers wherever possible. If you led a discussion group or taught a class as part of an assistantship, include the number of people involved. Record the titles of project papers and reports, even the number of pages. List all the courses you took that were related to your major or to a job field you now want to enter.

One recent graduate, using the three-step method of analysis for successful classroom experiences, wrote the following:

#2. Courses Which Were Most Challenging or Enjoyable:

1. FRENCH
Wanted to learn to think in another language.
Listened to records of conversation 3 times a week;
Started dinner club at college for students and French nationals;
Spoke only French at meals; held one every three weeks;

> *Exchanged letters with Parisian friend of a classmate for two years;*
> *Did assignments for class very fully, sometimes practicing silent-*
> *ly on the way to class.*
>
> *RESULTS: Was really thinking in the language by the time I*
> *finished French III.*

2. *ALGEBRA:*

> *Challenge—to learn enough of the basics to do well in an elemen-*
> *tary course in information science.*
> *Math is hard for me, so I spent extra effort preparing each assign-*
> *ment and set up 3 office visits with professor to go over exams (after*
> *he indicated he was open to that).*
>
> *RESULTS: Completed course with knowledge of all basic concepts*
> *covered; got a B+ grade. Bonus was that prof. offered to help me*
> *the next term if I got stuck in the information science course.*

Another young person analyzed a summer job not in terms of the physical work performed, like sweeping floors and scraping ice cream containers (activities she did not plan to use in her next job), but in a way that illustrated leadership and a sense of responsibility:

#5. Summer Work

Baskin-Robbins, Cream Street, Summer, 1989

RESPONSIBILITIES:
Handled cash & customers.
Rude customers push ahead on hot days; in this store, arguments
sometimes lead to fights.

ACCOMPLISHMENTS:
Learned to say things in a light manner without putting people down
—told one boy that "I'd be very happy to give him lots of time to make
up his mind when it was his turn, if he'd wait a bit now."
Served all customers in turn;
Earned the store some goodwill;
Very few fights during my shifts.

Accomplishments include learning. This is not the same as attending a class. If you really learned something in a class, chances are you can talk about it for a few minutes. Think about those kinds of classes and what you could say about them, for interviewers still ask people to, "Tell me about some of your classes."

Finally, if you feel concerned because you have formal education in a field but no job experience, remind both yourself and your potential employer that by successfully completing courses (for instance, in business management or retailing) you have demonstrated your abili-ty to learn in that *field of work.* Chances are that you can learn just as quickly and successfully on the job. Abilities are potential skills. They merely need the opportunity to be exercised.

SECTION 2: EMPLOYMENT HISTORY

Using separate sheets, provide the following data for each employer or position you have held.

1. **EMPLOYER'S NAME, ADDRESS AND PHONE NUMBER**

2. **DESCRIPTION OF EMPLOYER**
   What the organization makes, sells, services. Size, sales volume, branches, number of employees.

3. **TITLE OF YOUR SUPERVISOR**

   Name:

   Telephone:

   Address:
   If no longer with that employer.

4. **DATES OF YOUR EMPLOYMENT**

5. **YOUR JOB TITLE**

6. **DESCRIPTION OF YOUR JOB**
   Be as specific as possible.

Your Responsibilities	Accomplishments or Successes	Results for the Company

7. **PROMOTIONS**
   With or without a change in title.

8. **PAY RAISES**
   Especially those based on merit.

9. **EQUIPMENT USED**

Specific Equipment	Proficiency *if applicable*

Employment History

Use a separate sheet of paper for each employer or position you held. The main object here is to list the skills you've used in your jobs and the positive results you accomplished for your employer.

Don't shortchange yourself by falling into the trap of describing your work in terms of mere job titles like assistant director or secretary to the president.

Jean Summers, in her book *What Every Woman Needs to Know to Find a Job,* points out that if you write or say "for three years I was secretary to the president," most people will assume that you spent it typing, filing and taking coffee breaks. That is the general understanding of what a secretary does and, as a shorthand kind of language, that may be true. But in real life, it may be other skills that qualify you for the job. For instance, one Pittsburgh secretary to the vice-president of a large electrical firm has a skill list that looks like this:

1. *Screened calls to V-P; did customer relations work on the phone with large accounts.*
2. *Wrote monthly reports (for V-P's signature); gathered data from sales and financial management departments; developed statistics; composed summaries of year-to-date developments and matched them with goals set by board of directors. 20 page report each month.*
3. *Trained and supervised others on the V-P office staff: secretary, receptionist, 2 clerks.*
4. *Wrote letters for V-P's signature (20 some per week).*
5. *Responsible for office budget and authorizing expenses for office supplies. Develop estimated budget for approval each year.*
6. *Learned, then instructed staff and V-P in use of terminals and computerized filing system.*
7. *Organized V-P's travel and meeting schedule.*
8. *Took dictation from V-P (110 wpm).*
9. *Edited and typed confidential letters.*

Make sure that everything you really did on the job is included.

When you walk into the interview arena, a mere list of your work skills is not enough to set you apart as a candidate who is a "doer." You need to go one step further. You need to substantiate them. This means indicating how well you did something and how your employer benefited. If you want to say that you are good at writing reports, list at least one you are willing to talk about to a potential employer. Perhaps attach it to your data project.

Focus on the skills that you think are most marketable in your field or ones that are really strong. Use the three-step method described above. This part of one Pittsburgher's data project looked like this:

#6. Description of your Job: *Asst. Purchasing Agent*

RESPONSIBILITIES: Decided on purchases for 7 specialty steel products. ($2,500,000 annually).

ACCOMPLISHMENTS: Got complete authority in my area in less than 2 years (quicker than guy before me).
Really knew vendors, got "inside" them, could spot market changes coming (Feb. '89 price-break situation).

RESULTS FOR COMPANY: Maintained good balance between inventory and customer demand (impt. for profits).
Got hard-to-find items by knowing who to talk to in supplier firms (example: germ-resistant polycoating for Altoona Hospital's stainless fab-job).
Combined orders to get special-order price breaks.
Tapped into nat'l. trade group to swap 'dead' inventory. (New for company).

Again, if you are able to be specific, do so. Say that sales increased 15% at your company, if they did, and note the way your work contributed. If times were bad, did the sales increase 3% in a market where competition was going under? That, too, is an accomplishment. If sales and profitability are not applicable for your area of work, increased productivity, efficiency and better service to customers are all buzz words you can use. Don't neglect small items; they can be weeded out later. If you are an experienced worker, this part of the data project should take your greatest time and effort.

Life Skills

You may have skills that you have used effectively—but not for pay. Often these skills are of value in the world of paid work. Homemakers are one group of people who develop significant skills by doing unpaid work—skills such as scheduling time; budgeting money; organizing events; making sure people do their jobs; comparison shopping and so on. In addition, skills developed in parenting or caring for sick and elderly family members may be important sources of accomplishment.

You do not have to be a homemaker to have picked up life skills like driving, landscaping, sewing, gardening, refinishing furniture or fund raising, of course, but you do need to treat those skills and successes seriously. The experience you gather in the course of living your life

SECTION 3: LIFE SKILLS

1. COMMUNITY ACTIVITIES
Work backwards, most recent first. Include church, social, civic, etc.

**Organization   Dates   Its Purpose   Your Role/Responsibilities/
Accomplishments**

2. FOREIGN LANGUAGE ABILITY
Note level of fluency: excellent, good, fair.

Language   Speak   Read   Write

3. TRAVEL IN U.S.; OTHER COUNTRIES
Describe what you feel you gained from the experience.

4. HOBBIES, PERSONAL INTERESTS
Number of years pursued, classes or formal training, level of proficiency or success.

5. SPECIAL FAMILY RESPONSIBILITIES

6. MILITARY SERVICE
Treat work performed in service as part of employment history.

Dates   Branch of Service   Rank (entering, leaving)

Special Training, Courses   Accomplishments, Medals

7. OTHER

is valid experience. This is a case where maturity has its benefits—you may have an edge over the very young *because* you have lived longer. Whatever your age, the more of these skills you can claim, the better.

In this last part of the data project, use the three-step method of analysis for community and volunteer activities, both past and present, just as you did above.

Success in a hobby can occasionally be used to your advantage in a job search. In one case, a female lawyer stimulated greater interest from law firms here by mentioning her achievements in competitive skiing. Hiring attorneys saw her as a highly competitive person who liked to win, a valuable personality characteristic in litigation. But much of this information is for your personal reference only.

Do I Really Have a Skill...To What Degree?

Every skill is possessed to a certain degree, a level of proficiency. It is the degree to which you possess a skill that determines, first, whether it is good enough to be a paid skill and, second, the level at which you can claim expertise. For example, a North Hills woman re-entering the job market had always managed her family's budget and she listed financial management as a skill. However, when she went to a large bank and told them she felt qualified to work in financial management, she was dismissed with a barely concealed snicker. On the other hand, she did not have a totally unmarketable skill. When she approached a neighborhood cardshop owner who needed some help "running the place," she gave this description:

> I spent 12 years handling all the taxes, loans, bills and financial-aid-for-college forms for the family. I always planned for and scheduled payments on time and I developed a formal budget system that kept track of how much was spent monthly and yearly in 14 different categories such as clothes, auto maintenance, etc. .... *And* I have a sample to show you how efficiently and simply it works ...

Then her skill was both appropriately described and applied. She was a serious candidate and eventually got the job.

The degree to which you possess a skill will not be measured by any book. The marketplace will tell you. If you are not sure, you can base your estimate on the quantity and quality in your documentation. If you raised $55 on a cookie sale for a softball team, your experience in fund raising is at a lower level than that needed to raise $3,500 three years in a row from a neighborhood festival which included patron contributions, raffles, booths, competitions and entrance fees, even though both were volunteer projects. A professional in the job of your choice can give you a rough estimate of the market value to place on your volunteer skills, but do not take one person's word as gospel. Since this is a judgment, plan to ask several people for feedback.

Using the Data Project

Most of us are not trained to "talk up" our good points, but that is exactly what you need to do every time you write or talk to someone during your job hunt. The personal data project is basic training for writing about yourself in your resume, cover letters and on application forms, as well as for talking about yourself in interviews.

For instance, if you plan to apply to advertising firms for copy writing positions, note every instance where your writing skills were involved —in paid, unpaid or educational experiences. You can then select the most appropriate examples to use as you approach each advertising contact.

A review of the data project reinforces your positive attitude about yourself. It gives you the "ammunition" you need. If this way of talking about yourself does not come naturally to you, you must prepare more thoroughly so that you will not be disadvantaged in your job hunt. If requested to "tell me about your last job," (a frequent request), you need not be limited to saying, "Well, I did a good job. I was a good worker. I did a good job of it." Although this is exactly how one experienced Pittsburgher stumbled through his first interviews, after completing his personal data project, he was able to detail his job from an action-oriented point of view. He said:

> On my first couple tries I started talking about what the company does and what the people under me do—but that didn't hit the mark. Listening to myself (he used a tape recorder to practice), I saw that describing what I did, how I did it and the results of my doing it was a much more focused way. Since I had already done all these things—they were all on my data project—it really wasn't bragging. I didn't have to say I did a great job; let them decide that. I can readily talk about how I supervised 8 accountants and 14 support people through a 3 month period where we doubled our normal audit load for a special project and got the job completed on time without losing any of the staff and with a minimum of frayed tempers.

Indeed, when he got into talking about this part of his last job, his feelings of being ill at ease in an interview melted away. He became animated; the subtle elements of his style of management showed through and it was easy for an employer to make the judgment that he would *fit* and that the company wanted him.

Personal Characteristics

Personal characteristics tend to lie unrecognized as valuable job commodities. They include such traits as punctuality, grooming, dressing attractively, acceptance of supervision, care of property, friendliness, impulse control, etc. These are qualities that everyone *could* have, but not all people possess.

The list on the next page is not exhaustive; there are literally hundreds more, but this list contains many that *employers* consider positive in one type of job or another. Employers look for honesty in a cashier, for example. A model must be attractive; a physical therapist, patient. Traits that are good in one job may be undesirable in another. The ability to be deferential—to be respectful or ingratiating to another person— may be a real asset to a receptionist whose boss must keep powerful clients waiting for him in the office or on the phone, but the same trait serves no special purpose for a scientific researcher.

To turn the list into a useful job hunting tool, make several copies of it. On one, check off those traits you feel you strongly possess. Give other copies to co-workers or friends. Have them check off ways that you **appear** to others. Let them know that flattery is not the object here. The purpose is two-fold. First, it will catch any traits which slip past you because you take them for granted. Second, it will give you a glimpse of the qualities that you project in a first impression—which is how you will appear in an interview. By knowing your strongest personality traits, you can make certain that you display them during an interview.

Personal Characteristics

_____Adventurous
_____Alert
_____Ambitious
_____Assertive
_____Attractive
_____Broad-minded
_____Calm
_____Charming
_____Competitive
_____Confident
_____Conscientious
_____Consistent
_____Cooperative
_____Curious
_____Decisive
_____Deferential
_____Dependable
_____Detailed
_____Determined
_____Disciplined
_____Discreet
_____Efficient
_____Easy going
_____Energetic
_____Enthusiastic
_____Exact
_____Flexible
_____Forceful
_____Friendly
_____Honest
_____Humorous
_____Impartial
_____Independent
_____Innovative
_____Inspiring
_____Intelligent
_____Logical
_____Loyal

_____Mature
_____Mechanical
_____Moral
_____Motivated
_____Obliging
_____Optimistic
_____Organized
_____Outgoing
_____Patient
_____Perceptive
_____Persevering
_____Persuasive
_____Pleasant
_____Poised
_____Practical
_____Professional
_____Punctual
_____Realistic
_____Respectful
_____Responsible
_____Robust
_____Self-confident
_____Self-controlled
_____Sensitive
_____Serious
_____Sincere
_____Stable
_____Supportive
_____Tactful
_____Thorough
_____Tolerant
_____Understanding
_____Unique
_____Versatile
_____Verbal
_____Warm
_____Wholesome

Easier Said Than Done

Often employers have an image in mind of what the person who will fill a job should be like. Consciously or unconsciously they look for certain personality characteristics. One human resources manager in a local financial institution remarked,

> We hire hundreds of new college graduates each year and we look primarily at their personality qualities. We can teach them the necessary tasks but we can't change their characters.

At both high and low job levels when interviewing gets down to two or three final candidates, usually all of them are qualified. The differences among applicants lie more in their personalities. You cannot change your personality for each job interview but you can spotlight its most applicable points.

The regional sales manager for a large tool manufacturing company listed the following as the important personal qualities he looks for in new sales representatives:

Enthusiasm
Determination
Likeability
Neat Dresser
Dependability
Sincerity
Diplomacy
Self-motivation

Think for a moment. If you were seeking this job, how could he find out about these qualities in an interview with you? You would not be seriously considered for the job if you did not appear to have them. How *do* you show something like dependability or determination? This is where examples come into play, for past performance displays concrete evidence.

If you are a smart job hunter you will 1) identify the characteristics which are valued in the job beforehand. Then, 2) dig through your data project before each interview. Find instances from any area of your experience when you demonstrated that trait. If you choose examples which are appropriate to the job level you seek, you will be able to talk about your traits both indirectly and concretely.

You might demonstrate your honesty as a candidate for a registrar's office position did by saying, "I handled the cash register for three summers at a restaurant with 20 waiters. We never had a shortage while

I worked the register." Dependability shows in a statement like this: "I called my accounts twice a week, so all my customers got into the habit of waiting for me to call before placing their orders." A pleasant story can convey several desirable traits at once without being offensive or "hornblowing":

> Cold calls are a challenge. I remember making nine trips to Service Maintenance before they gave me a single order. It got to be almost a joke between the purchasing agent and me but they came around and they've become a good account.

You can also use a characteristic to dissolve possible problem areas:

INTERVIEWER: I see that you live in East Faraway.

YOU: Yes, but in my last position, I was even farther away and I missed fewer days of work because of weather problems than any of my co-workers. In fact, I even was given a key so I could open up.

Patterns and Matrixes

When you have completed the personal data project and exercises here, you are in a position to make some observations and decisions about your job hunt.

Look for a capsule description of your strongest points. Look for:

A knack,

An instinct,

An ear/eye or head for something,

A proficiency at something.

In short, answer the question *what does this person do well?* Do your successes come from using the same skills over and over? Do you work better in certain kinds of situations? One county manpower administrator realized that her special skill was implementing projects that had very tight budgets. Another saw perseverence and compiling skills used again and again in different settings. A credit manager captured his knack by saying: "I have more ways than anyone you've ever met to dog an account without offending people."

Another method is to pick out the *patterns* and *clusters* of skills in your background. This chart of skills groups some related abilities into general categories, like organizing skills or analytical skills. Underline the skills on the list that show up repeatedly on your data project. This is a quick way to see where your strongest experiences lie.

Skills

Numerical Skills: *from counting to accounting; financial management; evaluating numbers.*

Organizing Skills: *involving detail work or follow-through; accepting responsibility for the handling of things or events.*

Persuasive Skills: *influencing, selling, mediating or promoting.*

Performing Skills: *music, art, public speaking, etc.*

Leadership Skills: *also making decisions, initiating and directing.*

Management Skills: *developing, planning, executing policies, supervising others, team building.*

Communicating Skills: *either speaking or writing with clarity and effectiveness.*

Educating Skills: *specifically involving the transfer of some comprehension or skill to another person.*

Interpersonal Skills: *ranging from serving other people to caring for them; listening, advocating and representing—all human relations skills.*

Innovative Skills: *creating new ideas, imagining, applying theory, experimenting.*

Artistic Skills: *visual and spatial designing, styling, decorating.*

Observational Skills: *perceptive focusing, detecting, appraising.*

Analytical Skills: *problem solving, researching, investigating, systematizing.*

Manual & Machine Skills: *including operating, set up and repair; also, designing and crafting; hand dexterity as in typing or sawing.*

Athletic Skills: *involving bodily movement or eye-hand coordination.*

Outdoor Skills: *horticulture, farming, ranching, etc.*

Skills not included elsewhere: traveling, ——————————————

This kind of grouping will be useful when it is time to write a resume. The assistant purchasing agent for the steel jobber, mentioned earlier, found that his numerical skills surfaced repeatedly. He had processed statistical material, had been an honors math student in high school and liked figuring sports odds, too. His organizing skills were also heavily documented in his current job. He decided to use these groupings when he described his experience in his resume. You can do the same.

A Field of Interest as a Starting Point

If you have a specific field of interest, you have an obvious starting point for your job hunt. Perhaps your educational backgound is vocationally oriented—nursing or computer programming—and you want to continue building a career there. Perhaps your work experience has all been in one field, so you will stay in your specialty for financial reasons like the polymer coatings specialist who'd been thinking of change but decided against it. Make sure you haven't outgrown your early interest in your field before you put yourself diligently into the same job market again.

A long term interest in one field often does signal wide areas of compatibility with the people and the values of the field. However, some career changers and new graduates have no *strong* preference for any specific area when they start. If you have many interests which you find hard to choose among, narrow your focus to three or four fields first, even if you have to be arbitrary about your choices; next look at your skills to see whether they're reasonably compatible with each of those fields. Then, *explore each of these fields of interest one at a time.* Here are a few possible areas to help you get started:

Communications
Teaching
Social Service
Law
Medical Service
Public Service
Personal Service
Planning
Scientific Research
Applied Science
Mechanical
Technical
Production
Construction
Transportation
Agriculture

Outdoor Work
Recreational Leadership
Management
Supervision
Finance
Numerical Work
Clerical
Business
Marketing
Direct Sales
Computer-related Jobs
Military Activities
Fine Art/Music/Drama
Commercial Art
Religious Activities
Other _____

Developing a Job Objective

Wrap up this preparation phase by deciding which skills you want to use in your next job. Choose from among the highest level of skills you can claim and that you enjoy, choose ones that you think are most saleable or that are really your strengths. Select three or four. This is sometimes called setting a functional job objective. Consider the skills you select as tentative objectives, subject to change as you interact with your job market's realities, reshaping and realigning them.

A young Pittsburgh professional had entered the corporate world as a bilingual secretary for the company's South American branch. The list of job skills that she decided to market included: handling responsibility; interacting with customers and suppliers regularly (especially on the phone); using persuasive skills (she discovered she had many); Spanish fluency and the knowledge of exports she had acquired in her two years on the job. She knew of no other jobs as a bilingual secretary that were an advancement over the one she had. But the precise advantage of setting a functional job objective is that you are not limited by job titles. At that moment there were probably a half dozen jobs in Pittsburgh that used most of the skills she wanted to market. These options had diverse job titles and were in different fields. She pursued several. When a position in inside sales within her division did not materialize, she accepted an administrative job in customer relations for a growing exporter.

A Murrysville job hunter who had held several positions in industrial relations and personnel had multiple skills in management, staff development, writing and public speaking. He had been most highly paid for negotiating and resolving grievances, which had also given him five years of ulcers. The priorities for his next position placed manpower planning at the top. Supervising training and development came next, along with his desire to travel. Negotiating was at the very bottom. He realized that his salary requirements might mean some re-evaluation of his priorities, unless he found the right spot. Eventually he found that spot with a smaller corporation where his time was split between managing the expansion of the human resources department and developing the training programs to be used at the company's Puerto Rican assembly plant. Although little labor negotiating occurred, when it did the company wanted to have a seasoned professional on board.

The clearer **you** can be about the combination of functions you want to perform or skills you want to use, the more focused **your** job hunt will become.

Don't Blow It

This kind of preparation for job hunting takes up only a few pages but it can represent for you a significant amount of thinking and rethinking. It is worth your time.

Your world is full of people who would like to help you by recommending you for jobs or telling you about them. But time and again people waste the willingness of their acquaintances to connect them with the hidden job market because they cannot answer the question put to them: "What are you looking for?" Don't let that be you.

Even if you decide to skip doing the data project, don't move on in this book until you have prepared a short answer, at least, "for public consumption."

The answer should not be so vague *(Som'thin' in management)* that no one knows what you want, nor should it be so blase that it only evokes sympathy *(Guess I'll sit 'til my 'comp runs out)*. If you say, "I'll take anything" you will probably hear of nothing. Likewise a litany of negatives *(I don't want shifts. . . I refuse to type. . . I'll never work for a grouch like my last boss)* puts your contacts on the spot of trying to find something that will please you. People back away from that kind of a situation.

Make it as easy as possible for them. Tell them briefly about the kind of work you want to get or describe an interest or skills that you have. Also indicate your willingness to listen to any possible prospects they might hear about.

Such a two-sentence answer might sound like that of one Pittsburgh job hunter who said, "I've always been interested in photography, especially with set lighting. I have done some freelance portraits, but I'm open to any good prospects." Another person said, "I'm up in the air about my next job, but as a management trainee in a hardware store, I've gotten experience with customer service and money handling as well as with tools and repairs."

Incidentally, the person first quoted in the answers above took a job doing newspaper advertising layouts of photography and sketches for a small Carnegie advertising firm. Although this only involved her photography skills marginally, she really liked the work. She heard about the job when someone remembered her and put together the idea of photography and fashion pictures.

The author of the second quote was passing the time between innings of an Etna softball game, talking with the older brother of a friend who was on the team. The conversation moved to a discussion of the high cost of repairmen and of handling complaints and ended with the older brother asking Tom if he would like to manage an apartment complex for him.

It pays to learn how to say what it is you are looking for.

PITTSBURGH RESOURCES FOR PUTTING YOUR ACT TOGETHER BEFORE TAKING IT ON THE ROAD

This is a list of groups and organizations who may be able to help you to assess your skills and decide on a career direction. It also includes agencies that use counseling to help the unemployed find work. The inclusion of a group does *not* constitute an endorsement of their programs or services.

This list does not include "Executive Career Counselors," that is, firms that you pay to go through a job hunt with you or to send out your resumes. For something about these, see PART FOUR of this book. Nor does it include programs open only to laid-off workers from one company. Individual practitioners, also, have been omitted although a few have excellent reputations and have been in business for years.

This information was accurate at the time of writing, but agencies close, open and change frequently. This is not a complete directory. You will need to supplement it with your own research before you can make an informed decision.

For a lot more detail on how to be selective once you've decided to explore getting help, there is no better advice than that of Richard Bolles in his book *What Color Is Your Parachute?* (see his Chapter Four and his appendix on Professional Help). Remember that price is not necessarily an indication of quality. In this area the only thing that counts is the result: *Do you end up knowing what it is you do well and want to do next?*

College-Based Testing, Career Counseling & Job Hunt Help

Carnegie Mellon University, Career Services and Placement, *Oakland.* For alumni. Fee. Career counseling and job search help. Contact: 268-2064.

Community College of Allegheny County, Career Planning and Placement Offices, *on each campus.* For graduates and former students. No fee. Career counseling, job search help. Contact the campus you wish to use. Community College also has some spe-cial programs such as **AMAP** *(McKeesport)* and the **PACT** Program *(North Side)* for single parents and homemakers that offer supportive services through a 120 hour career planning course. Eligibility requirements, no fee. Contact: 237-2595. The **Workers in Transition** program for unemployed Allegheny County residents aims to enhance your employability by directing you to appropriate

113

free training at the college or elsewhere or through classes in job search skills. Contact their hotline: 237-CCAC.

Duquesne University, Career Planning and Placement, *downtown.* For alumni. Fee. Career counseling and job search assistance. Contact: 434-6644.

Job Advisory Service/The Center for Professional Development, Chatham College, *Shadyside.* For adults. Fee. Career and job hunt counseling, vocational testing, comprehensive programs for the job search, group

programs and job listings. Contact: 365-1142.

Point Park College, Placement Office, *downtown.* For alumni. No fee. Testing, career counseling and job search help. Contact: 391-4100.

Robert Morris College, *downtown.* For alumni. No fee. Counseling on careers and job hunt help. Contact: 227-6821.

University of Pittsburgh, Placement Service, *Oakland.* For alumni. Fee. Testing, career counseling, job hunt preparation. Contact: 648-7130.

Non-Profit & Community-Based Testing, Career Counseling & Job Hunt Help

Carnegie Library, The Workplace Room. For all ages. No fee. A computerized information system with school searches and career descriptions. Also job listings, books, videos, a public access computer and typewriter for resume writing and out of town newspapers. All available at the main library in *Oakland,* call about availability at other branches. Contact: 622-3133.

Employment Information Network, *Allison Park.* Church related service matching job openings with job seekers. No fee. Counseling, referral to other employment support groups. Contact: 487-3370.

Interfaith Re-employment Group, *Mount Lebanon.* For adults. No fee. Assists professionals with job search and career development. David Bates, Director. Contact: 531-1007.

Jewish Family and Children's Service, Career Development Center, *Squirrel Hill.* For unemployed and underemployed of all ages. Sliding fee. Career counseling, job search techniques, job training and placement. Contact: 422-5627.

The Pittsburgh Experiment, Employment Anonymous. For anyone confronted with unemployment or reemployment problems. No eligibility requirements. No fee. The program provides support and referrals. Meetings at several locations. Contact: 462-9961, 281-9578 or 366-1338.

Priority Two, Four locations: *Sewickley, Churchill, Wexford and Bakerstown.* For adults. $35 fee, scholarships available. Uses seven week program to help former salaried employees find a job that is right for them. Contact: 741-8368.

Psychological Service of Pittsburgh, *downtown.* For adults. Fee. Testing, career and vocational counseling, job search techniques, company outplacement. Contact: 261-1333.

Unemployment Project, *Braddock.* For Turtle Creek/Mon Valley area residents. No fee. Family counseling and job search techniques. Contact: 351-0222.

Urban League of Pittsburgh, *downtown.* For adults and youth. No fee. Job listings and interview with a counselor. Contact: 261-1130. Jobs for those over 54, *uptown.* Contact: 687-0140. Training for youths, *uptown.* Contact: 687-2257.

YWCA, Professional Development Department, *downtown.* For men and women. Fee. Provides testing, counseling, job hunt techniques. Contact: 391-5100, ext. 246.

Government, Social Service & Special Assistance Groups

Association for Habilitation and Employment of the Developmentally Disabled (AHED). For adults. No fee. Career goal planning and special assistance in the job search. Contact: 381-3313.

Bidwell Cultural Training Center, *North Side.* For adults. Must meet JTPA eligibility requirements. No fee. Testing, counseling, job hunt and job training. Contact: 323-4000.

Blindness and Visual Services. For adults with visual disabilities. Counseling, job development and job search techniques, all no fee. Other services based on need. Contact: 565-5240.

Braddock Training & Employment Center, *Braddock.* For Allegheny County residents who do not live in the city of Pittsburgh. Income guidelines. No fee. Part of the Dept. of Federal Programs. Testing, counseling, job training, job search help. Contact: 273-6450.

Office of Vocational Rehabilitation. For Allegheny County residents with physical or mental disability. Sliding fee. Assessment, evaluation, ancillary equipment, therapy, retraining and job search assistance. Contact: 392-4950.

Older Adult Employment Program, *downtown.* For those 45 and older who are Allegheny County residents. Income requirement. No fee. Counseling, job development, training. Contact: 281-4658.

One-Stop Shop, Allegheny County, *downtown.* Primarily for unemployed or dislocated workers in the city and county. Eligibility requirements. No fee. Testing, job search techniques, training in vo-tech schools or community college. Contact: 355-6617.

Open Doors for the Handicapped of Pennsylvania, *East Liberty and Mon/Yough areas.* For disabled individuals living in Pittsburgh and Allegheny County. Differing requirements. No fee. Job training, job search techniques. Contact: 362-6347.

Opportunities and Resources (OAR). For youth. Eligibility requirements for most programs. Testing, career counseling, job training, job development and job search assistance. Contact: 562-0614.

Pittsburgh Employment Alliance. For job-ready adults with physical or mental disabilities. No fee. Assessment and evaluation, job search techniques and placement. Contact: 281-4224.

Pittsburgh Partnership, (JTPA), *downtown.* For adults and youth in the city of Pittsburgh. Income guidelines. No fee. Testing, training, job search. Contact: 255-8914.

Quest and Invest, *East Liberty.* For those 17-21 who live in Allegheny County but not in the city of Pittsburgh. This program is a part of Dept. of Federal Programs. Job training, job search help. Contact: 361-6200.

Senior Employment Program Coalition (SEPCO), *downtown.* For those 50 or older. No fee. A group of 11 agencies that assist senior job seekers with their job search techniques. Contact: 355-5264.

VA Medical Center, *Oakland.* For veterans in need of employment or vocational training. Income guidelines. No fee. Testing, counseling, training, job search help. Contact: 363-4900, ext. 228.

Vocational Rehabilitation Center, *uptown.* For people with special needs. Various eligibilities, some fees. Evaluation, skills training and preparation for working, job development and job hunt assistance. Contact: 471-2600.

Useful Reading
For Career Planning & Deciding

Bolles, Richard N. *What Color Is Your Parachute? A Practical Manual for Job Hunters and Career Changers.* 10 Speed Press, Updated annually.

Catalyst, Inc. *What to Do with the Rest of Your Life.* Simon & Schuster, 1980.

Catalyst, Inc. *When Can You Start?* MacMillan, 1981.

Figler, Howard. *The Complete Job Search Handbook.* Holt, Rinehart & Winston, 1988.

Germann, Richard. *Job and Career Building.* Harper, 1980.

Hagberg, Janet, and Leider, Richard. *The Inventurers: Excursions in Life and Career Renewal.* Addison Wesley, 1978.

Loughery, John, and Ripley, Theresa. *Career and Life Planning Guide.* Follett, 1976.

Morgan, John S. *Getting a Job after 50.* Petrocelli Books, Princeton, NJ, 1987.

Pilder, Richard, and Pilder, William. *How to Find Your Life's Work.* Prentice-Hall, 1981.

Thain, Richard. *The Mid-Career Manual.* Prentice-Hall, 1982.

PART THREE
A CRASH COURSE IN JOB MARKET SAVVY

5

WHAT TO KNOW BEFORE YOU HIT THE STREET

Pittsburgh's job hunters have become increasingly savvy and your efforts will be measured against this higher standard.

What will it take for *you* to become savvy, that is, competitively knowledgeable about the dynamics of your job market? Some books suggest reading up on a company's products and finances. This should be one of the things you do during your job hunt. By no means, however, would this kind of reading alone give you the being-in-the-know you need to generate appropriate interviews for yourself, the real goal of all such preparation. The process recommended in this chapter takes some work on your part, but if followed will give you what you need to know "before you hit the street."

What SHOULD You Know?

Take a moment to think of what you need to know as you step out to job hunt. Most Pittsburgh job seekers start with a few basic questions:

1. Where should I go to get a job? Where do my best chances lie?
2. Where do I fit into a company?
3. Where is the grapevine for my field and how can I become part of it?
4. What are the current problems in my field? What kinds of people do employers hire to solve them?

121

    5. What salary is "ballpark" for my skills?

    6. How can I judge whether a job I'm offered is a "dog"?

Many other questions could be asked. All of them have answers. In fact, there is virtually nothing about your job hunt that you cannot find out if you are willing to work at it.

Who Needs to Know What?

Do you need to answer all these questions to get a job? No. **You only need to know as much as it takes to get the job you want.**

The more competition you have and the better your competition is, the more you need to know in order to spot, assess and capitalize on opportunities early—before they are widely advertised.

If you are a career changer, you can turn your novice status to good advantage and motivate people to be helpful by the skillful use of questions. Do this by learning as many of the elementary facts about your prospective new field as you can before approaching your contacts. When you've done solid, basic research first, you will have intelligent queries which will help to establish you as a dynamic, alert, quick learner—in short, an attractive candidate.

The longer you've been in your career field, the more knowledgeable you are expected to be about who hires whom, the profit picture, department biases, expansions and impending overhauls, etc. Be cautious, however, about operating as though the "truths" of yesterday still hold in the changing market of today. Check that they do first. This helps guarantee your appearance as a seasoned professional rather than an out-of-touch, old-timer.

How to Learn

The Two Ways. The two ways to increase your understanding of your job market are reading and listening. Richard Bolles says it well,

> You read until you need to talk to someone because you cannot find more in books; then you talk to people until you know you need to get back and do some more reading. (*What Color Is Your Parachute*, p. 122)

Effective job hunters heed Bolles' advice. They learn factual data from factual sources such as newspapers and magazines and use their time with people to explore more subtle aspects. People can tell you things

that could never be publicly printed, e.g., "That firm never hires lawyers from the University of Pittsburgh and they've only chosen two from
Duquesne." "The vice-president of sales there is a family brother-in-
law who has no power in hiring. Richard, the head of accounting and
finance, actually does most of that."

But whether the information comes from trade journals or belongs in
the category of hearsay and grapevine communications, Bolles also
cautions:

> . . . the *woods are alive* with people who will solemnly tell
> you *something that ain't true* as though they were sure of it
> with every fibre of their being. So, check and cross check and
> cross check again the information that books, people, and
> experts give you. Let no one build any boxes for you; and
> watch that you don't hand them any wood with which to build
> one for you, either. (*Ibid.,* p. 103)

Reading Your Way to Job Market Savvy

If the thought of doing research creates an image of endless hours spent
in cobweb covered nooks of a library, think again. Whether you do your
reading and research in a library, at a computer or from the comfort
of your own easy chair, gathering information related to your job hunt
goals can be a direct short cut that puts you ahead of the majority of
job hunters and shortens your sojourn in the ranks of the unemployed.

Perhaps you feel like Allison, a career changing social worker, did:

> Initially, I thought that doing research was a cop-out, just
> a way to avoid the anxiety of looking for work. But after the
> first half day I spent at the Oakland library, I realized how
> naive I really was. I had been applying for jobs in "personnel"
> without knowing the difference between various positions, let
> alone being able to tell someone whether I was better
> qualified to work in benefits, wages and salary, training and
> development, or industrial relations. Presuming I didn't have
> to know this because I was changing careers probably wasted
> a few of my first contacts.

Today, three jobs later, she is Branch Administrator in the customer
service department of a large communications firm and swears by the
research route. "Don't wait for someone to take you aside and explain
things to you," she said. "It might not happen."

The Art of Reading with a Job Hunter's Eye

The place to start is by focusing on a specific interest area. Too broad a career goal (for instance, "Sales") will diffuse your research. Concentrate on a specific job target like wholesale food sales or international banking so that you can accomplish real results. If you have several goals and do not feel ready to choose among them, it is better to pursue one at a time rather than to start exploring all of them at once.

You may not need to read *about* your career field like Allison, but even the experienced professional can use some of the information readily available to advance a job search. Reporters for Pittsburgh newspapers, for example, often interview people for features on home town industries and companies. They usually include names, titles and current information that could take you hours to duplicate.

Test your ability to read with a job hunter's eye now. The following short article is about marketing hospital services. If you were job hunting in this field, what could you learn from this article?

EXECUTIVE REPORT   November, 1987

HEALTH CARE

Hospitals, heal thyself
Health care providers turn to marketing for financial well-being.

By John Benson

To survive in a competitive market these days, hospitals can no longer rely on just being good healers.

"Today's hospital can no longer think in terms of its caring, maternal image, but rather must look to a consumer-driven, value-oriented reputation," said Richard McDonald, president of McDonald Davis & Associates in Milwaukee, the nation's largest marketing communications firm specializing in health care. "The staying power of a hospital's fiscal integrity is most likely going to depend upon its marketing acuity."

McDonald said he believes hospital marketers should hold the rank of vice president and deserve equal footing alongside chief financial officers.

"Operations, finance and marketing. It's a three-legged stool," he said. "Take away one leg and the business —the hospital—will fall."

U.S. hospitals spent $1.1 billion on marketing in 1986, a 56 percent jump from $700 million in 1985, according to a study by Chicago's SRI Gallup. The study also reported the average annual hospital marketing budget— excluding marketers' salaries—is nearly $227,000. Budgets approach $500,000 annually in the largest facilities (350 beds or more).

While Pittsburgh-area hospitals have stepped lightly into advertising, other local marketing efforts seem to be, if not matching national marketing campaigns in aggressiveness, moving in a progressive direction.

One marketing push is in the direction of "wellness" programs, including diet classes, stop-smoking classes, physical fitness courses, aerobic dance lessons, stress management programs and many other illness prevention and education programs.

"We're (hospitals) trying to increase our market share," said Peter Hughs, assistant administrator of marketing and planning at Franklin Regional Medical Center. "We started marketing here two years ago. In order to stay competitive, we've had to turn to creating new programs and repackaging existing services."

In the past year, Franklin Regional has introduced a Breast Imaging Suite, which is an outpatient mammography service, and a physician referral service, one of the most popular hospital marketing tools in use today.

Franklin also introduced its Weekend Guest Program, where people needing at-home care (normally elderly people) can check in for the weekend. "The benefits of the program are twofold," said Franklin Regional President James Reber. "Guests enjoy a pleasant stay with individualized care and activities that are geared toward their expressed interests. The families, confident that their elderly family member is receiving excellent care, can enjoy an occasional weekend away from their responsibilities.

Hospitals have always been conscious of guest relations. But a new emphasis on attracting patients has hospitals scurrying to make their facilities as comfortable and hotel-like as possible.

"A hospital is basically a big hotel that heals people," said Hughes. "The healing process is just one part of healing people."

At Sewickley Valley Hospital, surveys of inpatients are conducted to measure the hospital's quality of comfort and adequacy of guest relations. Sewickley Valley Hospital Vice President Marvin Wedeen said there's no reason hospitals should not be as concerned with providing comfort as car makers and airlines.

"The public has been trained to expect comfort from plush interiors in cars and service and comfort on airplanes. We're just responding to that trained expectations," Wedeen said.

Wedeen emphasized that the key to balancing good guest relations and quality health care is moderation.

"Some hospitals go overboard. If you start dressing your personnel in fancy uniforms, you're going overboard," he said. "I think you can offer affordable and effective health care and include a certain level of comfort and service without overdoing it."

In more progressive regions, hospitals are offering such unheard-of (for hospitals) amenities as candlelight dinners for new patients, doorman and bellhop services, gourmet menus and more stylish furniture for private patients.

This kind of packaging is evident in area hospitals also. St. Francis Hospital's "Lean Teen" and "Clean Teen" programs are designed to trim down teenagers and get them off drugs, respectively.

WELL-Stop is Sewickley Valley Hospital's newly instituted smoking cessation program. Cope-Well is its four-week stress management program for women.

Women's health services are the hottest marketing items going right now. Over 35 percent of marketers surveyed recently by SRI Gallup reported women's services are their most successful product lines. Most local hospitals now have complete birthing centers and many are now offering various women's health screening programs.

As part of their childbirth program, Citizens General Hospital offers prenatal, lamaze and parenting classes. They also have sibling preparation classes, freedom from smoking classes, CPR classes and regularly hold special events concerning health-related issues, such as medication awareness and updates on medicare coverage.

One question raised by this influx of new services and repackaging of old services at hospitals is: Are hospitals responding to a genuine need or demand for these services, or are they trying to create their own demand to attract patients and generate income?

Wedeen admitted some local hospitals create programs hoping to invent a demand and a need for a service.

"It's a way for some who are unable to attract a certain segment of the community to capture a share of the market," he said. Wedeen was quick to add, however, that any service that can provide the community with any form of health information is generally a good thing.

"Total health care involves more than just donating your body to a machine. We've become so technology oriented that prevention is sometimes overlooked. Any effort that promotes wellness and health education has a positive impact on the public," Wedeen said.

Bill Jennings, vice president of marketing at Montefiore Hospital, said there are boundaries between excessive marketing and a hospital's responsibility for quality health care, but that any tangible maintenance of wellness promoted by a hospital is a plus.

"Hospitals need to be in continuous contact with the public so they can determine what is needed or wanted in the way of new services. That way, a demand won't be created, it will already exist," he said.

reprinted with permission

Finished? Good. The article mentioned:
1. Names of five local hospitals.
2. Names and job titles of four persons responsible for marketing at three of the hospitals.
3. Three types of hospital services that are being marketed locally *(wellness, women's health services, outpatient services)*.
4. "Quality environment" is a marketing feature for some hospitals locally.
5. The fact that a large hospital is one with over 350 beds.
6. The statistic that nationally the average hospital marketing budget, excluding salaries, is $227,000 a year.

Sometimes a bit of history or mention of a trend is more valuable than the factual information an article contains. For instance, early in the article the head of an advertising firm in Milwaukee is quoted (actually, he is described as the president of the "nation's largest marketing communications firm specializing in health care"). Does this suggest to you a topic that is peripheral to the topic of the article, but that could help you as a job hunter? Namely, that hospitals can contract with outside firms rather than hire all their own marketing personnel. Do a whole series of questions now arise? Questions like: Which hospitals do that *here*? What firms are they using? Would *I* have a better chance, given my background, to go with a health care marketing firm rather than directly with a hospital? Moreover, if you already knew that Pittsburgh has 16 large hospitals (over 350 beds) and learned from the article that Pittsburgh hospitals are not yet heavily into all phases of marketing, would you still be encouraged about prospects for job growth in the marketing department even though you read in this morning's paper that, overall, jobs are not growing in hospitals?

Now for another example. Here, let us say that you have a business degree and eight years of experience in selling financial planning services. The article below comes into your hands. What can you pick up from it?

PITTSBURGH BUSINESS TIMES   October 12, 1987

FINANCIAL PLANNING

Financial planning grows
PNB joins Mellon in offering specific planning via new group

By Rick Stouffer

As this country's rich get richer, and the middle class continues notching up to a higher plane, increased numbers of individuals need financial planning expertise. And more players are on a daily business basis entering the financial planning field.

And why not. To get the biggest payoff on their investments, to prepare for the smoothest transition from working to retirement, to save the most for their children's education, to prepare financial security for loved ones when the main breadwinner is gone and to hold off the tax man, individuals are willing to spend millions on sound financial planning.

Today, insurance companies, brokerage houses, accounting firms, individual planners, CPAs and lawyers are in one way or another offering planning services.

Recently, commercial banks have come to play, armed with the resources of the financial institution and literally a captive audience—their depositors, credit card users and loan customers.

Banks are placing more emphasis on financial planning, segregating the service from traditional trust services offered and capitalizing on the ability to refer customers to other bank units rather than turn down requests for help in such areas as investments.

And despite the increased number of bank failures and bank troubles throughout the country, studies indicate that banks are still rated highly among all entities providing financial advice. Built-in trust (no pun intended)

127

is part of a bank's financial planning mystique.

"Banks have all along offered financial planning to their most affluent customers," said Lee Rowland, administrative manager for the Pittsburgh office of Merrill Lynch.

"I would have to agree that they do have a built-in clientele."

In Pittsburgh, Mellon Bank has been a strong financial planning player since 1983 and Pittsburgh National Bank, which tried in the late 1970s to put together a program but failed, last month went public with its newest financial planning unit.

Each organization has a slightly different slant in terms of client to be reached and methods used, but both know the advantages to using in-house services to garner clients and the role planning can play in bringing new customers to the bank.

Each has also taken a somewhat different tact in reaching the same goals. Mellon relies on a staff of seven lawyers and/or public accountants with its head man a former 12-year Big 8 accounting firm veteran, while PNB has actually placed two certified financial planners on staff, rounding out its seven-person staff with lawyers and CPAs.

Personal contact, not pounds of computer printouts, remains the basis of each program.

"Our organization started in January 1983 upon my arrival from Price Waterhouse," said Joseph Banko, Mellon's vice president in charge of the Financial Planning Unit, part of the bank's trust operation.

Banko was not exactly bullish on the idea of establishing financial planning within a bank; he actually laughed at the idea.

"I at first said no way, there was nothing at a bank to entice people to use it for financial planning," said Banko, who only agreed to head the new unit if he got exactly what he wanted, what he knew would work.

"I told them that they needed products interesting to non-traditional trust customers," said Banko.

Those services included such things as traditional money management and tax planning, but also outside real estate and oil and gas investment advice and the first thing the new unit concentrated on: tax shelters.

Banko said that from the start Mellon was commited to making his unit work. And it is his unit, it remains part of the bank but is run as Banko's personal business.

Ten years ago, PNB did not make that type of commitment. Not only was the timing bad, but planners were not part of the organization and trust department personnel were basically thrown into the breach, according to Joseph Grieco.

"Today, there is definitely a commitment to make this work," said Grieco, one of two CFPs hired to put financial plans together.

PNB spent 18 months planning the group's activities, according to Grieco, trying to figure the best plan of attack, finally deciding that having actual planners on staff was a better idea than trying to train bankers to be planners.

Mellon and PNB also let their units be objective; no customer is forced to use PNB's brokerage service or Mellon's trust operation, for example. The products are there, if needed, and are certainly recommended, but there is no hard sell.

"A customer well serviced will be drawn to other Mellon services," said Banko. "We're not trying to do everything in-house."

Planners know a little about a lot of different subjects and customers have to realize this," said Grieco. "If they have an insurance question, we can't (by law) sell them insurance, but we can tell them, 'here's a group of what we think are good insurance people. You pick one.' "

Both units tout personalized service, each relies on computers to help staff members weed through dozens of answers to in-depth, personal questions about a client, and each charges radically different base fees.

Mellon's retainer range is between $3,000 and $5,000, with an hourly charge pegged at $75 per hour. The numbers would seem to indicate that Mellon is targeting only the creme de la creme individuals and/or corporate executives, but Banko said that if someone can afford the fees, the unit will take that person on as a customer.

"We don't tell people they can't come in," said Banko. "We even have a couple of lottery winners as clients."

PNB, on the other hand, admits that it can't offer its service to everyone, and that it is looking for clients 35 to 65 years old, with a minimum family income of $60,000 to $70,000 and a minimum net worth of approximately $100,000.

The basic individual charge for a PNB plan is $800, which includes about 10 to 12 hours of time with a client. Above that the rate is $75 per hour, with yearly updates costing $250.

"Right now, the 10 to 12-hour figure is more than enough," said Grieco.

PNB's traditional middle market customer is the financial planning group's target, according to Grieco.

"We're after the middle 60 percent of a company," said Grieco. "We can do our plan for the top 1 percent or 2 percent by adding on to our base rates, but that is not who we are trying to reach."

Both groups use the computer, but printouts measured not by pages but by pounds do not good reading—or a successful financial planner—make.

"You know what would happen if I walked into a chairman's office with a 70-page report?" said Banko. "I'd be out the door in about 30 seconds."

"Planning is really creative solutions to a client's situation," said Grieco. "We use the computer to give us a printout of a client's situation, but then we take that printout and refine it, to fit that person."

Grieco said that PNB does use a five-page executive summary which provides information and recommendations.

"We identify the issues, what should be done, why a person should do it and why what we say should be done is better than the alternatives," said Grieco. "People don't want to read a document, but they do want to be told what to do.

"And we don't want to give them information, we want to give them intelligence."

Both Banko and Grieco stressed the personal touch of their operations, maintaining that the one-on-one communication was what set their work apart from the competition.

Mellon's approach is certainly working. Banko admitted that for the first three years the operation was a money loser, but that now gross revenues are growing at a 30 percent per year clip.

Currently, Mellon has 200 individual clients and has relationships with five major Pittsburgh corporations, which offer to their executives planning as a perquisite or benefit.

In operation for approximately two months, PNB's group has seen and completed or is in the process of completing plans for 12 to 15 people, according to Grieco. Corporations are also targeted.

"We believe that there are three markets for our services," said Grieco. "There are the customers who talk to the bank's employees at various levels, the customers of lawyers and CPAs that we will talk to, and the corporations."

One corporation was particularly important to Banko, for the first group of executives his unit had to sell were the top executives within Mellon.

"We reasoned that if we couldn't sell our service to our own executives, we couldn't market it outside," said Banko.

The top 20 to 30 people within the bank were offered the service as a perquisite, with the then head of human resources serving as the guinea pig.

"Within three years, 95 percent of all executives within the bank were part of our program," said Banko.

Even with a built-in audience and the outside clout that Mellon and PNB carry, financial planners contacted were naturally taking a wait-and-see-if-it-flys attitude toward the new competition.

"We'll just have to wait and see how they do, but the outcome will be dependent on the capabilities of the people that they hire," said Karen Greb, a cer-

tified financial planner with the local Merrill Lynch office.

"If they get good people they could be very successful."

One planner compared the entry of banks into financial planning to another rush by new players less than a decade ago.

"Four to seven years ago, the brokerage houses got heavily into financial planning, then bagged the idea when they determined that it wasn't worth it," said William H. Humphries III, chief policy officer in Pittsburgh for AYCO Corp., a subsidiary of American Express.

"Margins are razor-thin (concerning financial planning), it is a very labor intensive operation and not a big moneymaker."

Banko sees his operation as successful and so do a lot of competitors. According to the Mellon VP, accounting firms now come to the bank to find their planning people.

reprinted with permission

You could read this article and absorb nitty-gritty information such as how much your competitors—the banks—charge for services and the number of pages to which they condense their computer printouts. However, if, at this moment, you were tired of being an independent financial planner and the thought of working under the umbrella of a bank sounded appealing, you would read with an eye to some different aspects of the article. You would think about the following:
1. Which of the banks would be more receptive to your rather decent financial planning credentials?
2. Which bank would be more receptive if your experience was primarily with upper income clients?
3. Besides banks, what other firms are mentioned as doing financial planning? As employing financial planners?
4. Given the differences in the client profile that each bank describes, what differences do you think would be found in their marketing to those clients? In their hiring of people with personalities compatible with those marketing images? Where do you fit?

Information of the kind in these articles is time sensitive. That is, if it is more than a few months old, you had better reconfirm who works for whom and who has been merged with whom.

Did your initial reading register the wealth of information mentioned in these articles? Could you remember it all six weeks from today? One tip every good researcher mentioned was: *clip everything you might want to use; date it; and keep it in a folder for future reference.*

Local News

The *Pittsburgh Press* and the *Pittsburgh Post-Gazette,* our two daily newspapers, and business newspapers like the *Pittsburgh Business Times* and *Allegheny Business News* yield information every day to those who read them with a job hunter's eye. Browse through a few issues of regional magazines like *Executive Report* and *Pittsburgh Preview* to determine if they are oriented toward your field of work. The *Wall Street Journal* and business sections of the *New York Times* are also good sources for business and commercial trends, but it is hard to beat the hometown news.

Articles like the two above with their contact names and local data are not the only valuable reading to be found in local newspapers. There are also the want ads, the "moving up" columns and meeting notices.

Want Ads. These are an obvious place to look for job openings but they also play another role in your information gathering. You can find job descriptions, titles and salary ranges there. You can also ferret out career paths by checking out ads for jobs one or two levels above the one you seek. Clues to non-published jobs are abundant. If one bank looks for a community events planner, you might assume that similar-sized banks maintain such a position, too.

"Moving up" Columns. Run regularly in Pittsburgh's newspapers and magazines, "moving up" columns list some of the local people who are being promoted or hired. Rather than being envious, look at these features as sources of information about names of potential hiring managers, job titles, as a clue to organizational structures, opportunities for unfilled slots and, when the articles are longer, as descriptions of career paths in your field. One job hunter made a practice of sending brief congratulatory notes to all people in her field whose names appeared in these columns. When she called for an appointment (about her job hunt) later, her thoughtfulness was often remembered.

Meeting Dates. Trade and professional associations' meeting dates are usually run once a week. In the Business and Labor Section of the Sunday *Press* (at this writing) and in each issue of the *Pittsburgh Business Times,* you'll find names of many active associations' scheduled events.

Typical Newspaper Listing of Meeting Dates

The Pittsburgh Chapter of Robotics International will open its fall season with a meeting Thursday at 8 p.m. at the Engineer's Club, William Penn Hotel.

Guest speaker is Lester V. Ottinger, president of Robot Systems Inc., Atlanta. His talk, entitled "The Application of Robots in Industry," is a review of the state of the art in robotics and the diversity of skills required for personnel working with robotic systems.

Other scheduled events are:

PITTSBURGH AREA COMPUTER CLUB will meet today at 1 p.m. in the Community Room of the Northway Mall, McKnight Road.

FINANCIAL EXECUTIVES INSTITUTE members will hear a talk by Dr. Jerry Jordan, a former member of President Reagan's Council of Economic Advisers, at its meeting tomorrow at 5:30 p.m. at the Duquesne Club.

SOCIETY OF PACKAGING & HANDLING ENGINEERS will meet tomorrow at 5:30 p.m. at the Holiday Inn in RIDC Park. Al Bayless and Dave Selway, Signode Corp., will present a program on plastic strapping systems.

AMERICAN FOUNDRYMEN'S ASSOCIATION will meet tomorrow at 6:15 p.m. at the Moose Club in East Pittsburgh. Peter Grazlotto of Dale Carnegie Courses is the guest speaker.

AMERICAN SOCIETY OF WOMEN ACCOUNTANTS will meet tomorrow at 6:15 p.m. at the Pittsburgh Hilton. Rick Ficher, of Rockwell International, will speak on "Time Management."

AMERICAN PRODUCTION AND INVENTORY CONTROL SOCIETY meets Tuesday at 5:45 p.m. at the Allegheny Club. "MRP Implementation" is the topic of a talk planned by Harvey E. Field, executive vice president of R.F. Alban Associates, Inc.

DATA PROCESSING MANAGEMENT ASSOCIATION will meet Tuesday at 6:30 p.m. at the Parkway Center Terrace Room. Jackie Horne, human relations consultant and trainer, will speak on "Effective Listening Techniques."

NORTH AMERICAN SOCIETY FOR CORPORATE PLANNING has invited G. J. Tankersley, Chairman of Consolidated Natural Gas Co., to speak at its meeting Tuesday at 5:30 p.m. at the Pittsburgh Press Club.

NATIONAL MICROGRAPHICS ASSOCIATION will meet Wednesday at 5:30 p.m. at Froggy's. Dale Carnegie marketing associate Peter Graziotto is the speaker.

MERCER COUNTY LEGAL SECRETARIES ASSOCIATION will conduct its fourth "Business Machines Show" from noon to 8 p.m. Thursday at the Sheraton Inn/Shenango, West Middlesex.

AMERICAN SOCIETY FOR TRAINING AND DEVELOPMENT is conducting a one-day workshop on "Enhancing Your Presentation Skills," Thursday from 8 a.m. to 5 p.m. at the Pittsburgh Hyatt. Lee Kraus, manager of Jones and Laughlin Steel Corp.'s Education Center, and Sarah Schreider, a private consultant, are in charge of the program.

GREATER PITTSBURGH CHAMBER OF COMMERCE is sponsoring a workshop on the unemployment compensation system Thursday, beginning at 9:30 a.m. at the Alcoa Theatre, Alcoa Building.

UNIVERSITY OF PITTSBURGH Graduate School of Business Alumni Association has scheduled a social event Thursday from 5 p.m. to 7 p.m. at the Pittsburgh Press Club. Special guest is Foge Fazio, head football coach at Pitt.

Books

There's a wealth of career field information to be found in books. If you know very little about your intended field, the place to start is with the "bible" of career field information, the *Occupational Outlook Handbook*. This book describes 300 occupational fields. It tells you what workers do on the job; the training and education required; earnings; advancement opportunities; working conditions; related occupations and employment outlooks. Although its data is based on nationally averaged statistics, which smooth over some of our local factors, it's an excellent resource for novices.

Once you've touched base with the *Occupational Outlook Handbook* you can move on to books that provide information specific to your career field. Although many of these are designed for young adults, there are some, like the *Jobfinder* series and the *Career Directory* series, that are useful at every skill level.

The *College Placement Annual* with its addresses of the 1,200 companies that recruit on campuses is especially useful to recent graduates who, for one reason or another, did not get to see those recruiters. *Inside Management Training* is good browsing for those looking for management training programs and the *Peterson Guides* offer a general look at major employers in different career fields.

Serious explanation of one industry (such as banking, or electrical machinery manufacturing) may call for using the industry surveys of *Standard and Poor* or *Value Line*. Because of their cost (subscription rate per year for *Standard and Poor Corporation Records* is $745), such directories are usually only available in larger, business-oriented libraries.

The Business Branch of Carnegie Library reports that the *Directory of Corporate Affiliations* (Who Owns Whom) is well used by job hunters, so is the *Standard Directory of Advertisers* and *Dunn's Guide to Health-care Companies*. The library has annual reports on publicly owned companies. If you are looking at companies that are privately owned, annual reports won't be available. Instead, try *Ward's Business Directory* or the *Macmillan Directory of Leading Private Companies*.

All the books mentioned are available either at the Business Branch or the new Workplace Room of the Oakland location of Carnegie Library. Other libraries, especially college libraries will have some, though not all, of these materials.

Magazines and Journals

Take a look at current trade journals in your field. If you do not know which ones are best, look in the *Encyclopedia of Business Information Sources* or the *Encyclopedia of Associations* at Carnegie Library. Listed under the names of trade associations and professional societies will be the titles of any journals they publish, the subscription cost and address of the editorial office. You can write to request a sample copy or to purchase a single back issue. If subscribing, request that your subscription begin with several back issues so you can obtain recent information without having to wait for future issues.

Magazine articles are useful for the job hunter who wants to do a quick study of a particular topic—like zero coupon bonds or focus selection interviewing. To find articles in magazines to which you do not subscribe, you can ask for assistance at the library or browse through recent volumes of the *Business Periodicals Index.* This index catalogues articles from magazines like *Business Week, Forbes* and from major trade journals, such as *Iron Age* and *Personnel.*

Carnegie Library of Pittsburgh carries about 5,000 magazines and journals. Some are bound; others are kept in microfilm form. The Business Branch subscribes to 80-100 magazines with a business orientation. University libraries often subscribe to esoteric journals in a wide range of fields. Many libraries now have computerized lists of every magazine received by every public library in the state.

Carnegie Library of Pittsburgh also has computerized access to the *New York Times* information bank and has the capacity for searching several other data bases such as DIALOG and Dow Jones News Retrieval at modest cost. You'll find terminals at the Business Branch and the main library and a very helpful reference staff.

Newsletters of Local Professional Associations

A superb source of home town data is to be found in the literally hundreds of newsletters published by local groups. They range from hand-stapled copies to full scale glossy issues. No library keeps a complete collection of them, but you can find out about them by asking people in your field. Practical information ranges from the names of people in local companies to opinions expressed by people you might meet in interviews. They may list local activities, noted speakers coming to town or illuminating surveys (especially salary surveys) of the local membership. In addition, they sometimes provide opportunities for you to write letters to the editors or articles which will raise your visibility.

The Best Kept Information in Town

The time will come when you want to know everything you can about one specific Pittsburgh company. That time most often will be shortly before a job interview with them. That's when you will want to know about the "clipping files" of Carnegie Library. Since 1970 they've been performing an invaluable public service by clipping newspaper articles about local businesses. They keep them at the Business Branch and, more recently, at the PA Room of the Oakland branch. Today they clip the *Press, Post-Gazette, Courier, Business Times* and *Wall Street Journal.* Give an information librarian the name of the local company you want, he or she will tell you if it is one of the hundreds they have on file. You can do this by phone. (Business Branch: 281-5945; PA Room, Oakland: 622-3154) It takes a few months for articles to get from the newspapers to their clipping files, so read on your own, too. There are some differences in the contents of the two collections. Also, the Business Branch is located in the downtown area while the Oakland location is open some evenings. To encourage your usage, you don't even have to have a library card or live in Allegheny County to use their materials in the library (only to take out books).

As an example of the kind of job hunting help you can get, a librarian recounted this story:

> A gentleman was going to be interviewed for a job in financial administration with the Pennsylvania Department of Transportation. He came into the PA Room, here, one evening and asked if we had anything about "the State." We were able to give him a *Commonwealth Phone Book* so he could see all the divisions of the state's Department of Transportation, their locations and the names of people there. We also had a copy of the *State Budget.* He could see how much was allotted for this year for each department and for major projects within departments. We showed him that part of the *State Planning Report* that describes the main transportation projects that are planned for future years. He got so much more than he had expected and we were delighted to be helpful.

Of course, not every story has such a good ending, but printed information is always there, waiting for you to tap into it. The other source of job market savvy—people—are there, too, but it takes a little more effort on your part to approach them properly.

Learning From People

Talk to people is at once the most obvious and complex admonition. There are whole books written on networking and using contacts to learn about the hidden job market.

Three critical guidelines should direct your gathering of information from people.

Know what it is that you want to learn. Get it into one or two simple sentences before you venture out.

Ask questions that can be answered. Questions like, "Who will hire me?" don't get many answers. Nor do questions that put others on the spot: "Is that company prejudiced?" "Does your boss play politics in hiring?" Answerable are questions like these: "In your opinion, which are the top three CPA firms in town that are not branches of the Big 8?" or "Is anyone you know doing focus selection training?" or "What's the name of the department manager there? Is he local?"

Ask the question of the person who can best answer it. If you want a detailed description of a job for which you are a candidate, you would best ask an acquaintance who is familiar with both the job and the manager who will be doing the interviewing. If your question is properly phrased, he can give you valuable tips. If he does not have answers, he may direct you to someone who does.

If you are not a newcomer to the field, you might wonder, as did one local marketing assistant, "How can I ask questions without appearing to be a dummy?" You can ask someone about a company's benefit program and power structure without appearing incompetent. You can display confidence in your work skills while soliciting advice. "Would you have this resume typeset?" A person with strong writing skills might ask, "Will my lack of formal technical writing courses hamper me in competing for jobs in today's market?"

Remember though, few people are vitally interested in whether you get a job or not. To only a few very close associates can you openly state, "I'm looking for work. Do you know of a job for me?" Set out with a different goal, however, namely, to find your best job opportunities by becoming well informed about your job target. Note the trends, the needs, the issues, the comings and goings of personnel—all this you can get from many, many people who need not know you intimately or be in a position to hire you.

Who to Talk To

People who are active in your field are your richest source of current information about your job market. Talk directly to people who are doing what you want to do and talk to their bosses. Seek out the individuals who've been recommended to you as someone-who-knows. The people who know the most are likely to be in positions of authority in their own organizations. They may also be active members of trade or professional groups or speakers at seminars and meetings.

When you're already working in a field, you're part of a ready-made grapevine or network. You probably bump into people who share your interests during the course of work or meetings. It can be natural and easy to explore current issues or concerns with them, as long as you're not asking to be let in on their organizations' secrets. Finding out what's going on may be as simple as asking, "What's new?"

If you're new in town or if you're changing careers, you will need to work harder to make your opportunities happen. But you're really just a phone call or a letter away from anyone you want to talk to. If you can get a referral from someone to your potential contact, fine, but if not, you can still reach key people. Let them know you're new in town or interested in a career change to their field. Say (or write) something like, "I understand you're very knowledgeable about what's going on in this field locally. I'd like to meet with you for twenty minutes to discuss some questions which have come up during my exploration of the field."

Fred, a former secondary school teacher and vocational guidance counselor, explored his market this way. Initially, he planned to respond to ads for college and trade school recruiters but concern about his qualifications held him back. He decided to check first with some of the recruiters who came to his high school. From observing and talking to them he learned three important facts: 1) Schools picked people whose personal style reflected their images; 2) Starting salaries ranged widely and some recruiters' paychecks were tied to the number of students they enrolled; 3) Recruiters came from a variety of backgrounds, some from teaching.

Fred ruled out the pay-on-commission jobs, but explored further. He came up with a name from his past—a former department chairman from graduate school, with whom he'd had good rapport. He reintroduced himself by phone and set up an appointment.

The former department chairman, who was now a dean, confirmed some of his research. "Yes, the recruiter's image does reflect the school's marketing strategy. Further, from what I hear, everyone who ever went past high school feels qualified to become an admissions rep." Fred was secretly glad he had held back on mailing out his resume.

The most important thing that came out of Fred's interview with the department chairman-turned-dean was the suggestion that he look into the community college system. "I think someone with your polished skills in assessing academic ability might be a real asset over at CCAC." When Fred inquired if the dean knew anyone there who might tell him how their programs operate, the dean replied,

> Well, the director is pretty much a local expert. He might talk to you. Also, I'm friendly with a person who's just set up a program on the West Mifflin campus. Tell Karen I told you to call her—and say, "Hello" for me.

Fred got the names and one phone number and went on from there. As he talked to both these people, he began to see what types of positions were realistic for him. He eventually applied for and got a job assessing the academic aptitude of CCAC apprenticeship program applicants and developing remedial educational programs tailored for each student. He got the lead for his new position from Karen, who told him about it as they talked about programs on other campuses.

Fred became savvy about his market by using the classic technique of interviewing for information. His initial conversations were very different from job interviews, yet they were not merely social. He was looking for information. He knew it and he made sure the people he spoke with knew it also. He was able to create a relaxed atmosphere. He was not on the spot, nor were they. He was successful in every interview because his goal was to obtain information and he got it. He was genuinely appreciative and let people know *this*, too.

Notice that Fred did not ask the dean if he knew anyone at Community College who could give him a job. (Actually, the dean would have had to say *no*, because Karen was not in a hiring position.) The dean didn't give Fred a job or even give him a lead to one, but he did inform him of another person to contact.

In its pure form, an interview for information is distinguished from a referral interview, or a courtesy interview as it is sometimes called, by the fact that in the first, the content centers on questions which you want to have answered. It shades into a referral interview when you want that person to sponsor or hire you and you turn the attention onto your own qualifications. Weave your way carefully between these shoals. Differentiate, if you can, between the people who can give you information and those who can give you jobs. If you want a job, don't begin by saying, "I'm not looking for a job; I just want to talk to you." If you tried a job pitch halfway through your conversation, you would appear to have lied, because you did. On the other hand, when you want information, you can state up-front that though you will be looking for a job later, right now, you do not expect them to know about any openings. You will get more positive responses this way.

Not everyone lands a job while exploring his or her market, but a large proportion (56%) of all successful job hunters do.

Other Roads to the Hidden Job Market

Go to local, state and national **conferences** and **conventions** in your chosen field, regardless of how boring the speakers or the location (York, Pennsylvania in February, for instance). At these gatherings you will find a bigger collection of people—who work for or are potential employers—than you could personally get around to seeing in at least a month.

"Talk shop" a lot and listen even more. If nothing else, you'll learn names of new people. Be alert to news about companies' recruiting efforts or new projects which may be a tip-off to good jobs later. Some conferences are out-and-out meat factories where everyone knows that resumes are to be freely exchanged. Most are not, so, when in doubt, jot down names and addresses while you're there or get business cards. You can let them know you're job hunting later. Call them after a week or two to set up an appointment, or write.

Most fields have **professional, trade** or **union associations.** Attend local meetings of the groups which provide you with the most up-to-date information and the most contact with potential employers. Although there are some associations that are not open to people outside the field, most provide an opportunity to attend a trial meeting, at least.

Attending association meetings is a non-stressful way of being with the people whom you want to contact later in your role as job hunter. Here, you can spend time with them as a peer.

If you are wondering how to act, Richard Bolles offers good advice when he says, "Dress well and conduct yourself as *quietly confident that you will be an asset to any organization you ultimately decide to serve in.*" (*What Color Is Your Parachute,* p. 101)

Much has been said about *using* professional and trade associations to springboard a job hunt. There is a fine line between use and abuse —a line which often becomes blurred. Some people have stomped on the line, to their own disadvantage, because collaring members at

139

meetings to ask for a job becomes counter-productive quickly. After all, these groups have a ready-made grapevine.

There is a lot you can glean from the right side of that invisible line, though. You can learn what kind of dress is standard; topics of interest; attitudes of members; new trends; the structure of departments in various companies (gotten by noting the titles of members); which levels of people attend the meetings; movement of people from employer to employer; which companies are *not* represented in the membership, and other "news." If you have not been a member of a group, you might consider joining now.

One Pittsburgh job hunter who had let her membership in a professional society lapse, rejoined when she was unemployed, saying, "I have more time now that I'm not working, so even while I'm job hunting I'll be able to do some things for the organization that I've always wanted to do." She raised her visibility most effectively. People became aware that she was looking for work but she also *gave back* something to the organization. The quality of two programs that she put on for the group displayed some of the qualities of the work she could do. Job leads really did come to her. Of course, that is never guaranteed. Nevertheless, the key to operating with integrity is to give as well as to receive something from the group.

Finding Associations

The most comprehensive listing of local associations comes from the Greater Pittsburgh Chamber of Commerce's publication: *Chambers of Commerce and Civic Agencies, Trade and Professional Organizations and Women's Organizations.* It is by no means exhaustive because small groups start up every day and others disband or become dormant for a year or two. In some cases the only way to get in touch with an organization is to phone officers (who are newly elected each year) because the group does not rent separate office space.

Occasionally a local magazine like *Pittsburgh Magazine* or *Pittsburgh Preview* will run a partial listing of associations with phone numbers. Local papers publish calendars of meetings each week. Of course, you can ask people in the field which groups they belong to and who the current president or membership officer is. That is another reason to talk to people.

You can find listings of national groups and inquire if they have local chapters. In addition to the Chamber of Commerce publication, Carnegie Library has three other helpful directories:

1. The *Encyclopedia of Associations,* three volumes. Presently the best available.
2. *National Trade and Professional Associations* directory.
3. *Directory of State, Regional and Commercial Organizations.* A 1,350 entry listing of Pennsylvania municipal organizations.

Miscellaneous Opportunities

You may find that **seminars** or **continuing education** courses in your field are fertile ground for meeting peers. When you go, preserve the attendance rosters. Call the people later, if appropriate.

If you are a recent graduate, do not forget that *instructors of classes in your career field* can be a good source of job market information. Look for people who currently consult or work in the field while teaching part time and those who are part of the job placement committee at your school. You need not be currently in their classes, although the more distant the relationship you have with them, the more useful it is to have a third party who will refer you to them. One bright young Pittsburgher, who was completing her degree work at a small Christian college in southern West Virginia got her professor to give her the name of a department head at the University of Pittsburgh. Through him she was routed to no less than three other teachers, the last of whom gave her a lead to a summer spot at the firm where he worked part-time. She was in competition with students from the university, but it was a competition she would never have known about otherwise.

An Ongoing Process

Information is the basis of all good decision making. Once you get the information you need for your job hunt, keep it coming. Determine to establish a regular reading and participation program. If reading articles related to your work bores you, perhaps you are not in the right field or are so knowledgeable that you should consider writing one yourself. See yourself as both a giver and receiver of the expertise exchanged in professional associations and alternate those roles as you move upward in your career.

From Theory to Practice

Reading that all these information resources are available may seem like a theoretical exercise—at least until you have a real question that
141

you need to answer. That is when you will want to be already proficient at drawing together all your sources of information. In the example that follows, you can see how printed materials and information from people can be intermingled to arrive at the answer to a frequently asked question.

Example #1: What Salary Can I Ask for?

This is something you may want to research *before* you get into a job interview. The salary that a company is willing to pay and the salary you are willing to accept depends on numerous items, both tangible and intangible. Some of the considerations that go into the final figure are:

> Current supply of your specific talent in your job market
> Current demand for your talents
> Size of the company
> Industry in which the company participates
> Financial strength of the company
> Hiring manager's ability to alter pay scales set by policy
> Trade-off between salary and benefits
> Potential for increased earnings
> Living costs in the area
> How well you have sold yourself for the position.

Think first about what you need to know. Probably you want to know an appropriate salary *range* with a 10% variance for your intended position. Second, look at your resources for answering that question and begin your research with the most promising. Your resources include the following:

1. *Your own earnings.* Except for career changers and people switching from the public to the private sectors of the market, the first and most obvious source is your current salary. If you are changing careers, the *Occupational Outlook Handbook* is the universal starting point. Follow by asking a local person to confirm a wide salary range for the Pittsburgh area.

2. *Want ads* are an easy-to-reach source for salaries in some jobs, especially if you read them over a period of weeks.

3. *A contact or friend who is working in the company* is another source of information. He or she may not know the salary for *your* position but can probably give you some idea about the benefits package offered by

the company. Further, an employee can tell you whether the company pays a higher or lower salary than others in the industry locally.

4. *Directors of employment agencies* can help if you have used them at some point in your job hunt. They are usually well informed about salary levels in their areas of expertise. Headhunters and executive recruiters won't be pinned down, but you can probably get a range confirmed.

5. If you belong to a *local professional association,* see if they conduct periodic local salary surveys of members.

6. The "Index to Salaries" in the new publication *Business Rankings and Salaries Index* (Gale Research, 1988) doesn't give the actual salaries, but tells you all the known sources of salary information for any particular occupation. Five minutes with this book can put you onto the right track if you haven't found any answers yet. It is especially good for finding trade magazines that publish salary surveys. There's a copy at the Business Branch of Carnegie Library. To get the trade magazines, you can call the editorial offices of the magazine and see if you can purchase the issue you desire. You can also see what other local libraries have a copy of it by using Carnegie Library's computer access to the holdings of public libraries across the state.

7. The *American Management Associations* publish salary surveys in eight areas: top management, middle management, professional/scientific, supervisory management, sales personnel, technician, office personnel and hospital and health care. Some of the fields list national or regional salary averages. Others are specific to one of 80 metropolitan areas of the country (Pittsburgh is one of these areas). Costs of the surveys range from 80 dollars up, so they might be a good co-operative investment for members of a local professional association.

8. If you still have not come up with any answers, you might try the *American Almanac of Jobs and Salaries* (John A. Wright. Avon, 1984.) at Carnegie Library's Workplace Room, Oakland branch. You could also look at the *Almanac of American Employers* (1985) at the library's Business Branch. It lists salaries and benefit packages at 500 of the country's largest firms. Or you could ask to look at the most recent U.S. Department of Labor's *Area Wage Survey* for the Pittsburgh area.

9. Finally, if you are relocating to Pittsburgh from another major city, you can review the relative cost of living. Carnegie Library of Pittsburgh has a *Cities File* (Second Floor, Main Reference Room) which has costs of living index information about major cities.

Example #2: _____
(put your question here)

Here is an opportunity for you to consider a question you have about *your* job search. List the various people and written resources you can tap for an answer.

1. _____

2. _____

3. _____

6

DEVELOPING YOUR JOB MARKET

A job hunting accountant was a CPA and had four years of experience. He was lamenting over his job search:

CPA: *There are no jobs.*
Q: *Where do you want to work?*
CPA: *I thought a bank or medium-sized accounting firms would be good places.*
Q: *Where have you been?*
CPA: *I've been everywhere. The banks aren't hiring and I went to all the accounting firms where I had leads. Nothing.*
Q: *How many of the banks did you get to?*
CPA: *Mellon and Equibank. I sent my resume in.*
Q: *What about the professional firms?*
CPA: *I had leads to two and there was a third one that I decided to try.*
Q: *What happened with those? Did any of them look good?*
CPA: *Oh, yeah—two of them. But I never heard back from them.*
Q: *Oh.*
CPA: *Do you think I ought to go back to school and learn computers?*

There is no sense in giving up on a job hunt until you've exhausted all your real possibilities. The CPA above has lots of untried opportunities. Two banks certainly do not exhaust the number around; there are more accounting firms than he has considered; these are not the

145

only organizations that employ CPAs and he has yet to follow up on any of his prospects.

The single major reason that many job hunters fail to "turn over all their stones" is that they simply are unaware of how the job market operates and how their personal job market relates to it.

How the Pittsburgh Job Market Operates

Jobs open up every day. Openings come about when a new job is created or when people retire, leave town, die or are fired. The chart of *Average Annual Job Openings* in this chapter gives you a rough idea of job openings in your field. These figures are the tip of the iceberg, however, for they don't take into account the movement from one job to another within the same occupation. These openings that don't get counted increase the real number of opportunities available to you. Together, the total is more in line with the study mentioned earlier which suggested that perhaps up to one third of all jobs are open in any given year.

Naturally, some fields have more openings than others, but a large number of openings does not guarantee that a job is easy to get or that there is no competition.

A field like mechanics is a good example. In 1988, there was an estimated average of 1,216 openings in the greater Pittsburgh area for mechanics. Of these, only 29 were expected to be due to growth. When you consider the large number of qualified people who are seeking work in this field, you have a classic example of a tight job market.

Markets Within Markets

At the same time, there is a local shortage now of mechanics who can repair data processing machines. This points out that there is not just one job market in which everyone jostles for elusive jobs. Engineers, for example, do not compete with MBA job seekers. Even package design, ceramic and mechanical engineers are not in competition with one another. Rather, every field has its own job market and within that market are specialties and sub-specialties, each with its own market ebb and flow.

Annual Average Job Openings for Selected Occupations

Pittsburgh PMSA (includes Allegheny, Fayette, Washington and Westmoreland counties only)

Occupation	1995 Employment Projection	Annual Average Job Openings		
		Due To Growth	Due To Labor Force Separation	Annual Average Openings
Total, all occupations	957,882	5,585	36,932	42,517
Managerial & administrative occupations	62,427	540	2,754	3,294
Management support occupations	30,841	306	950	1,256
Engineers, architects & surveyors	13,288	70	394	464
Natural scientists, computer & math scientists	6,839	116	108	224
Social scientists	1,217	12	29	41
Social, recreational & religious workers	10,570	94	561	655
Lawyers & judges	5,374	68	318	386
Teachers, librarians & counselors	54,534	536	1,637	2,173
Health diagnosing & treating occupations	37,213	716	1,192	1,908
Writers, artists, entertainers & athletes	9,106	60	326	386
Technicians occupations, including health & engineering	37,178	402	719	1,121
Marketing & sales occupations	114,479	1,222	5,749	6,971
Administrative support occupations including clerical	162,485	401	5,458	5,859
Service occupations, including cleaning, food & health	180,346	2,290	8,618	10,908
Agricultural, forest, fish & related occupations	12,557	−9	704	695
Blue collar worker supervisors	12,446	−149	511	362
Construction trades	29,274	121	870	991
Mechanics, installers & repairers	39,234	29	1,187	1,216
Precision production occupations	18,760	−186	810	624
Machine set up, operators & tenders	25,561	−532	975	443
Hand working occupations, including assembly	12,115	−240	475	235
Plant & system occupations	1,869	−13	93	80
Transportation & material moving operators	43,607	−44	1,500	1,456
Helpers & laborers	29,969	−261	839	578

Source: For complete listing see *Pittsburgh PMSA, Occupational Trends & Outlook for Total Civilian Employment 1984 and Projected 1995.* Department of Labor and Industry, Harrisburg, PA, 1987. Sequence of occupations listed follows line numbering system of *Trends & Outlook* chart. Data may not add to total due to rounding.

Your Personal Job Market

Your personal job market is defined as **all those jobs for which you are qualified in all the organizations where you could work.** The number of jobs in that pool varies with your work specialty. A radiation therapy technician, for example, may have a pool of 54 positions in this geographic area. A secretary with an insurance firm would have a much larger number of potential positions in her job market.

Learning about the entire Pittsburgh job market is an impossible task. You can, however, learn a great deal about the intricacies of a small, well-focused segment of it. That is the way to tap into the hidden job market for your field.

Developing a Job Market Profile

A health administrator and planner who had worked for six years at the largest hospital in town felt her market was *Hospitals* and that she didn't have many other options. She changed her opinion when she drew up a list of *all* the places she could think of that employed people with her background or interests. The list looked like this:

> Hospitals: profit, non-profit and health systems
> Nursing homes & extended care centers
> Community health departments
> Voluntary health agencies
> Benefits departments of large corporations
> Schools: public systems and colleges
> Mental health centers
> Rehabilitation centers
> Research centers
> Group medical practices
> Women's health centers
> Armed forces
> Emergency medical services

Personal preference determined which part of the market she would concentrate on first. Her interests tended strongly in the direction of community health or voluntary organizations and she had well-developed communication skills. From her list she selected two types of organizations that seemed most attractive and began writing down names of actual employers that she knew. She included even those she thought she might eliminate later because of distance, salary or working conditions. As she began thinking about hospitals, she decided her

148

strongest interest would be in those that had close ties to their communities, so "Hospitals as Community Resources" became the title of another grouping. At this point her lists looked like this:

COMMUNITY HEALTH DEPTS.	VOLUNTEER AGENCIES	HOSPITALS AS COMMUNITY RESOURCES
Allegheny Cty. Health Dept.	Cancer Society	
Health Information Center	Lupus Foundation	St. Francis
	Western Penna. Safety Council	South Hills Health System
	Myasthenia Gravis Assoc.	
	American Parkinson's Disease Assoc.	

The next step was to identify *all* the potential employers for her job market. She could have paged through the yellow pages of the phone directory, but she was aware of a local directory of health, welfare and community organizations called *Where to Turn*. From it she came up with names of 22 voluntary health organizations and four sub-departments of the county health department that were interesting possibilities.

To find which hospitals were actively servicing their communities, she followed her hunch that these would be hospitals with outpatient facilities. To confirm that she had listed all of them, she used a directory of area hospitals that indicated which had outpatient services.

At a one-day seminar on community health services the previous year, she received an information packet which included a list of participants and their organizations. The people who had attended that seminar either shared her interest or were sent by agencies who were concerned about the subject.

As she dug through the packet information, she noticed that some participants were from third-party organizations such as insurance companies and Blue Cross-type organizations. The thought clicked that these groups, too, had an interest in preventive health care, at least among their own subscribers. So a fourth list evolved,—"Third-Party Organizations"—and she resolved to find out something about how they hired, too.

At this point you may well be saying she was "conveniently lucky" (for the purpose of this book) to have those directories. But there are an amazing number of lists and directories about. Some are public, some are quasi-public and others are only in the possession of the members on the list.

Most of them, however, are accessible to the determined, creative job hunter. The collection of publicly available directories of Pittsburgh

149

employers at the end of each of the job fields in Chapter Two identifies many, but by no means all, of the directories that you can use in developing your own list of potential employers.

Your Job Market Profile

You can take the following steps to develop your own list of potential employers.

1. Be clear about the skills you want to use; have a job target.
2. Identify all the *types* of organizations where you might work (like the health planner's original list).
3. Select two or three (initially) of the most interesting/realistic types for you.
4. Using a sheet of paper for each type, list the names of actual employers where you could work. Use directories, the phone book, other people's suggestions, *all* your sources. Allow some time to do this. Don't eliminate at the start. Put addresses and phone numbers in, if you like.
5. Add to your list every time you think of, hear of, or see the name of another potential employer.

If your list of potential employers is drawn well, you have a concrete look at your personal job market as it stands at this particular moment. While it does not guarantee you a job, it is a very selective list—chances are good that you will work at one of the places on your list.

Narrowing Down

You may be in a general field like social work and have a specialty like counseling drug and alcohol addicts. You can create an extremely narrow job market for yourself by deciding that your next job, for example, will be with a profit making firm rather than a non-profit hospital. There may be only three or four employing firms in this market, but you'll have the advantage of concentrating your energies totally onto this small area.

Or Opting for Expansion

However, it makes sense to expand your job market when things are taking a lot longer than you anticipated; when positions in your field are really slow to open or it's overcrowded, and when you feel upbeat and positive about the area of expansion.

To be successful, expanding your job market must be more than exploring one field, getting discouraged and looking for another kind of job, and then another, and on and on. There must be some kind of system to your thinking and decision making. Two systematic ways to expand your job market are by increasing the range of positions you are looking for or the geographic area in which you are willing to work.

When you increase the range, look at related positions first. Think about your area of specialization. Where does it fit generally? If you did production management in extruded plastics, you might expand your search to firms that use other methods of manufacturing plastic products. A secretary with an insurance firm could expand her options by considering law firms, universities, construction firms, and so on.

You can also consider work in adjacent fields. A local engineer who designed specialized cardboard packaging saw a tighter market ahead and moved into his company's sales department. He judged correctly that in a downturn production staff might be laid off, but the sales force would be retained to work even harder and he would become doubly valuable.

Choosing to work in related fields needs careful forethought, however. Most of the time people get hired to do exactly what they have done before, or something quite similar. Nevertheless, you may find that you can expand your potential work settings considerably if you look at the skills that are involved in a job rather than just its job title.

A Greenfield woman worked as a technical writer of training manuals used by educators. She wanted to investigate related job opportunities. Since her educational background was in psychology and research, she began by looking into opportunities in a large mental health research setting. She found there were three types of research and technical writing jobs there that she was capable of doing because of her current experience. Without an advanced degree, however, she would probably stay at one salary level. Dolores then began investigating whether hospitals needed people to develop instruction manuals and evaluation programs for departments that were introducing sophisticated diagnostic equipment. In this nascent field, she felt, degree requirements would not be so important for advancement. Conversations with people in some hospital departments and a referral interview with a local equipment manufacturer made her conclude that jobs would be very limited in number. Around the same time Dolores began looking into the computer area. She suspected that computer consultants could use someone with her skills to adapt documentation (the teaching manuals) to individual business applications whenever software systems were changed. She found some part-time opportunities in this area but she is holding out for full-time work with full benefits before changing jobs. Expanding her market meant looking across fields to see positions where her skills functioned.

Expanding Geographic Area

A simple thing like increasing the geographic area in which you are willing to work can also bring increased opportunities. Given Pittsburgh's topography and roads, your personal geographic map will probably not be a mere circle drawn five miles around your home. An actual trial run by auto or PAT bus, even if you are a native, can answer doubts about distance and put misconceptions to rest. A Dormont job hunter who is willing to travel to the Greater Pittsburgh Airport vicinity has more opportunities for jobs than if he limits himself to the downtown area alone. The RIDC Industrial Park on Route 28 is closer to many people in Penn Hills than the Golden Triangle. Consider your geographic boundaries—both mental and actual. See if their expansion is an option you want to exercise.

Where Do I Fit in an Organization?

Armed with your job market profile of potential employers and knowing what skills you have to offer them brings you to the starting gate of active job hunting. But some job hunters are stopped short because they aren't able to say how they fit into a company. Especially in large firms, a frequent screening question used by the personnel office is, "What department would you like to work in?" You must show at least a rudimentary understanding of how that company is structured in order to be considered.

The work done in all organizations can be broken down into functions or parts. Whatever the organization does—whether it manufactures beer or provides family therapy—different employees will be designated to provide it, sell it and bill for it. Although the words used to describe these functions may differ from company to company, the essential work of each function remains the same.

To see how the different functions interrelate, look at the model of organizational structure. This is a simplified framework for figuring out where you fit.

Functional Structure of Organizations

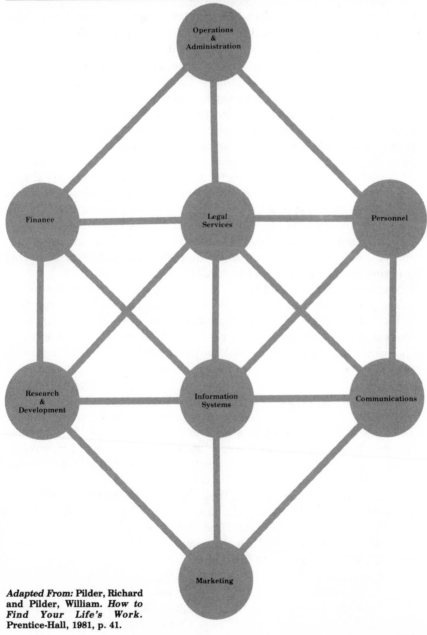

Adapted From: **Pilder, Richard and Pilder, William.** ***How to Find Your Life's Work.*** **Prentice-Hall, 1981, p. 41.**

Each of the six basic functions on the outer rim of the diagram are distinct although they are related to the other parts. Legal services and information systems are cross-functional, which means they are used by all the other departments. In smaller companies, one person may informally carry out several functions. In larger companies, each function tends to become a whole department.

Operations/administration is the function that distinguishes one organization from another and differs markedly from industry to industry. The operation of a company means the printing or the beer making, the filling of teeth (for a dentist) or the holding of classes (for a university). The finance department, on the other hand, does essentially the same work in a manufacturing company as it does in a large law firm. The same is true of personnel, communications and marketing.

The information systems area is the newest and most rapidly changing of the work functions. Computers are its keystone. While computers began to be used first in the finance departments for billing and accounting work, their use is expected to spread until all functions will have computerized tools incorporated into their work. Today, companies vary considerably on whether they have computer/information systems that function as independent departments.

Management is not indicated on the chart, because it is a role that takes place within *all* the functions of an organization. Management skills, which include planning, organizing, decision making, communications and leading have a role to play in each function. A 3-dimensional diagram of an organization would be pyramidal and would indicate one manager heading each department. There may be several layers of managerial hierarchy leading to a single chief executive officer.

Unless you have past management experience, your management entry position must come on the level of one of the departments. This is why so many job hunters show their lack of knowledge when they vaguely state their job objective as "management." However, an objective such as "a management position within finance" or "within marketing" begins to be meaningful.

Richard and William Pilder in their book *How to Find Your Life's Work* have written a brief, excellent chapter "How Organizations Function and Where You Fit." It summarizes each functional area and the kinds of positions within it. Within the communications area, for instance, jobs fall into several classifications:

Customer Relations	International Relations
Government Relations	Creative Services
Investor Relations	Employee Communications
Media Relations	Community Relations

After reading it, a Bloomfield graphic artist who wanted to work on annual reports or brochures in a big corporation overcame an initial hurdle at the personnel office by describing his functional objectives in terms of corporate organization. His objective, he explained, was "to work in corporate communications using my graphic design and layout skills to produce striking and attractive investor relations materials." Once he got in the door, he was able to discuss his design ideas and elaborate on his willingness to consider other corporate areas where his skills could be used.

Look at your own work skills to see where in an organization you might fit best. Using this kind of research can help prevent the old screened-out-blues.

PART FOUR
WHATEVER IT TAKES

7
PLANNING A JOB HUNT

Finding a good job rarely happens by accident. An effective job hunt operates within the framework of a plan that focuses on the objective of the job hunt—getting you in contact with the greatest number of people who could hire you.

How Successful Job Hunters Operate

Sometimes one method of job hunting—networking or mass mailings —is proposed as the only route to follow. But most successful job hunters use several routes, following up on the ones that produce interviews or leads and falling back to others when one path dries up. They readjust and adapt their plans a little every time they uncover another potential employer or get a new insight into how their particular market is operating.

In reality, job hunts do not unfold in a series of distinctly separated steps. For instance, you don't need to decide precisely which job you want before you can begin to write a resume or research your market. You need not practice interviewing techniques until you are perfect before attempting to answer a want ad or have a "real" interview. In actual life, people make the decision about the job that is right for them *while* they are hunting and they perfect their interviewing skills by doing real interviews.

This is not to suggest that you begin job hunting with *no* idea of what makes a good job for you. Neither should your very first act be to set up a job interview with the president of a firm where you want to work. Innumerable job offers are lost by people who aren't really ready to job hunt. Do enough preparation to avoid wasting early opportunities, but expect to put the finishing touches on your decisions and your skills in the course of your job hunt. That is how successful job hunters operate.

Visualizing It All

When you job hunt you carry out a number of activities simultaneously. Looking at a time line can help in grasping the relation of these overlapping activities. Consider Richard, a job hunting chemist who was selective about his next job and whose job hunt took place without any particularly "lucky breaks." His job hunt looked like the time line here.

Not every job hunt is lengthy, however. At any point after his first step into the job market, Richard could have learned of a job opening and—being prepared to interview and able to recognize and follow up on a good job for himself—gotten it.

Phases of the Job Hunt

The work of job hunting falls into several general phases. The first phase is mostly one of preparation. You are looking around at yourself and your field; you are learning techniques; developing a current resume and getting together a couple of outfits to wear on interviews. Shortly after this you begin investigating some possible routes, checking to see which methods besides the "grapevine" look promising. Perhaps you'll be replying to want ads and learning which employment agencies handle your specialty. You sharpen your awareness of your own job market; begin networking and spot where you belong.

The next phase involves an initial foray into the job market. The main goal here is to make sure your perceptions of where you belong in the job market are correct, i.e., that you could actually be hired by employers for jobs at the level at which you are applying. You can do this by making contact with people who can confirm your impressions of the market (although sometimes people do this the hard way—by being continuously turned down for jobs). Another goal is to contact people who can provide leads to available jobs. Although you are modifying your strategies as a result of what you are discovering, you need to be ready

A Job Hunt Time Line

	September	October	November	December	January

1st-4th week

PREPARATION
Personal Data Project
Resume 1st draft
Contact Resume references
Interview practice

3rd-10th week

INVESTIGATE JOB MARKET
Renew magazine subscriptions
Go to local meetings
List potential employers
Research articles on companies
Lunches with professional friends
Polish Resume

5th-14th week

INITIAL JOB HUNTING
Reply to open ads
Get referrals to preferred employers
Use direct contact after researching

10th-20th week

ADVANCED JOB HUNTING
Selection interviews
More referral interviews
Follow-up letters and calls

ACCEPT JOB

to meet a real job opportunity, should a serious prospect appear, as it could at any moment. You want, by this phase, to be able to handle an interview with composure, to submit a polished resume and to write a memorable thank you letter.

In the advanced phase of job hunting, you have fine-tuned your techniques as a result of phase two. Your job hunting hits a peak of efficiency; you know and pursue the methods that bring results; you know which jobs to go for. The surest sign of this phase is that you are considered a serious candidate for most of the jobs for which you apply. Now it is just a matter of time.

Action Plans

If you operate effectively from "a gleam in the eye," fine. But for most people, a written plan is a way of "getting it all together." It clarifies what has to be done and allows you to measure the successes in all the intermediate steps you have to take to get to the final objective of a good job.

Keep a notebook or diary to record your job hunting activity. In it put names, addresses, dates and identifying notes about people you see or interviews you go on. Keep descriptions of jobs for which you apply and copies of letters that you send.

To develop a plan, do a quick overview of the tasks involved in the current phase of your job hunt. Consider direct activities such as interviewing and indirect ones like going to meetings and reading articles. Make your list of what you feel you have to do. It might include:

> Completing a personal data project,
> Writing a resume
> Deciding whether to widen your job target, etc.

Next, translate these goals into a specific plan. That is, break each goal into smaller parts. Note the action to be taken at each step of the plan. Set out for yourself—on paper—not only the longer term goals, but weekly activity goals. Richard, the chemist, began each Monday by reviewing where his job hunt stood and setting what he thought would be realistic accomplishments for the coming week.

Goals which you see as "hard for me to do" deserve special attention. Richard, for instance, dreaded calling people on the phone, so he broke the activity down into smaller parts:

Deciding whom to call (Randy, at Heinz);
When to call (before lunch tomorrow);
What to say (a small achievable objective, such as asking
"Are you going to the meeting next Thursday?"); and
Thinking of a response to each of the possible answers.

He overcame the larger obstacle of calling people by breaking it down into parts that he could handle. Approach your obstacles the same way.

How Much Time Do You Need?

Realistically, you need at least five hours a week to devote to job hunting in order to produce measurable results. Most experienced people feel that spending 25 solid, prime hours a week on job hunting is equivalent to working full time. You will be doing more than most job hunters do if you spend this amount of time.

Even if other activities crowd your day, you can make time to job hunt. One Pittsburgh area woman worked in the suburbs as a psychological tester. She also went to school for an advanced degree two nights a week, had two young children and yet wanted to get a better job. She decided to *make* time for her job hunt. She laid specific plans:

Take one day off every three weeks for interviewing.
Go to a monthly professional meeting.
Lunch with a colleague in a different company.
Set up an "I'm interested in your kind of firm" meeting
by using a referral.
Contact a working classmate to learn what's happening.
Read an article associated with my current class or about my
field. Keep notes on it.
Clip and/or reply with resume and cover letter to a want ad.

She worked them into her schedule at the rate of one per week. After three months she was still confident that this patient approach would work and, after a while, all the elements began to jell. She said, "I would have given up if I hadn't paced myself." For someone under more pressure to get faster results, the one-a-week goals could become one-a-day goals. Whether you are employed or have the task of finding work as your main job, set realistic goals and reach for them.

METHODS PITTSBURGHERS USE TO GET JOBS

A nation-wide survey asked people what job search method actually led to their obtaining the job they currently held. The results showed:

34.9% applied directly to employers
26.2% asked friends, relatives and others
13.5% answered newspaper ads
 5.6% used private employment agency
 5.1% used state employment service
 3.0% used school placement office
11.7% other

Source: Jobseeking Methods Used by American Workers. **Dept. of Labor, Bureau of Labor Statistics, Bulletin 1886.**

A look at these statistics—even if they are only roughly applicable to Pittsburgh—suggests that employers regularly are approached by two streams of job seekers. The first are those who decide, for one reason or another, to come to this employer and ask for work. The second are those who do the same thing based on the suggestions of friends, relatives or other people with whom they have had contact. More than 60% of the jobs are filled this way. If these two kinds of contacts do not satisfy an employer's need, only then has he any reason to pay for a newspaper ad, use an employment agency or even tell people in his company that he is looking for candidates for some particular job.

The contact route is also the major way "quasi-jobs" are filled. These are jobs that do not formally exist as openings until an employer sees across the desk the right person at the right time. It's been estimated that as many as one in five professional and management jobs are filled this way.

For this reason, jobs listed in ads and with agencies tend to be unrepresentative of the full range of available openings. In disproportionate numbers employers list jobs calling for specialized technical skills that are hard to fill or list jobs in low paying, low status or high turnover occupations.

If you add to the percentage of jobs filled by contacting employers (the first two on the list) the percentage filled through other means that are not fully open to all of the public, it is easy to understand how experts come up with the statistic that over 80% of the jobs are "hidden," that is, not known to everyone.

What Methods to Use

Use the methods and approaches that give you control of your time, money and energy; the more power you have over these elements, the more you gain in motivation, confidence and success. Use the methods that generate the largest number of productive contacts with employers and, of course, use the methods that result in the most job interviews. After you've tried several methods, you'll get a feel for the ones which are most productive for you.

All of the job hunting methods work in Pittsburgh *sometime* for *someone*. It is not a question of which method but which *combination* of methods will fit your unique mix of time, energy, personal style, career field and the level at which you're seeking work. Each method will be discussed in this chapter. We begin with the referral method because Pittsburgh, without a doubt, is a "contact town."

USING YOUR CONTACTS— THE REFERRAL METHOD

When asked, "What method would you use, if you had to start job hunting today?" every person interviewed for this book mentioned using contacts, usually as the first, often as the only, approach. Said one personnel director succinctly, "Oh, I'd tap in."

If ever you've heard, "It's who you know, not what you know" spoken in anger or disgust, you've heard a frustrated job hunter talk about someone else's effective use of this method to become a sponsored candidate.

Being a sponsored candidate does not *have* to mean getting the job through under-handed pull. You do not have to have high ranking personal connections through your relatives, old-school ties, membership in posh social clubs or being in the "right" part of the corporate community (though we'd be lying if we told you that they don't sometimes make a difference here).

To be sponsored for a certain job may simply mean that you've presented your credentials at the right time to a person who has some connection to the selection process for that job. It works at every level, from the lowest paying to the highest paying positions all over Pittsburgh and the Tri-State area.

It worked for Gene, a newly hired messenger/mail clerk at one of the downtown headquarters offices. He was working as a bus boy, part time, a month after his high school graduation. At a rainy wedding reception for a cousin, talk turned to jobs. Gene mentioned his need for a better job with a future and how hard he'd work at one. One fellow mentioned his brother-in-law who was bidding on a promotion, saying,

> "Even if he doesn't get it, one of the other entry-level guys will, and they'll have to bring in another person at the bottom rung."
>
> Gene asked, "Would it be okay if I called him to find out more about it?"
>
> "Sure."

When Gene called, the brother-in-law was helpful, giving him a lot of information about the company and the kind of employees they liked to hire—people who wanted to stay on with the organization and advance. They hired primarily at entry level and promoted from within. He gave Gene tips on getting that across. The most important thing he said to Gene was at the very end of the conversation:

> I'll send you an application blank and when you get it back to me, I'll turn it in for you. They always try to give an interview to someone who is referred by an employee, so when you come to the last line on the application blank, where it asks where you learned about the job, put my name down.

Gene didn't get the *job* because of a referral. What he got was a better chance to obtain an interview. He was sponsored by an employee in a company where employee referrals are given weight. He got the job on his own merit with a little help from a friend.

Who Are Your Contacts?

An initial reply is "I don't have any contacts." Or "I know people, but nobody important." As with Gene, you don't have to know important people, you just have to know how to get to the people who are important because they can hire you. You may be hired on your own merits, but you need the opportunity to get there.

Ask yourself: how many people would I have to go through in order to have a short handwritten note of mine placed in the hands of the President of the United States? A typical thought-through response might be: I would talk to a state representative or local politician whose name I could use with the administrative assistant at Senator Heinz's home office. Then I could deliver the note for him to carry into the bi-monthly breakfast meeting that the President holds with ranking Republican senators.

If the President is only three or four people away from you, others are equally accessible; and the route is the same: **You can get to the people who can hire you through other people.**

Your contact list begins with your family and extended family, friends of the family, classmates, workmates, neighbors, people at parties, members of social clubs. You can tap into networks of people you do business with—druggist, bank manager, barber, dentist—especially people who have contact with a lot of other people. Include those active in your field of work: professional and trade association members, speakers and lecturers, professors and prominent professionals.

You are, of course, only one step away from all the employers for whom *these* people work and all the contacts *they* have. It is estimated that the average person knows 200-400 persons and each of these 200 people has his or her own circle of acquaintances. Of course, you must let these people know what it is they can do to help. They cannot tell you of opportunities unless they know you are looking for them. But, potentially, if they all knew about your job hunt, there could be 40,000 people on the lookout for an opportunity for you.

Few job hunters, of course, use all of their contacts; but they are there nonetheless.

How to Help Your Contacts Help You

1. *Start by separating your wishes from the reality of what you can get.* You might wish that somebody would tell you what to do or give you a job. But you actually can learn which companies are good to work

for; you can find out who's looking for applicants even if they are not publicly advertising the fact; you can get referrals to hiring managers.

2. *Make it easy for your contacts.* Indicate clearly that all you need is a suggestion, a lead; you'll take it from there and do all the work. You will get more action if you ask not only if they know of actual jobs but if they also know of *someone* or of a company that might be good to check on. You will hear of more opportunities if you don't make them vouch for you (that puts them and maybe *their* job on the line). Try to approach it so that people who do not know you well will have nothing at risk in helping you.

3. *Know what to ask for and how to ask for it.* You can ask for procedures for applying and names of people to contact. Present yourself as interested in a promising job but not as a desperate person (*I'll take anything*). Don't forget to find out how your present contact has come to know the person to whom he or she is referring you—a vital detail. Also, stay open to others' advice and suggestions even if you eventually decide not to follow them.

Do let them know that you are experienced or skilled. One woman applied at the plant where her brother worked only to find that a job for which she would have been a good candidate had been filled the week before. When she said, "Why didn't you let me know, when you knew I was looking for work!" he replied, "Oh, yeah, I would have; but I didn't know you did *that* stuff."

4. *Thank people.* Most of the time the only reward they get from helping you is your thanks. Keep them in touch with how your job hunt is going and follow up. In this method, things pay off later, later, and still later.

The golden rule of using contacts is to **be as thoughtful and helpful to them as you would like them to be to you and then do it for others.** It is a misconception that the contact method is a way of *using people.* It need not be a using, it can be a *letting*—letting people give what they are willing to give you. If they don't want to, they won't. You need ask only for what they willingly give. This book does not recommend *using contacts* (although the term is used) but treating them as human beings. The contact method is not an impersonal formula for job hunting; it is making relationships between people.

Advanced Contact Using—Networking

Although you can use your contacts to suggest firms where you should put in an application or to tell you of jobs that are unadvertised, there is another way your contacts can take you into the hidden job market. This is through what is commonly called "networking."

It frequently means moving from an informal contact to a more formal one. Veronica, an accountant, began by talking with her neighbor who worked in the marketing department of a bank. She asked her neighbor for a few minutes of his time to discuss her interest in his job and what he knew of opportunities for accountants in banking. He had known her for years, so it was easy for him to suggest that she call one of the people in banking operations to discuss opportunities there.

This second contact was a formal contact, someone she had never known before the courtesy interview she had with him. But from him she got specific information about the types of jobs she might qualify for in the banking industry. She asked for the names of people who actually performed the work she was interested in doing. She then contacted them, using the formal contact person as her introductory reference. At each interview, she asked her contacts for permission to use their names when she called or wrote to the people they mentioned to her. Her later contacts began providing her with ideas for job leads and names of people in other banks who would be good to see. One person invited her to attend a meeting of the Society of Women Accountants, as her guest. There she met the person who later hired her.

Networking is a very sophisticated, but natural, approach to job hunting. The object is to get interviews with the people for whom you want to work. You get there by referrals. You are not held back because you do not *have* direct contact to these people, because you *make* new contacts each time you are referred to another person. The goal of each interview is either to be considered for a job there or to get a job lead. This happens when your interviewer suddenly remembers someone who was looking for a person like you or, in a quieter vein, suggests you call so-and-so "who is always looking for people with good backgrounds." If neither of these goals is obtained, ask at least for the name of another person to whom you could talk.

You can choose people whom you want to meet from the list of potential employers that you developed earlier and work to get referrals to them or you can just follow the suggestions of your contacts.

The situation is sometimes described by employers as a "no stress look" at candidates because there is no pressure on them to do employee selection. However, you must make sure that you get an opportunity to display some of the qualities that would make you a valuable employee. The more people in your field you get to see, the more successful you are likely to be. If you keep in touch with all these people over the period of time that you are looking for work, there you will be—available, qualified and with your name fresh in everyone's memory—when a job comes up.

Does it work? Not invariably, but it is one of the best things going.

How to Get In

With some exceptions, local hiring managers and personnel professionals are willing to see people when they have no openings *as long as they have time and job hunters are honest with them.*

True, some people are too rushed to talk to anyone. Others don't want to be part of this kind of networking and their wishes must be respected. But some people may only be temporarily hard to get to and your perseverance and willingness to wait until they can see you will pay off.

Honesty is a key element in the referral process. Everyone dislikes being tricked, and it really backfires on job hunters who mistakenly believe they can get a job if only they can somehow "sneak" into the interviewer's door. As one professional in human resources said,

> I like to take the time to see possible candidates as often as I'm able, to talk about my field or even with the possibility of referring them to someone else. But I don't like to feel tricked and I know most of the ploys by now—the senior who wants to discuss a term paper topic, but who can't give me the name of the engineering professor who assigned it, and so on. It's a shame: we do like to see interested people who might fit in somewhere, because we like to keep a talent pool. It makes our job easier when a manager decides to gear up. And, from what I can tell, the managers in our company try to make time to talk shop with interested people, too, because they never know when they'll be needing someone as a replacement or a new hire.

"What I like to hear on the phone," said the advertising director for one of Pittsburgh's major corporations,

> is a statement such as "I know you are not hiring anyone right now, but Bill Jones suggested I call to arrange a time to talk with you about general developments in the field. He thought you could steer me in some good directions." I will try to fit that person into my schedule somewhere, especially if Bill Jones is the kind of guy who does not usually waste my time.

Honesty works best in letters requesting referral interviews, too. The following letter's beauty is its directness. The job hunter here tailored the letter to his reader and kept the work and initiative on his side by promising to call. When he did call, he was already expected and recognized.

171

24 Executron Avenue
Pittsburgh, PA 15212
September 23, 1989

Ms. Jane Smith
Manager of Employee Training
Tangent Corporation
444 Cosine Drive
Pittsburgh, PA 15222

Dear Ms. Smith:

    Bill Jones of the Sandwich Wrapping Company suggested that I write to you. He mentioned that you were the President of our local ASTD chapter and that you knew just about everyone in the field.

    I am relocating to Pittsburgh after an absence of six years. In that time I gained experience in planning, organizing and managing Quality Circles--which I understand are of continuing interest in several Pittsburgh area companies.

    I particularly need advice from active professionals who know the local scene, not because I expect you to know of any specific openings. Jim mentioned that you keep up on new developments as they break, so I hope we can meet to discuss trends. Perhaps you'd be interested in my experiences in Milwaukee, where the labor climate has greatly improved because of innovative training programs.

    I will call your office next week to see whether you can arrange time for a meeting.

              Sincerely,

              Joseph O'Hara

              Joseph O'Hara

You may ask for an interview on the basis of your referral alone. You may ask for an interview on the basis of discussing some special, newsworthy trend in your market or an idea you have to share (this is sometimes called a proposal interview).

The Interview Itself

Begin with a clear explanation of why you are there. Discuss the field; present your qualifications; solicit their insight into your particular job market as they see it today. Look for a satisfying meeting between both parties as an immediate objective and, in the long run, hold to the expectation you will be considered for a job or will get a referral.

Your attitude frequently determines how much you will get from the interview. If you explain your purpose openly, with an expectation that the contact person will want to help, you will often get what you expect.

The referral method blends elements of gathering information, which was talked about earlier in this book, and of presenting yourself as a job candidate. As a way of sharing information about yourself, you may mention how you got to know the person who referred you to your present contact or how you got his or her name. You can describe your job and career objective along with a few of the steps you've taken so far. You can give information about yourself in a positive, non-confrontive way, perhaps by asking for feed-back on your resume or discussing the feasibility of one of your ideas.

You might get advice on the current job hunting scene or how a company's departments are organized. In every case you will receive the benefit of sharing time face to face. During your first few referral interviews, you will be requesting more advice and information, your questions will be less sophisticated and you will be relying more on your contact's altruism for obtaining referrals.

Follow-Up

In every case, maintain relationships with the people you meet. Show your continued interest in their work and encourage their continued interest in your progress. Your job hunt is not a one-afternoon event. Keep them aware of you through follow-up letters, clippings of interest, thank you notes and occasional phone calls or progress reports, when appropriate. They may learn of something later and tell you about it *if you get back to them.*

People who are active in referral networks tend to see lots of people who are "in the market" just like you. The quality of your follow-up separates you from the people who are just trying out a technique suggested in a job hunting book. Your thank you letter after an interview may well be the single most important type of letter you write during your job campaign. In this sample thank you letter, note that Catherine

173

leaves ample opportunity for further communication. You can do this after every contact during your job hunt, with good effect.

2556 Alport Road
Pittsburgh, PA 15212
October 22, 1988

Mr. David Magnusen
Marketing Manager
Videot's Delight, Inc.
323 Bakersfield Street
Pittsburgh, PA 15222

Dear Mr. Magnusen:

I came away from our interview yesterday with a wealth of useful information. When you showed me the early figures from your national media campaign, I began to understand your marketing strategies better and to see why your company is doing so well. I would love to hear how Phase II and Phase III go.

I've begun revising my resume according to your suggestions and after incorporating some of your ideas, I can already see substantial improvement. I'll send you a copy shortly.

When the resume is ready to go, I'll begin to approach the marketing managers whose names you gave me, starting with Sandra Green and Gordon Smalley. You've given my job hunt a real boost. I'll keep you posted on what happens when I talk to your friends and colleagues.

Thank you for all your help.

Sincerely,

Catherine Poskin

Catherine Poskin

Care and Feeding of Yourself and Your Professional Contacts

To successfully carry out a referral campaign, you must maintain your integrity and honestly believe that the people you talk to will benefit from the time they spend with you.

What do you have to offer a contact person? According to them, one thing is an exchange of information. You may know about a new process or service that your contact hasn't had time to read up on. You may carry "grapevine" information, as did the job hunter who was referred to an agency director by a former colleague. The job hunter was able to tell her about her colleague's prestigious move to a new employer.

A key person at the center of one of the bigger referral networks in town offered this reason for his involvement and the energy he spends seeing one or two job hunters a week:

> If a person approaches me with a good letter of request, plus a resume, I have trouble saying no, especially if I think I can help. I remember when I was just starting out and how much other people's interest helped me. Now that I have attained a certain position, I am very pleased to be able to use it positively...I feel great when one of the people I refer gets a job, either directly or indirectly.

This Is a Lot of Work

The referral method *is* a lot of hard, imaginative work. And, there is no guarantee you will get a job this way. But since *most* jobs do not become publicly known, it is wise not to ignore this vast hidden job market.

Does the referral method work in Pittsburgh?

Every day.

JOB HUNTING WITH THE WANT ADS

Only 10-15% of all job openings are ever advertised. Despite those figures, almost every local job hunter we've ever talked to began searching by sitting down with the Sunday *Pittsburgh Press* Want Ad Section. As one woman said, "It just seemed like the right way to begin."

One small ad in the Sunday *Press* may draw 5 or 500 applicants, half of whom are well qualified. If you use the want ads as a job hunting method, read them carefully and respond selectively.

175

An ideal ad would give you all the following, essential information:

Job title, duties and responsibilities
Educational requirements/preferences
Experience or skill requirements/preferences
Salary
Benefits
Advancement opportunities
Additional requirements (travel, relocation, car, etc.)
Name of company or employment agency
Desired method of response to ad

Not every ad does. Sometimes, when an ad is designed to attract a large pool of candidates, only the glamorous features of a job are mentioned. In other cases job requirements are unnecessarily inflated so only the most qualified persons will apply (they hope). Other times, ads have just been poorly written.

Learn the language of the want ads. Read between the lines. Pay special attention to the skills or experience they *require* as opposed to what they *prefer*.

Read Your Way to Better Responses

The following ad appeared some time ago in the *Pittsburgh Press.*

Director—Community based internship program for re-entry women. Administrative and supervisory experience in business or non-profit. Funded salary in low teens. Resume to Job Advisory Service, 300 South Craig Street, Pgh., PA 15213

If you study the analysis of this ad, you can see how someone's skills and personality can be related to advertised requirements. Then you can apply the same approach to a want ad that interests you today and be prepared to write clear, well-targeted cover letters and cue cards for a telephone reply. Here's how:

Step One. List each of the responsibilities or duties mentioned in the ad. Opposite each item, list all your matching qualifications and accomplishments. Include material from all aspects of your experience and education, using your resume or personal data project as a guideline. At this stage, the winning candidate for the job might have had an outline that looked like this:

Actual Requirements	My Accomplishments
Administration/supervision	ran program; supervised 35 volunteers plus CETA staff; now supervise 12 f.t. employees; managed budget; planned and carried out complete program.
Business or non-profit experience	both: non-profit was very similar in nature to current program needs.
Knowledge of re-entry women	worked with them; saw they needed to develop or uncover their skills and build confidence; helped them make transition to paid work.
Knowledge of community based programs	usually involves some recruiting and field work; public relations efforts like public speaking and presentations.

Step Two. After you've matched all your relevant accomplishments to the requirements listed in the ad, read between the lines. Muster everything you already know about the industry, the field and the type of position described. It's time to identify the. *implied requirements.* If you don't already know a lot about the nature of this type of organization or position, take time to do a bit of quick sleuthing before you formulate your response. Use some of the reference books listed for your field if you have the time or check the company clipping file at Carnegie Library, otherwise, call the organization and request a brochure or annual report to obtain some background information about the implications of the words in their ad. In some cases, there is a full job description available and only a scaled-down version was placed in the want ad space. Often a call to the office (if the name of the company is published with the ad) with a request for "more details about the requirements...so I don't waste your time," pays off. In this case, the office manager would have read you a 2-page job description which had a lot of clues as to how to frame your response. Continuing with the internship director position as an example, step two might look like this:

Implied Requirements	My Characteristics or Skills
Non-profit programs often funded by grants; operate within timetables established by funding sources	need to be able to jump right in and "do."
Limited budgets	wear many hats; don't need assistants; financial management skills—living with low budgets already; willing to go the extra mile for something I believe in; get along on salary in the low teens.

177

| Get along with existing staff (assume it's a small staff) | flexibility; work independently; friendly; professional attitude; enjoy working with others who are committed to helping people. |

The Story Behind a Want Ad

The internship director ad drew 94 replies over the ten day period that followed. Two people called to find out to whom to personally address their reply. One person stopped by to see what/where the agency was and then wrote a tailored cover letter, and one called and was given a full job description. This improved each of their chances.

After the bulk of the replies arrived, the agency executive director completed a rough sort. She eliminated four resumes as totally unacceptable and divided the remaining 90 into three stacks: the first contained all the *best* ones; the second, *excellent* candidates, but with a few questions regarding their suitability; and the third, less desirable, but *qualified.*

In responding to the ad, about 25 did not use a cover letter but, in the words of one of the readers, "merely dumped their resumes into envelopes." Only one of these made the *best* stack.

After a couple of days, the first two stacks were reviewed again and reduced somewhat. At that point, the resumes in the "Best" pile were read again and ranked. In this important phase, their written words were all that represented the candidates in the silent competition taking place. Cover letters carry a lot of weight in determining who will be called for an interview. That's why it is necessary to show some of your personality in your writing. Instead of saying things in stilted business language, try writing as though you're talking to a respected friend whom you like and want to impress with your obvious talent.

Two actual cover letters are reproduced here, with the comments of the agency's executive director who read them. Assuming that both these applicants were well qualified, who would you pick to interview?

Eleven candidates were selected to be interviewed. Of these, two were not reached easily and were dropped. Appointments were set up with nine others. One canceled her first interview and when she called back, interest had already focused on the two top contenders, so the interview with her was really a courtesy. Of the eight interviewed, three replied with thank you letters and one (the runner up) called after four days to inquire whether she might answer any lingering questions (this clinched her for the job if, by chance, the first choice turned it down). The first choice candidate was the writer of the second cover letter.

555 Anystreet Drive
Pittsburgh, PA 15235
555-1212

May 5, 1982

Job Advisory Service
300 South Craig Street
Pittsburgh, PA 15213

Dear Job Service,

    Please accept this as my letter of application for a
position as Director within your program.

    I feel fully qualified to perform professionally in
this capacity through my past supervisory work experiences
in human services within non-profit agencies.

    Enclosed is a copy of my resume. Any additional
information can be supplied to your office promptly.

    Thank you.

                        Sincerely,

                        Barbara Monesson

                        BARBARA MONESSON

O.K., but quite brusque. Get the feeling this is one of 10 such letters she dashed off that day with no special care.

Tells me she feels qualified; no support to her claim.

Appears to think she is applying for position as director of the whole agency — my job! Shows no personality or knowledge of the type of program.

Incorrect. Doesn't know anything about our agency.

802 Nonesuch Avenue
Pittsburgh, PA 15261
May 4, 1982

Job Advisory Service
300 South Craig Street
Pittsburgh, PA 15213

To whom it may concern:

Please accept this letter as my application for the position of Director
of your Re-entry Program for women. I recognize how vital this service
can be because I ran a similar program, geared to volunteers, for the
St. Mary's City Commission. Many of the women were contributing
outside the home for the first time in years; most had to rediscover
their skills and reestablish their confidence.

In addition to this direct experience I feel that I am well-qualified
for other reasons. Most of my career has been spent with non-profit
organizations; therefore, I have proven my success at running a program
on a tight budget while "wearing many hats." I've been responsible
for everything from initial planning to final publicity, and have put
to good use my experience in writing, public speaking, graphic arts,
audio-visual presentations, etc. I currently supervise twelve full-
time sales/stock women, and while working in St. Mary's City had a 35-
person volunteer staff as well as CETA employees. Finally, I am
willing to work long and hard to meet a challenge, and I enjoy contributing one hundred percent of my energy and enthusiasm to a service
that I feel is important.

I hope that I impress you as favorably as the opportunity to be Director
of the Re-entry Program for the Job Advisory Service has impressed me.
I would like to meet with you to discuss the position and the overall
program. I am usually very difficult to reach during the day (office:
444-1212), but a message can be left with my mother, Mary Almenda, at
333-1212.

Thank you for your consideration. I look forward to hearing from you
soon.

Sincerely,

Bonita A. Perry

BONITA A. PERRY

Nice tone.

*Hones in on the issues relevant to all
non-profit agencies — budget, flexibility,
motivation and commitment to a
service. Has skills in all phases; can
wear many hats; enthusiastic.*

*Shows understanding of the program
and its clients.*

Almost, But Not Quite All They Ask For

Can it be a good use of your time to apply for jobs that ask for more or different experience and education than you have? Yes, *if* you take it upon yourself to show how your background is relevant to the requirements *and* give special attention to the results produced. This shows, by implication, the valuable contribution you can make to that employer's work force.

Creeping job-requirement inflation has been rampant locally. A financial firm looking for a bookkeeper placed an ad requiring a college degree. "We never asked for one before, but we figured we wouldn't get swamped that way," said the hiring manager. Would they look at someone without a degree? "Sure, if the background looked good," was the reply.

Working up a sample presentation can give you a basis for deciding whether to pursue a want ad for which you are almost, but not quite, all they ask for. The job hunter in the following case did reply by phone (as the ad had requested) and was called for a selection interview.

Example

Ad Requirements:

3 years business mgmt. & suprv. experience. Degree in Bus. Ad.

Job Hunter's Experience:

6 years experience at a hospital (non-profit); senior standing at local university; major courses in business and accounting are completed; attended while working full time.

Presentation Points:

I've been in purchasing at Presbyterian-University Hospital for 4 years and before that was an assistant for purchasing at Mayview State Hospital. The department has a staff of 14. I have spent considerable time implementing new materials management systems that have reduced inventory levels 35% and achieved measurable savings over previous purchasing costs.

I have completed most of the coursework for a business degree at Pitt while I've been working. Only 2 electives need to be taken. My QPA in business and accounting courses is 3.4.

Where to Look for Want Ads

In addition to the *Pittsburgh Press* Sunday classified ads, both daily papers run help wanted ads and occasional "career opportunity" sections. A proportionately smaller number of listings are to be found in Pittsburgh's wealth of ethnic, racial and religious publications, like the *New Pittsburgh Courier, Jewish Chronicle* and the *Byzantine Catholic World.* Fewer still and more scattered are job listings in the university newspapers, advertising tabloids and "green sheets," as well as church bulletins and civic organization newsletters. If you are a regular reader of certain publications, your characteristics may be just what the employer was looking for when he placed the ad there. Some local professional associations list job openings in their newsletters, another reason for you to initiate or reactivate your membership.

The Workplace Room of Carnegie Library in Oakland has as good a collection of job want ads as anywhere. In addition to the two daily newspapers, they receive job listings from the State Civil Service, the Allegheny County Health Department and the city of Pittsburgh. They have a copy of the state Job Service's microfiche of local jobs and of the Interstate Job Bank which is a selective listing of skilled jobs from state employment services across the country. At this writing they subscribe to the *National Business Employment Weekly,* a regional roundup of want ads from the *Wall Street Journal;* the *National Job Market,* a bimonthly of professional positions that includes a "Federal Job Guide" section; the *Career Opportunity Update,* a monthly that advertises management and technical openings for experienced workers and the *Affirmative Action Register* which posts jobs for exempt government positions, university upper level administration and some medical and scientific research directorships. The Science and Technology section of the library sends over the *Weekly List of Openings* published as part of the American Chemical Society's journal, which is actually a compilation of want ads for scientists clipped from 19 different published sources.

These are all at the library, for you to use or to see before you spend any money on them. Those not for sale, like the Job Service listings, can often be found free at non-profit agencies that offer employment assistance.

Posted Jobs. Although not strictly want ads, posted jobs fall into this classification, too. Posted jobs are just that: typed descriptions of job openings which are literally posted on the walls of the firm—often as a way of informing current employees of job openings. The local universities,

182

the city and county, often hospitals and utility firms do this. Some large firms (but by no means all) also post. A few, like a bank with many branches, publish internal memos of job openings for the use of their employees. If the jobs are posted, usually on the walls near the personnel office, it is legitimate for you to be there and to return, perhaps every ten days, to keep on top of things. If you ask someone you know who works there to look for you, plan to thank your contact and reward his or her efforts by checking back often.

OTHER DIRECT APPROACHES TO EMPLOYERS

All the rules for finding a job boil down to two: get an interview with the person who is able to hire you and present yourself well enough in the interview that you are offered a position. The most direct method of getting that interview is telephoning a potential employer and requesting one. If you have a contact or referral whose name will serve as an introduction, this is your best bet. But not every case works this way. Sometimes you know who you would like to work for but have no contact there or you cannot get through by phone. Then you might want to consider being your *own* contact and writing a letter to introduce yourself. This is the origin of the "employment sales letter."

A decade ago, such letters were uncommon, written by "creative" job hunters and they enjoyed a degree of success. In the job hunting field few successful techniques remain secret. Sending introductory letters mushroomed into a profitable third party business. Job hunters purchased "direct mail campaigns," paid someone to write them a catchy sales letter and mass mailed to companies they knew nothing about. The uniqueness attached to the letter approach disappeared when companies received dozens of them a week. This happened in Pittsburgh when the official unemployment rate was over 10%.

Consequently, two critical cautions now attach to writing such sales letters. First is to avoid the "canned letter" or "mass mailing" appearance. Do this by writing your own letter; mail it to a company you want to work for because you already know something about them and address it specifically to a person whose name and position you have confirmed yourself. If you do this you probably will observe the second caution: always follow-up your letters. Call "to see if the letter was received" and if a meeting is possible and, if not, then could you "call again in a few weeks?" Not following-up your letters is like putting bait on a fishing rod but never checking the line.

183

A word about replies. The days of sending out letters asking for work and sitting back waiting for eager responses from employers—if they ever existed—are long gone. Some employers might be mildly interested but wait to see if you "really mean it" by proving it with a call. Furthermore, employers generally don't acknowledge resumes and requests for jobs, not because they are rude or want to be mean to you in particular, but because the direct and indirect cost to a business of sending a single letter has mounted to well over $20.

With these cautions, letters to employers can be part of a comprehensive job hunt campaign.

Letters to Personnel Specialists

Sending letters to personnel departments, without doing any research, may use up a good deal of your time and money. Although some personnel specialists mention that they read every application and letter they receive and answer them all, many good people get lost in the rush. As one typical personnel specialist pointed to a 4-inch stack of resumes, cover letters and applications on the corner of her desk, she sighed,

> Those came in within the past two days. I will divide them into smaller stacks, probably after lunch. Most of their senders will receive form letters which say, "Sorry, your qualifications do not meet our needs." A few will get one saying "We will keep your application on file" (mostly technical people or entry level professional applicants) and a third group will be sent a letter requesting them to call for an interview because we foresee possible openings within the next month or so. For one, maybe two, I'll arrange an interview because I know one of our managers is looking for someone with those particular skills. I process a group like that every couple of days *and so does everyone else in my department.*

She went on,

> Those latter applicants will compete against "sponsored candidates" in our regular selection process, perhaps our own employees or people who've been referred by a colleague or friend of the hiring manager. If they haven't been referred by anyone, the quality of their cover letters and their answers on the application forms are two keys to possible success. I also pay particular attention to what an applicant tells me on the phone and how he or she sounds. I listen especially for eagerness, poise, self-confidence and willingness to provide

some information. When a candidate has all those *plus* the necessary qualifications, I'm pretty sure we're not wasting everyone's time.

With a numbers' game like that, you need to maximize your effectiveness. You can call the switchboard to obtain the names and correct titles of key managers and the personnel specialists who hire for your type of position. You can also request an application form, recruiting information and general brochures which describe services or products before you make your direct approach to your targeted contacts.

If you run into a policy of "We do not accept phone requests for application forms," you can use the opportunity to politely ask more questions about the application process. You can learn a lot in a few minutes from the personnel department's receptionist—hours to apply, tests given, whether you will have opportunities to meet with an interviewer when you go in to fill out the application forms. (If you are asking increasingly sophisticated questions in a courteous, interested manner, you may be referred directly to someone with the authority to invite you in for an interview.)

Writing to a Hiring Manager

Another way to increase the effectiveness of this method is to direct an introductory letter to the manager of the department in which you want to work rather than to the personnel department.

The introductory letter reproduced on the next page got the writer an interview that led to a job. Note the way Robert related his skills to the employer's needs, which he had uncovered by careful listening during a phone conversation with the company receptionist and by reading through feature articles in a professional magazine and some clippings from the *Pittsburgh Post-Gazette*.

Not all sales letters need to be as detailed as this one to be effective. The best ones home in on an organization's needs, though, or are directed to department managers rather than human resource professionals and are followed by a phone request for an interview. When drafting your sales letter try to put yourself in the hiring manager's shoes by writing out a job description or an imaginary ad for a person who could solve some of the department's problems. Then answer the imaginary ad, using the technique described in the want ad section of this book.

Occasionally a hiring manager who does not have time to see you will forward your letter over to personnel. You're still in the ball game, so follow up to check on the status of your application and request an interview with the personnel representative.

38527 Bear Creek Road
Pittsburgh, PA   15206
September 15, 1989

Mr. Vincent E. Vincent
883 Saarinen Road
Pittsburgh, PA   15213

Dear Mr. Vincent,

I understand that you and your partners plan to develop several commercial
and residential properties in Oakland over the next five years. If so, I'd
like to talk to you about some of my recent accomplishments as an apprentice
architect in a 10-person office.

I have taken a 96-unit condominium through 5 programmatic changes and
designed and drawn details for another 40-unit condominium. In addition,
I programmed architecture to accommodate urban non-nuclear families, which
involved describing and drawing 50 potential architectural patterns under 4
headings.

Some other projects which might interest you include: planning 13 apart-
ments in a dormitory remodeling project and designing 5 work areas for a
community health and recreation center. I designed a 750 square foot
addition to a 6-room ranch house, which involved working with the owners,
programming and proportioning the new spaces and responding to the clients'
evaluation of the completed work.

In the course of these projects I have designed kitchens and baths; worked
with bearing wall and precast concrete structural systems; connected three
kinds of extruded sections to each other and to columns; planned plywood
cuts to economize on the number of sheets needed in major projects and
solved many other design and architectural problems.

I am a graduate of Carnegie-Mellon University with a Bachelor of Architecture degree and am presently working for Seymour Ellis, Architect/Planner.

-I will call your office next week to see when we can set up a meeting.
Your ideas for Oakland are tremendously exciting to me and I think I have a
great deal to contribute to your plans.

Sincerely,

Robert A. Millvale

Robert A. Millvale

Pounding the Pavement

In some fields, such as commissioned sales work, calling on employers without an appointment is an accepted way of job hunting because it is so similar to actual working conditions. In other fields, your cold calls on receptionists in personnel departments may result in very few job interviews. You probably will be able to put in applications at several organizations in the same day and, in doing so, you may learn some helpful things about pursuing your application further, but don't expect to be invited in for anything deeper than a quick screening interview while you're there. Look at the visit as an opportunity to observe other employees in action and to pick up the brochures, company literature and other information you need. Otherwise you may feel that you've been wasting your time. As one man who'd recently completed his A.A. degree in computer programming from CCAC put it,

> I decided there just had to be a better way to get a job! I wore out my shoes and spent hours filling out job applications. I also spent tons of money on PAT bus fares only to feel like a non-person. It wasn't that the personnel people were unfriendly. They just didn't seem to need me. I'd go home and wait for days to hear from them. I began to get the feeling that NO ONE was ever going to hire me. It was awfully hard on my ego, to say nothing of my feet!

Alex, the computer programmer just quoted, then began to plan his approaches more carefully. He felt most comfortable using direct approaches to employers so he decided to combine using the telephone and sending letters to heads of data processing. In many cases he had to go to a company to fill out an application anyway, but at least he knew whether they would accept it before he put on his suit and tie and made the effort. As he talked to more people, he began to realize that he should *not* start any phone call by asking whether they were hiring. The person on the other end of the phone almost always said, "No."

After many phone calls, letters and applications, Alex began follow-up calls to people who had talked to him. He used all the information he'd been able to gather in his pavement pounding/brochure-gathering days to target his job hunt. It took him five months to strike pay dirt, but he is working now in the data processing department of one of Pittsburgh's savings banks.

LET SOMEONE ELSE DO IT— EMPLOYMENT AGENCIES

Finding a job takes time and energy. For some people, using agencies can shorten or ease the task. If you are willing to play the percentages (5.1% got jobs through state employment agencies, 5.6% got them through private employment agencies) or if you're in an occupation where agencies are frequently used for filling openings, then this method may be one that will be successful for you.

The Public Employment Agency

The Bureau of Employment Security's Job Service is the state employment agency. There are a total of 18 Job Service offices in the eight-county area, at least one in your county. To use its free services, simply go to the neighborhood office nearest you and apply.

In Allegheny County, the current locations of Job Service offices are:

Regional Office—Job Service
300 Liberty Avenue
Pittsburgh, PA 15222
  565-5337

Carnegie Job Service
140 E. Mall Plaza
Carnegie, PA 15106
  429-2809

McKeesport Job Service
627 Lysle Boulevard
McKeesport, PA 15130
  664-6940

North Hills Job Service
300 Cumberland Road
Pittsburgh, PA 15237
  366-3121

Pittsburgh Job Service East
6206 Broad Street
Pittsburgh, PA 15206
  645-7010

Pittsburgh Job Service North
1122 Western Avenue
Pittsburgh, PA 15212
  565-2631

Pittsburgh Job Service South
918 Park Avenue
Pittsburgh, PA 15234
  565-3607

West Hills Job Service
1020 Beers School Road
Coraopolis, PA 15108
  264-5514

After completing their application forms, you can examine job listings on the bulletin boards and in the microfiche viewer. Once you have found jobs that interest you there, an interviewer will help you decide whether you have the necessary qualifications and will arrange referrals to the employers who listed the job openings. The offices are all interconnected by the computerized job bank system, so you can be referred to jobs listed in other offices as well. It is your responsibility to return frequently to pick up on new job openings. The state employment agency also deals in volume. When a mall or a new plant opens up, Job Service sets up an office on the site to interview applicants. They will advertise, usually in the local newspaper as to when applications will be taken. For these opportunities, it's important to relate well to people and to look neat.

If you meet income, age or background guidelines, you may be accepted into training programs like the Job Training Partnership Act (JTPA) or be able to bring a government rebate to an employer who hires you, as well as getting placement assistance. Displaced workers, blue and white collar, should avail themselves of such services through the One-Stop Shop (355-6611) or the Pittsburgh Partnership (255-2397).

Because their services are also free to employers, some good jobs for technically experienced people can be found in their listings. However, the most frequent kinds of jobs are those listed here.

Jobs Most Frequently Listed at JOB SERVICE Offices in Greater Pittsburgh and Average Starting Wage

Cleaner, Commercial	$3.46	Kitchen Helper	3.49
Salesperson, General Mdse.	3.51	Cook (restaurant)	3.62
Material Handler	4.82	Secretary	5.28
General Office Clerk	3.66	Laborer, General	4.28
Sales Clerk	3.46	Nurse Aide	3.88
Waiter/Waitress	3.37	Tractor Tlr. Truck Driver	5.20
Packager, Hand	3.60	Clerk Typist	4.77
Sales Clerk, Food	3.46	Receptionist	4.06
Cashier	3.54	Stock Clerk	3.96
Construction Worker	4.34	Cook, Short Order	3.62
Hotel Clerk	3.39	Telephone Solicitor	3.48
Fast Food Prep. & Serve	3.37	Automobile Mechanic	4.94
Bagger (retail)	3.60	Administrative Clerk	4.23
Sales, General Hardware	3.51	Carpenter	6.18
Security Guard	4.00	Cleaner, Housekeeping	3.45

Source: Labor Market Job Guide, **Spring, 1988, for the quarterly period ending December 31, 1987. This data collected when the minimum wage was still $3.35 per hour.**

Private Employment Agencies

There are at least 134 private employment agencies in the Pittsburgh area, ranging in size from one person offices to branches of national chains. They vary widely on how well they serve job hunters. In fact, their success rate is estimated variously at from 5% to 25%. How well a given agency will serve you depends upon how many jobs it has in your field; how completely the staff person describes a job before sending you on an interview; whether the agency does much screening for the employers whose jobs it lists; and how much advice the staff tailors to your needs, since much of the advice offered is designed simply to make a placement.

Who Are They For?

It's been said that employment agencies are for those changing employers, not for those changing careers. Employment agencies work best for: people with well-defined job objectives, working people with absolutely no time and energy to job hunt, and those who are willing to pay for a possible shortening of the length of their job hunts. Employment agencies can also be a conduit to jobs that are outside the reach of your own personal contacts.

Caveat Emptor. Job Advisory Service conducted a research project on the quality of employment agencies in Pittsburgh several years ago. Investigation revealed that state legislation, licensing and membership in professional ethics committees were of little use in determining the quality of an employment agency. Even lawsuit provoking word-of-mouth judgments were not uniformly helpful.

All employment agencies are businesses—there to make a profit. The money must come from you, an employer (the "fee paid" jobs), or from both. When you fill out an agency application form, you may be signing a contract, so check any forms carefully before completing them. You must sign a contract before a staff person will send you on any interviews, anyhow. Read the contract very carefully, for it sets out your legal obligation to pay. It will include terms and amount of payment required if you take any job offered you by employers to whom they refer you or mention to you.

Pittsburgh fees vary. The lowest seem to be equal to two weeks salary. Others range from 9% (for a salary of $5,000 or less per year) to 20% for a $20,000 annual income. You cannot spread payment of the fee over one year. Usually one-third is due within 15 days of starting your new job; the rest, within ten weeks. EXAMPLE: $15,000 job; fee = 15% or $2,250. Within fifteen days $750 is due. Check the want ads for a week to determine if the position you want is usually "Employer Fee-Paid."

A contract should state that you can cancel at will, at no cost to you. It should also clearly state that if you do not accept jobs that are offered to you, no fee will be due. In no way should you ever pay money before getting the job or for registering. Watch out for the paragraph covering your leaving a job; it can be very costly. If you quit before the full fee is paid, some contracts commit you to paying the remainder within a week even if you had accepted a "fee paid" position.

Another caution is not to freely relate to employment counselors the names of all the companies and positions where you have recently interviewed. Sharp-dealing agencies may quickly contact the company and send out candidates who are better qualified than you as soon as you leave. Assure them that you will promptly inform them if they begin to set up an appointment with an organization with whom you have already interviewed.

In spite of all these warnings, people get jobs every day through agencies and some of our best friends work for them.

If you have a question or want to register a formal complaint about employment agency practices, you can phone the Better Business Bureau (456-2700). It also sponsors a free TEL-TIPS series of taped telephone messages on employment; find these listed in the human service or blue pages of the phone directory.

If you use an employment agency, you will still need to have a good resume and polished interviewing skills. When you apply, be prepared to present your best side to the employment agency's interviewer.

In Pittsburgh there are general agencies that take job orders in all fields and others that specialize. Some people favor using a well-established, medium-sized specialist firm in the belief that they will get concentrated market coverage that way. There is no guarantee, of course, and you can also register at more than one agency. A quick survey of the area showed agencies claiming expertise in no less than 37 specific fields.

Executive Search Firms

If you are conducting a nation-wide job search for a position at the district manager, general manager, vice-presidential or presidential level with a company employing more than 500 people, you are a candidate for executive recruitment.

Elite executive search firms are retained by a company and paid on an annual basis; 15-20% of management positions above $35,000 are filled through recruiting firms. Such search firms project an image of "don't call us, we'll call you." Usually they are looking for specialized talent and will not interview unless you are an especially interesting candidate. Their success is based on knowing who are the best candidates, whether currently happily employed or ready for a change. They may accept resumes from qualified candidates but don't expect their help in finding you work. You may never hear from them, or may hear from them a year or two later.

Executive Recruiters Located in the Pittsburgh Area

Amansco, Inc.
  generalist; $40,000+
Becker Norton & Company
  generalist; $40,000+
George B. Bowers
  generalist; $50,000+
Boyden Associates, Inc.
  generalist; $40,000+
Denny and Company
  senior management; $75,000+
Fagan and Company
  international; $50,000+
Ketchum Inc.
  non-profit fund development; $40,000+
The J. Kovach Group
  real estate and construction; $40,000+
Roy Morris Associates
  generalist; $45,000+
O'Connor, O'Connor, Lordi Limited
  management; $50,000+
Reese Associates
  metals and capital equipment; $60,000+
Resources for Management, Inc.
  generalist; $50,000+
Daniel Stern & Associates
  physicians; $50,000+
The Walcar Partnership
  real estate & construction; $50,000+
Wolfgang & Dobbs, Ltd.
  (formerly Human Resource Consultants)
  generalist; $45,000+

Note: includes only firms said to operate on retainer.
$ = salary level at which search begins.

Seven different firms usually show up on the lists of the "Big Six" of executive recruitment firms in the nation:

Boyden Associates

Egon Zehnder International

Heidrick & Struggles

Korn/Ferry International

Russell Reynolds Associates

Spencer Stuart & Associates

Ward Howell International

Of these, only Boyden has a Pittsburgh branch, but at this salary level, the search firm's location is not an important criterion. There are about 14 other firms in Pittsburgh who are said to operate only on a retainer basis. They are included on the chart; but you may want to learn more about them and uncover the names and specialties of other national firms. To do so, the best resource is the *Directory of Executive Recruiters* (published by Consultants News, Fitzwilliam, NH) available at Carnegie Library's Business Branch. It has 92 different classifications and is updated frequently enough to catch the many changes that take place in this field.

If you are considering approaching these firms, be aware that it is not a task for the naive. Essential preliminary reading is *Executive Pursuit: The Insider's Guide to Finding Super Jobs through Headhunters* by Charles Fleming. Despite the title, it offers practical techniques while recognizing that the best way to get hired is to perform outstandingly in your present job. (It is available for $3.95 + $2.00 handling from Consultants Bookstore, Templeton Road, Fitzwilliam, NH 03447.)

One Pittsburgher, who formerly hired through executive recruiters, remarked that if he wanted to get himself into the files of an executive search firm, his first attempt would be to have an acquaintance of his who is in demand contact one or two firms and recommend him. Sending an unsolicited resume in the mail is a less effective choice.

Besides search firms, the general management consulting firms (like Drake Beam Morin) and large public accounting firms play roles you should know about. Management consulting firms, working with their regular clients, may conduct searches (they may also do outplacement for "downsizing" firms). Not all are in the business, however, and others are getting out. Four of the "Big 8" accounting firms have been active in executive search:

Arthur Young

Coopers & Lybrand

Ernst & Whinney

Peat, Marwick, Main

If you have a contact with any of these firms and confidentiality is not paramount, use it as your opening to get a referral to a search specialist.

The title *executive search firm* describes a range of agencies. Those who deal only with jobs paying over $60,000 are clearly at one end of the spectrum.

Management recruiting firms are a middle ground between executive search firms and employment agencies. Some operate on a retainer basis, like the search firms. Others are on a contingency fee: they are paid if they supply the candidate who is hired. Contingency firms may not be supplying all the candidates and may not know who your competition is. They are, however, easier to find and approach. There are a dozen or so of these firms in Pittsburgh. They have a higher profile and sometimes advertise in the want ads or phone directory. Check to find out which firms get a lot of assignments in your field. Take a low key approach when you contact them; be well in advance of when you actually want to make a job move.

CIVIL SERVICE/GOVERNMENT

A government job can be attractive. Benefits are good, pay is comparable or close to what private, small companies pay and agencies need a full range of workers. Hiring freezes notwithstanding, vital spots and legally required job positions must be filled.

Getting work with the government at any level usually means going the Civil Service route. There is no charge to apply, but it does take time to wade through all the red tape and tests that are sometimes involved. For that reason, don't expect to get results in a week or two. For that reason, also, lots of qualified people don't bother applying or don't follow up. Long term persistence can pay off here.

James E. Hawkins' *The Uncle Sam Connection: An Insider's Guide to Federal Employment* (Follett Publishing Co., 1978) is valuable. Although it is written for those seeking federal employment, it is useful if you are searching for jobs in any level of government when you do not have someone sponsoring you.

Each Civil Service agency—federal, state, county and city—has its own set of rules and procedures for applying. You will need to learn the steps for each level; call and ask questions until you understand how it works.

United States Civil Service

Employment is handled by the Federal Job Information Center, Federal Building, 1000 Liberty Avenue, 15222. The center no longer is open to visitors but operates by phone or mail. You can learn what jobs are open for application and which tests are being scheduled in the Tri-State region by calling or writing for the *Opportunities Bulletin.* If interested, you can also request an application form (#S-171); a general booklet (BRE#67); a booklet on your field of work, describing skills needed and where jobs are located nationwide; and information about current salaries (#AN-2500). The opportunities bulletins are also posted in state Job Service offices.

Pennsylvania State Civil Service

Many of the 85,000 Pennsylvania state employees are covered by Civil Service. The local branch employment office is in Room 411, State Office Building, 300 Liberty Avenue, 15219. Walk in and ask for the *Summary of Civil Service Exams,* which lists positions expected to open. It is usually issued the last week of each month. You can pick up a specifications booklet (extremely helpful) for currently open positions. Hours are 8:00-4:30, M-F.

Allegheny County Civil Service

In Allegheny County, apply for jobs at three different places:

Allegheny County Civil Service, located at 1520 Penn Avenue, Pittsburgh, 15222, handles applications for the Police and Fire Bureau *only.*

Allegheny County Health Department, Personnel Administration Department, 3333 Forbes Avenue, Pittsburgh, 15213, handles hiring for the wide range of jobs in the Health Department, including: air pollution control, environmental health, solid waste management, medical services, nutrition services, restaurant inspection, Department of Federal Programs positions and pre-employment services for the Adult Services Agency Commission on Aging. Jobs are posted at each of the five district offices and job descriptions are available at the Personnel Administration Department.

Employment Relations Department of Allegheny County covers all hiring not done by the other offices. Its jobs and those from the other three offices are posted outside the office door, Room 102, County Office Building, corner of Ross Street and Forbes Avenue, Pittsburgh, 15219. Hours are 8:30-4:30, M-F.

Adjacent Counties

These have a smaller number of employment opportunities and Civil Service positions. Here again, call the general number of your county office; be connected with the personnel/civil service department. Find out the hours of the department; hiring procedures; where jobs are posted and the name of an individual they would suggest you contact "just to get information" about general opportunities in your field with the county.

City of Pittsburgh

The Department of Personnel and Civil Service Commission is located in the hallway of the 4th floor of the City-County Building, 414 Grant Street. Hours are 7:30-5:30, M-F. Applicants must be city residents or, for some positions, willing to relocate prior to appointment. Jobs are posted on bulletin boards on the front and back doors of the building. If interested, go to the 4th floor counter for a full description and application form.

SCHOOL PLACEMENT

If you have had any recent training at a school or college, use that school's placement office in your job hunt. Their primary concern is with the current crop of graduates, but they are not hostile to "old grads" who are not imposing and who have not yet found a job. A creative job hunter went back to his old school and obtained its listing of companies that hired graduates in the past. He used the information as an opening line technique in contacting these local companies to request an interview.

Many students, especially liberal arts students, see their college placement office primarily as a place where recruitment interviews with large corporations are set up for engineering and business majors. The story is told locally of the physical education major who yearned to work in a big corporation but recruiters wanted only to see computer majors. He patiently waited in the placement office through days of interviewing until one of the students did not show up for an interview. He quickly offered to take the student's place and to be brief. His ingenuity was notable. He currently runs an employee recreation/fitness program for a national firm in rural New York.

If you do not fit the requirements commanded by on-campus recruiters, or the school has none, all is not lost. Make yourself familiar with the people in the office and with procedures, long before graduation time. Then they may help in arranging interviews for you, off-campus, at two or three companies where you really want to work. They'll be more willing if you give every indication that you are knowledgeable about the companies and will interview well.

In addition, placement offices, especially the larger ones here, can provide you with some good job hunting techniques. For a start, you may be surprised to find that they have libraries with books on career fields and job hunting. They frequently maintain information on the companies that have recruited there (the University of Pittsburgh's is extensive). You can usually get help with your resume. Several schools locally have VCRs and can tape practice interviews with you.

In no way is your placement office able to do all the work for you. Expect to use it in conjunction with other methods, unless your field is really in demand. Finally, when you have found your good job, remember your alma mater's placement office when you have a job order.

SPECIALIZED EMPLOYMENT ASSISTANCE

There are some special agencies locally which assist job hunters with handicaps—physical, mental, medical or visual—to find jobs. These include agencies such as the Bureau of Blindness and Visual Services and the Vocational Rehabilitation Center. A number of these agencies are included in the resources at the end of PART TWO of this book. Some of them now share their job listings in a common job bank. While at times limited by the number of jobs to which they can exclusively refer, these agencies can offer reality-tested advice and techniques on how to focus a job interview to your advantage. Coupled with other resources, they may provide just the boost you need.

If you want to know whether you fall into a special job hunting category, *Helpline* (255-1155) is the place to call. This free local telephone information and referral service has a comprehensive listing and can help you determine an appropriate agency.

CAREER COUNSELORS

Executive Career Counselors do not provide placement. Their work is to help you polish your job hunting skills. Regardless of what their ads imply, the contract you sign binds you to pay for services you receive and is not contingent on your finding a job. For-profit agencies can charge a healthy fee, from a few hundred to several thousand dollars. Locally, three are frequent advertisers in the classified ads of the newspaper.

Job hunters who are attracted to them hoping to be transformed into instant high-level corporate executive material will be disappointed. A real caution, for those who are already skilled professionals, is succinctly noted by Marge Rossman, an executive recruiter:

> I am suggesting that you avoid those with slick packaged presentations. . . look for professionals who want to teach you the career planning process and how to implement it whenever you need it. You may want help with your resume, letters, interviewing techniques or other aspects of job-finding activity and a good counselor will teach you to do these things for yourself. Your presentation will be unique and suited to you. It will not come from a package on some one's shelf. (*When the Headhunter Calls.* Contemporary Books, 1981. p. 17)

Community-based Counseling. In response to high unemployment, some local church groups and community colleges initiated support services and offer advice, assistance with parts of the job hunt and job hunt clubs. Colleges, too, may offer counseling and job hunt help. Many of these are listed in the resources at the end of PART TWO of this book. You will also find private practitioners whose value to you may vary greatly. There are no licensing requirements for career counselors in the state of Pennsylvania.

Getting assistance with career planning at a particular time in your life can be very effective. Learning techniques and how-tos before you tackle the job market can save you from losing out on valued opportunities. It can be expensive to learn from your own mistakes.

SCAMS

In times of high unemployment, questionable practices and practitioners arise. Some of these offers to help job hunters—for a fee— are absolutely legal but totally worthless. The fact that they pretend to have what every job hunter fondly wishes for (the most common request of job hunters is for a complete list of available jobs) or mimic methods that are helpful when done properly makes it hard to single out individual areas of abuse. Other kinds of employment assistance, like indiscriminate mass mailings of your resume, cause "no harm" (unless your current employer receives one) but don't produce enough results for the money invested.

No one has an exclusive contract on job hunt savvy. Acquire whatever you can, whenever you can, and incorporate it into your personal body of wisdom, checking it against common sense and your personal needs.

PART FIVE
COMMUNICATIONS: PITTSBURGH STYLE

9
RESUMES THAT WORK

Most job seekers have a resume of *one sort or another* at the start of their job hunt. This chapter is not designed to write your resume from scratch but to help you to evaluate yours against the expectations voiced by Pittsburgh hirers and polish it into a version that reflects you as a desirable candidate.

An effective resume is a *focused* summary of your education, your strongest skills and your experience. It is *not* your life history or a list of your strengths and weaknesses. Neither should it be a simple rundown of your job titles, employers' names and the dates when you worked for them. Although many people think a simple job outline is a true resume, it reads like an obituary and may serve as one for the job hunter who uses it.

The focus for your resume should be on employers' needs as well as on your own objectives. If you show an employer that you have 1) saved time or money, 2) added to profits and/or 3) contributed effectively to the production of goods or services similar to his own, you'll be on the right track. If you completed the Personal Data Project, your resume will follow logically from its basic format. Choose the skills and accomplishments which support your objectives and tell the employer, "I can do what you want to have done and I can do it well." Then present them in order of their likely importance *to the employer*.

What Employers Expect—the Basics

Hirers in our part of Western Pennsylvania say that resumes are getting better and better. They expect all the basic information to be there and they pay greater attention to the other, more subtle messages which resumes communicate. If certain information is missing, you may not get called for that all-important interview, so be sure to include these essentials:

- Your name, address and telephone number (at home and at work).
- A description of your work experience, with the employers' names and dates of employment included (whether your work was paid or unpaid).
- Your formal and informal educational background.

Telling What You Do

Many recruiters expect you to give greater emphasis on your resume to your last three jobs or your past ten years of experience. Beyond that, a simple listing is adequate for their needs, although *you* may wish to highlight some earlier experiences for your own purposes.

One successful job hunter highlighted all the sales experiences throughout her career, including a four year part-time job at Joseph Horne Co. which she had held 14 years earlier. As she put it,

> I've used many other types of skills during my career, but I wanted to change the focus of my work more into sales, so I reinforced my long-standing sales experience that way. Of course, the further back I went, the shorter my statements became. By the time I got to the Horne's job, I simply listed the title and dates.

And What You Do Well

Employers want you to *show* them *how well* you've performed your jobs. Saying you answered the phone for the sales department is not enough. They are only attracted to those who describe themselves as *good* phone answerers. They also prefer to be the ones who make the judgments about you, rather than having you evaluate your own skills. For instance, if you wrote, "I am an excellent fund raiser who coordinated the Alumnae Fund annual phonathon, which is the main source of outside money for the college...," a reader might think, "Prove it." However, you could show your excellence the way this Squirrel Hill woman did:

> Organized and executed an Alumnae Fund campaign that tripled the number of previous donors, doubled the amount contributed and won first place in the U.S. Steel-CASE Awards Program.

The content is quite different in the two examples although they were descriptions of the same job. The second version elicited comments such as, "That's terrific!" and "I want to meet that lady!" from local fund raisers who weren't interested in interviewing her when she sent them a resume with the first version in it.

This accomplishment appeared in context with her other skills. Although they were not all of "star" quality, they all showed measurable results and she used percentages and quantities to good effect. Here are two additional descriptions of her work duties:

> Initiated successful phonathons that reached 80-85% of the audience and brought in 45% of total annual funds.

> Created manual record keeping system to track income from various solicitation techniques; compiled statistics from this system to produce weekly, monthly, quarterly and annual reports.

Resumes that contain appropriate use of numbers impress many Pittsburgh employers with their aura of solidity. One human resource specialist from Dravo said,

> In our setting particularly, I look for measurable data, but I've *always* found that figures create a sense of credibility. Look at this bit of experience from one applicant's resume: "Supervised 20 operators as technical foreman for a 300 ton per day coal liquefaction plant." Although I may not have a spot for this person, I can quickly assess his current level of skill from these figures.

In addition to being influenced by the subtle message of strength that comes from quantification, employers are affected by the kinds of words you choose; your spelling and command of grammar; the way in which you organize critical information and by the physical appearance of your resume. All these factors combine to create an impression of you as an individual, so be selective about what you write.

Think about what you are saying to people when you allow long-winded versions of your skills to go straight from your data project pages to your resume. Will you seem wordy, disorganized or careless? You might if you choose to say too much, even if your skills are good ones. "A cluttered resume equals a cluttered mind," say the personnel professionals. In this first draft, a would-be marketing/communications manager fell victim to the overkill syndrome:

> Developed public relations plan which increased sales to the public by 25% through use of effective marketing and personal communication techniques such as color slide and narrations; advertising campaigns (for which I prepared copy); a new sales brochure and many appearances on local radio and TV programs such as AM Pittsburgh and Pittsburgh 2Day.

Looking at this material critically, she realized that most professionals in her field would be interested in knowing two important things about her: 1) she had planned and carried out a successful campaign and 2) she could do the design work also. She ended up with this shortened version:

> Designed marketing materials and a full-scale public relations campaign which increased sales by 28%.

She found that her contacts always asked her what kinds of materials she had developed and gave her an opportunity to explain which aspects of the marketing campaign were most effective, reaffirming her belief in "less is more."

Judge your resume's effectiveness by the principle of selectivity. Clarify what to keep and what to omit by reading yours and asking whether you'd hire a person with these skills for the job you want. Your resume will be read by someone who will probably skim it to identify quickly the kind of job you want and what qualifies you for that position. If you list the 28 different tasks you performed in your last job, you're likely to lose your reader. As one local employment specialist phrased it,

> I'm seeking people who understand priorities. I prefer not to waste my time digging through trivia to find the "good stuff" and, second, I'm concerned that a person like this really doesn't *know* what's important and will waste our time all down the line... I like to find the most important responsibilities needed for the job I have to fill clearly highlighted in an applicant's resume. That's the match I want to see... I

also *hope* that within three minutes I will know what this person wants to do for my employer.

This also raises the question of whether to include a job objective on your resume.

What About an Objective?

Every resume writer is familiar with the job objective—the statement placed near the top of a resume summarizing your career goals or the kind of a position you seek. Most Pittsburgh hirers don't *require* an objective but say that one is helpful. However, a vague job objective seems to be worse than none at all. As one personnel interviewer said, "This (a vague objective) gives me a negative feeling right away. Either you don't know what you can do or you don't know anything about our organization." Others stressed that you don't need to present a specific job title (which may be too limiting) but that you do need to find a way to let your resume at least imply what you want to do; otherwise you will spend a lot longer looking for a job.

If you do include an objective, use some of your functional objectives, rather than a simple job title. Instead of writing *POSITION WANTED: Sales Representative or Management Trainee* at the top of your resume, back up those titles with some skills or experience. The management trainee objective might read like this young job hunter's:

> MANAGEMENT TRAINEE in marketing where my direct sales experience and business administration courses will enable me to make an early contribution to company profits.

He keyed in to one of an employer's biggest questions—how much money will I need to spend on training this person before he or she becomes a productive employee? Your objective can serve as a little advertisement of what you do best.

An objective stated in terms of skills will rarely eliminate you from jobs for which you are qualified. However, if you are concerned about the risk of losing out on some opportunities by specifying what you want to do, omit one from your resume and use your cover letters to describe your job objective. That way you can use the same resume while highlighting aspects of your ability that are appropriate in different job settings.

Optional Information

Some of the most common categories of optional information include foreign language skills; travel experiences; memberships and offices in community or social organizations; professional memberships and personal interests. List only those which can help to make you more employable.

In many resume writing manuals, the authors adhere to a strict, one page only rule, which they follow by, "When in doubt, leave it out." In the Pittsburgh area, two page resumes are fine and, although you might agree with the when-in-doubt statement, *for the first draft* you should leave in everything that might help set you apart positively from other candidates. One recent M.B.A. graduate who wanted to work in international banking included a statement about his language fluency and extensive European travel during his young adult years. He sold himself to a large, local bank on the basis that this could provide a long term advantage to his employer after he'd learned the intricacies of banking operations.

If you have a college degree or advanced degrees, you may eliminate mention of your high school education. Recent graduates should list all summer or part-time work, though, along with a statement about the percentage of their financial contribution to the costs of their education (if they contributed 25% or more).

When Omission Is Not a Sin

Most job hunters find that deciding what to eliminate is the hardest part of writing a resume. Since length is one consideration, you may find that you have some excellent facts to present which you can hint at without going into detail. Some things are *no no's* anyway, for a variety of reasons, so eliminate the following details:

> reasons for leaving past jobs
> references to salary
> photographs of yourself
> your age, marital status, height, weight, race, religion and
>   political beliefs (whether or not they seem guaranteed to
>   weigh heavily in your favor)
> names and addresses of your references.

Salary information and reasons for leaving past jobs can hurt you. In addition to taking up valuable space which you could use to show your skills, they may price you out of your market or make your reader wonder why you focused on your exit from each job. If you have held several positions in a short time period, you may offer a brief explanation in your cover letter or during an interview, but not in your resume.

As for photographs, age, height, etc., it is illegal for employers to ask for information which has nothing to do with the job you are seeking. For at least one hirer, "Photographs are a real turn off! If a person has to count on looks, I figure there isn't much else there to sell." Some personnel specialists stated that they routinely black out all illegal information with heavy black marking pens. Unfortunately that destroys the appearance of any resume on which it appears.

A Note about References

The time to provide references' names is during an interview, preferably after you have gotten some indication that an employer is interested in you. Leave them off your resume since they are often contacted routinely when you provide their names.

To avoid reference burn-out, prepare your references ahead of time. Usually they will be asked to answer several questions (sometimes in writing), such as:

1. How long have you known this applicant, or how long has he or she worked for you?
2. What was the quality of his or her work? Would you recommend him or her?
3. How did he or she get along with co-workers? Clients? Customers?
4. What were his or her responsibilities?
5. Why did he or she leave your organization?
6. How would you describe this person's character? Please include information about honesty, motivation and dependability.

When you ask former employers, co-workers. college professors and respected community leaders to serve as references for you during your job hunt, give them the equipment they need to go to bat for you. Spend a little time with them reviewing the length of time you have known them, the extent of your responsibilities, your actual position title and positive reasons why you left that job. Don't forget to let them know when your job hunt is over and thank them even if they were not contacted.

Making It Work: How to Choose a Good Format

Although there are many possible style variations listed in resume writing books, in Pittsburgh only three basic resume formats appear regularly on hirers' desks. Two of these are readily accepted—the chronological and the combined chronological/functional formats. The third—the pure functional format—is less acceptable in Pittsburgh's relatively conservative business community.

Rather than present you with a lot of sample resumes (there are other books that do that), this chapter urges you to consider using a format that best shows your qualifications for the kind of job you want to get.

Your background may lend itself naturally to a particular format, but you can also "package" your skills in a variety of ways. The two resumes used here show this. Donna Johnson, a fictitious name for a local job hunter, used the first resume when applying for accounting jobs and the second when she was pursuing sales-oriented positions. Both resumes generated interviews. Both are honest descriptions of her skills, but consider how inappropriate she would appear if she presented the chronological format to a recruiter for Kaufmann's Executive Sales Training Program.

Weigh the following advantages and drawbacks of each format as you imagine how each one could showcase your talents.

CHRONOLOGICAL FORMAT RESUME: List and describe each job in order, starting with your most recent position and working backwards. Your education can go before or after your work experience, depending upon how recently you earned your highest degree and how relevant it is to your goals.

Who should consider it: job hunters whose objectives are clearly identified from looking at a description of their past jobs and people with an unbroken progression of increasingly responsible positions.

Advantages: 1) professional interviewers are most familiar with it; 2) the interviewer can use it like a map to follow your experience down a straight road into the past; 3) it's easy to prepare since it is listed job-by-job.

Disadvantages: It may emphasize positions or skills from recent jobs that you hope to minimize. It reveals all gaps in employment and any "job hopping."

Comments: For Donna, a chronological resume emphasizes her accounting skills in her education and job experience sections. She used

CHRONOLOGICAL FORMAT SAMPLE

DONNA JOHNSON
130 Swann Road
Pittsburgh, PA 15200
(412) 555-7777

OBJECTIVE: An entry level auditing position with a
public accounting firm. Seek to use my
accounting skills in a training program
leading to certification.

EDUCATION: B.S. Business Administration, Duquesne
University. December, 1981. Dean's List.

Course Emphasis: Accounting (27 credits),
computer science, law, economics,
statistics, finance, management.

Honors and Activities: Beta Alpha Phi,
honorary business fraternity; Phi Chi Theta,
professional business sorority--Fund Raising
and Social Chairperson; Junior Achievement's
Treasurer of the Year in Western Pennsylvania;
Degree of Excellence in Extemporaneous
Speaking.

Financed 80% of all college education.

EXPERIENCE: Assistant Controller, Marriott's Camelback
Inn Golf Club and Resort, Scottsdale,
Arizona. January 1, 1982 - Present.

- Supervised computerized accounting
  system (accounts receivable and
  payable); credit and collections.

- Interviewed, hired, trained, supervised and evaluated a staff of six.

- Prepared monthly financial statements
  and regularly scheduled reports.

- Monitored hotel's expenditures.

- Assisted with special projects and
  inventories.

- Prepared and delivered weekly presentations at hotel staff meetings.

(Continued)

211

Continued Resume of Donna Johnson   Page 2

EXPERIENCE - continued

> Manager, Duquesne University Federal
> Credit Union, Pittsburgh, Pennsylvania.
> March, 1979 - January, 1982.
>
> - Organized and managed Credit Union
>   office.
> - Maintained manual accounting system:
>   prepared monthly financial statements,
>   general ledger, payroll, loan trans-
>   actions, dividends, taxes and insurance.
> - Reduced loan delinquency rate by 20%
>   within a 6-month period.
> - Hired and trained staff.
> - Prepared and delivered monthly presen-
>   tations to Board of Directors.
>
> Bookkeeper, Roboro, Inc., McKnight East,
> Pittsburgh, Pennsylvania. June, 1978 -
> February, 1979. Summer and part-time.
>
> - Responsible for all phases of manual
>   accounting system for three McDonald's
>   franchises: general ledger, cash dis-
>   bursement journal, EDP payroll, accounts
>   payable, taxes, insurance and regularly
>   scheduled reports.

her two jobs to back each other up by repeating the skills they had in common. Employers could readily see the relationship between her education and her level of responsibility with this format.

Although Donna had worked at Gimbels for four years as a summer and part-time employee, she did not include that experience on this particular resume. Her main consideration was space and the sales experience was not relevant to the job she sought. However, she did include that job on every application form she completed.

FUNCTIONAL RESUME: Pure functional resumes leave out all dates and employers' names. Your experience is organized under functional headings instead of beneath each job title. The functional headings are listed as broad categories like management, training, communication, sales, data processing, etc. The goal is to select categories which support your objectives and place them in order of importance, level of responsibility and relevance. An example of a pure functional resume is not illustrated here, but if you drop the experience and education sections from the combination format resume that is shown next, what you have left is a pure functional resume.

Who it's for: A functional resume is used frequently by job hunters who have made several job changes or who have gaps in their employment history. It also is used by career changers whose job titles often don't reflect their qualifications for their current job objective.

Advantages: You can stress your marketable skills and emphasize professional growth rather than job titles, and you can de-emphasize positions or skill areas which do not relate to your current job objectives.

Disadvantages: Some employers are suspicious of the pure functional resume. Also, you can't highlight the names of employers or industries if you adhere to the format strictly.

Comments: Lu Chamberlin, a personnel relations administrator, who values honesty very highly, says that she doesn't eliminate candidates who use it, ". . . if certain skills jump out at me from the page." However, when she spots one she does suspect that there are gaps or a problem somewhere in the applicant's history. "It really doesn't help the job hunter much. The dates will show up when I look at the application and I just wonder why the person hasn't been 'up front' in the first place." What Lu and other hirers do like about the functional format is the ease with which they can relate your skills to the skills required in the jobs they have to fill.

You can obtain the advantages of both the functional and chronological formats by combining the two.

213

COMBINATION FORMAT RESUME: Present your functional skills in a separate section of your resume titled "career summary," "experience," "major skill areas" or something similar. After the summary of your experience, list company names and dates under a work experience or employment history heading.

Who it's for: It can be for everyone, really, but especially job hunters who have been employed in one or two firms for many years; for people who have been using all the needed skills at a high level, but without the title to go with them; and for career changers who desire to show the relationship between their current skills and the ones needed in their new field, without stimulating the reader's hang-ups about direct experience.

Advantages: By listing employers' names and the dates, you will reassure readers that nothing is being hidden or deleted. Because your important accomplishments and skills are listed first, readers are less likely to fit you into a box titled "social worker" or "teacher" or "blood technician."

Disadvantages: It may take longer to read unless you write very succinctly and lay it out with extreme care.

Comments: Local hirers value well-done combination resumes. They say that the outline formation, with indenting and clearly designated headings, helps them find the information they need quickly. When comparing it to the chronological resume, hirers say that the key is in the presentation—both styles work well when the job hunter lists skills and relevant responsibilities in order of importance.

Writing a combination resume involves a little more work than writing a straight chronological resume. If you want to use marketing skills, communication skills and management in your next job, like Donna Johnson did in her second resume, review each past job and your data project to pick out instances where each skill was successfully used. For your first draft, include *all* of the instances to see their quantity and quality. Then be selective.

Donna deliberately avoided references to her accounting skills and experiences because she had determined that she wanted her next job to be focused more on work with people than with figures.

For this sales-oriented resume, Donna reframed her approach. She included her direct sales experience at a department store for obvious reasons, but note the way she made use of her college activities. All of this data was on her personal data sheet when she sat down to prepare both of her resumes. However, she was careful to select only the achievements from her experiences which supported her specific job objectives.

```
COMBINATION FORMAT SAMPLE

               DONNA JOHNSON
               130  Swann Road
            Pittsburgh, PA  15200
               (412) 555-7777


Objective       An entry level sales position which includes
                a training program and offers opportunity
                for career progression in the field of
                marketing.

Major Skill
Areas
                Marketing
                  • Sold merchandise in a variety of depart-
                    ments in a large retail operation.
                    Commended on competence and versatility.

                  • Coordinated successful fund-raising
                    campaigns for college sorority--
                    developed and supervised marketing plan;
                    trained members in marketing techniques;
                    established and exceeded quotas.

                  • Increased Credit Union's membership by
                    15% and sorority's membership by 60%
                    through personal recruitment efforts
                    and advertising.

                Communications and Public Relations
                  • Prepared and delivered monthly presenta-
                    tions to Credit Union's Board of
                    Directors.

                  • Designed and produced newsletters and
                    brochures for Credit Union's membership
                    drive.

                  • Conducted telephone polls as a campaign
                    volunteer.

                Organization and Administration
                  • Organized Credit Union's entire office
                    operation.
                  • Responsible for computerized and
                    manual accounting systems, prepared
                    monthly financial statements, budgets,
                    and special projects.
                  • Supervised staff of 6--interviewed, hired,
                    trained and evaluated.

                                          (continued)
```

```
Resume of Donna Johnson
Page 2


Experience

        Assistant Controller    Marriott's Camelback Inn
                                Golf Club and Resort,
                                Scottsdale, AZ.
                                1/82-9/83

        Manager                 Duquesne University Federal
                                Credit Union, Pittsburgh,
                                PA.  3/79-1/82

        Bookkeeper              Roboro, Inc., Pittsburgh,
                                PA.  3/78-2/79

        Salesperson             Gimbel's North Hills,
                                Pittsburgh, PA.  12/74-6/78.
                                Summers and part-time.

Education

        B.S. Business Administration, Duquesne
        University, 1981.

        Course Emphasis:  Marketing, Management, Computer
                          Science, Accounting, Economics,
                          and Oral Communications.

        Honors and Activities:  Dean's List; Beta Alpha Phi,
        honorary business fraternity; Phi Chi Theta,
        professional business sorority--Fund Raising and
        Social Chairman; Junior Achievement's Salesman of
        the Year finalist; Degree of Excellence in Ex-
        temporaneous Speaking.

        Financed 80% of my education by working full-time
        and part-time while attending college.
```

Variations

The CURRICULUM VITAE is the one other type of resume which is widely used in Pitttsburgh because of the city's role as a center for higher education. This special kind of chronological resume may run to several pages since the faculty members who use them are expected to list their scholarly publications and the courses they've taught in addition to their professional positions.

The organizational problems that poses are easily solved:

1. When you list a position title, state your primary and secondary fields of specialization before you list the courses you've taught.
2. Use separate headings for books, published articles and papers you presented at professional conferences. Select on the basis of quality since search committee members will be on the lookout for puffery.
3. Date your curriculum vitae.

Your writing will be held to the highest critical standard, so you cannot afford even a single example of poor grammar, inaccurate spelling or punctuation error. Otherwise, follow the same advice that any other job hunter should heed. Emphasize results and accomplishments and be scrupulously honest.

Variations of the combination format include the targeted resume (see *The Perfect Resume* by Tom Jackson); the situation resume, a complex arrangement which shows large problems you've solved in a case study format; and the resume alternative, described in some job hunting books as a sales letter or broadcast letter.

These variations are not commonly used here in Pittsburgh. Perhaps one or two a year will appear on a particular hirer's desk. You take a bit of a risk in using them. If one comes at the right moment, it may seem like a breath of fresh air to the reader and win you an interview, but it could just as easily ruin your chances because it's unfamiliar.

The bibliography at the end of this chapter lists books which contain additional samples and information.

Hire Someone to Write It

Almost every individual who selects employees gave some version of the following quote which comes from Stan Schiffman, Executive Director of the Jewish Home for the Aged,

> I can spot a "professionally prepared" resume at once now, and I am usually unimpressed. In one recent search we received four different resumes printed on yellow paper, each one containing flowery, vague career objectives and a qualifications summary which told nothing about what the job hunter could do—it was mostly adjectives. Now I don't know who prepared those, but they sure didn't work with me.

Not all professional resume writers turn out work that so obviously misses the mark but they all have the disadvantage of knowing the job hunter only superficially. As in all parts of the job hunting process, completing the work yourself will add to your competence (at analyzing information, organizing data and writing concisely, in this case) and your confidence. Not every job hunter makes this effort. There are two pages of resume writing firms listed in the phone directory. But if you have any writing ability, write your own resume because it results in a direct communication of yourself that comes through to the reader. Says one executive for a health management firm:

> I use the resume to see how an applicant thinks. Is he or she logical? Organized? Concise? Expressive? Detail oriented? In different jobs I seek different traits. I don't expect technical applicants to write resumes the same way that administrators or public relations job seekers do. They are held to different standards.

Even if you have little faith in your writing ability, you can *prepare* your resume carefully before you take it to someone who will polish the wording or design the spacing. Make it your own as much as possible first so the professional can reflect what is most unique about you. Once the resume writer does his or her part, again exercise your own judgment about final wording and appearance. Make sure you are completely comfortable with it *before* you send it to employers.

If you do write your own, plan to do several separate drafts with a day or two between them. One job hunter who got stuck on the first draft because he was uncomfortable "blowing my own horn," found that each time he worked on the resume he thought of a new skill or a better way to say something. At the end of two weeks, he said,

> I found that my resume showed what was unique about the way I solved problems and met challenges in my work. I'm convinced that writing my own resume gave me the confidence to come across well during my interviews and helped me land my job here at Xerox.

Make It Work for You

Resume writing is action writing. Instead of putting down complete sentences, you start with action verbs and follow them with direct objects. Look at the following example from a Monroeville teacher's data project and resume.

> *DATA PROJECT: I made up educational games and re-*
> *source materials for teachers to use in*
> *fifth grade classrooms and then demon-*
> *strated the games for teachers, principals*
> *and supervisors in several schools.*
> *Results: all of my materials were adopted*
> *to be used for every 5th grade class in the*
> *district.*

> *RESUME: Created and demonstrated elementary*
> *level educational games and resource*
> *materials which were adopted district-*
> *wide.*

In another example from the same resume, Shirley wrote, "Managed movement of consultants, volunteers and observers through model open-classroom settings while maintaining an effective learning environment." If you analyze her statement, you find the three stage notation of a success is implicit. Problem: large numbers of adults invading these model classrooms. Action: managed (organized and scheduled). Result: maintained student learning in addition to providing reasonable opportunity for adult observation. She aimed to create a verbal picture in her readers' minds—a picture of someone who was much more than the stereotypical elementary school teacher.

To help you to write in this resume style, we present a short list of resume action verbs. You can do even better. Develop your own list by underlining all the verbs in your data project—then use a good dictionary and thesaurus to find strong, striking synonyms for them. Additional verb lists appear in many resume writing books.

A caution about language: because so many job hunters use resume books or consulting services, some words or phrases have become over-worked locally. Look for verbs to substitute for *communicated, developed* and *implemented,* if you can find more specific ones. Readers say they sometimes inadvertently skip over accomplishments because the initial verbs are so familiar.

Resume Skill Words

PRODUCTION

Shaped
Reshaped
Molded
Adjusted
Guided
Defined
Constructed
Repaired
Operated
Assembled

CREATION

Initiated
Created
Developed
Implemented
Conceptualized
Invented
Planned
Established
Performed
Dramatized

ORGANIZATION

Compared
Measured
Estimated
Calculated
Computed
Analyzed
Evaluated
Investigated
Researched
Examined
Inspected
Observed
Perceived
Interpreted
Translated
Forecast
Budgeted
Assessed
Appraised

Audited
Treated
Monitored
Anticipated

ADMINISTRATION

Arranged
Organized
Coordinated
Negotiated
Contracted
Delegated
Improved
Expanded
Enlarged
Strengthened
Stimulated
Promoted
Persuaded
Achieved
Produced
Attained
Presided
Chaired
Governed
Administered
Supervised
Directed
Managed
Controlled
Maintained
Approved
Applied
Recruited
Selected
Enlisted
Distributed
Sold
Demonstrated
Displaced
Represented
Motivated

COMMUNICATION

Spoke

Taught
Instructed
Presented
Trained
Conducted
Moderated
Led
Mediated
Facilitated
Encouraged
Guided
Counseled
Communicated
Motivated
Interviewed
Edited
Wrote
Reported
Reviewed
Advised
Translated

DETAIL-ORIENTATION

Updated
Scheduled
Tabulated
Systematized
Sorted
Straightened
Classified
Compiled
Assembled
Indexed
Recorded
Summarized
Processed
Programmed
Grouped
Catalogued
Operated
Filed
Detailed
Collected

Source: **Job Advisory Service**

When you stick to action verbs and direct objects, you create a concise, yet detailed, picture of your skills and accomplishments. To avoid vagueness or too much detail, look at the adjectives and adverbs you've used. They may create feelings of artificiality or overkill. One value of writing several drafts is that you can spot and weed these out.

Evaluating What You've Written

Once you've completed your second or third draft, you can use this checklist to evaluate your resume.

1. Have you been specific each time you listed an accomplishment or responsibility? Have you used numbers and percentages where they were appropriate?
2. Does each skill relate directly to your objective? Did you list the most important ones first in each section?
3. Are there any other achievements you should include?
4. If you have started with an objective, does it tell the employer what you want to do without being too limiting?
5. Does each statement start with an action verb? Is the tone positive?
6. Have you removed all confidential material regarding your past employers?
7. Does the format make the most of your experience and play down any disadvantages in your background, without being dishonest?
8. Does the language reflect the jargon used in your field?
9. Did you state your willingness to travel or relocate in positive terms?
10. Have you eliminated every error and awkward phrase?
11. Can you skim it quickly and pick out three skills that stand out? Do you know immediately what this person can do?

Once you can answer all these questions positively, you are ready to ask one last, different type of question. How does it look? This question moves you into the design stage. Most Pittsburgh hirers demand brevity. They expect you to be able to say everything important about your experience in two pages, unless you are in the academic community where the longer curriculum vitae is used. In addition, each hirer responds very strongly and personally to the way your resume looks. Although some employers are more sensitive to appearances than others, most people prefer not to interview people who allow sloppy looking resumes to represent them. To check your resume's layout and appearance, ask yourself a few more questions...

1. Is your resume easy to read because you've left plenty of white space on the page? Are the margins wide and well-balanced?
2. Do your headings stand out clearly? Have you used indentation, punctuation marks and other techniques to separate items and sections for easy reading?
3. Do your name, address and phone number appear prominently at the top?
4. Is every word spelled correctly?

Now is the time to show your resume to a reader or two who is "in the know." Talk to someone in your field who will be an honest and constructive critic. Do this *before* you make many copies so that you won't have a big investment in keeping the status quo. Each reader will want to change *something,* no doubt, but that's a good sign—it means people are reading it carefully. Look for the points of agreement among your readers; identify all the comments which make sense and integrate the best ones into your final draft.

Typing and Producing Mechanics

We live in a visual world today. If you could browse through a stack of 50 resumes and cover letters from people who were applying for the same positions as you are, you would quickly see what looks good, what doesn't and what you want yours to look like.

One of the first things you'd notice was the typing paper. See-through paper, called onionskin, comes off poorly. (Use 25% rag content or all cotton paper.) A manual typewriter that strikes the letters unevenly or a low quality 9-pin computer printer that shows the dots of its dot-matrix letters are also not good enough today. You do not want to associate being out of date or low quality of any kind with your job hunt. Likewise, avoid wild colors, pearlized paper or bold graphics unless you have an extenuating excuse such as being an advertising or graphics genius. Most employers are comfortable with a conservative style; besides you will be hired because you, not the appearance of your resume, are outstanding. (So use white, cream, ivory or very light grey paper.)

Browsing through that stack would make you aware of another fact of life: resumes usually do not stand alone. Since it is unacceptable to mail a resume without a covering letter, some forethought must be given to harmonizing these two companion pieces of paper that represent you in your absence. (For the content of those cover letters, see the Methods Chapter in PART FOUR of this book.) A resume on tan paper and a cover letter on see-through white paper are distracting. Glaring differences in the kinds of typefaces used on the two pieces also send negative messages, much like mixing plaids and stripes in an interview outfit. Think about the ways you will use your resume and about the paper and typing machine you will have available when you suddenly decide to answer a want ad or write a thank you note. This may influence some of your decisions about details of typing and reproduction.

Today it is easy and inexpensive to produce a good looking resume due to the proliferation of word processing programs, laser printers and the improved quality of photocopy machines. Once you have a final draft of your resume the next step is to get a perfect original that you can then copy. There are three usual ways to do this: typing, word processing and typesetting. Since it takes real skill to get a manual typewriter to produce clean even copy, use an electric one. Word processing programs have the advantage of being easy to change; you can have two or three versions with little effort and you can use different sizes of letters much like typesetting for a better layout of the resume page.

You can use your own, use public access machines, "private access" ones or pay someone to do the work. Access to machines is increasing: the North Side library of Community College has typewriters for its students, as do many of the colleges. Carnegie Library's Workplace Room for job hunters has a computer available for resume writing. You can rent the use of one: Kinko's Copies in Oakland (open 24 hours), for example, has three Macintosh computers that rent for $8 an hour, charged by the minutes used. Private access—a brother's computer, friend's unused typewriter, sister's secretarial connection—is well worth looking into as long as you keep in mind compatibility with the other written materials you will generate in your job hunt. You can find someone to type your resume through the yellow pages, or local and college newspapers. Some copy shops will do it too. (Kinko's will word process a one page resume for $13.)

Typesetting is another way to arrive at a "perfect" original of your resume. This is usually done by smaller printing firms and "instant" printers. New Image Press, for example, will take your rough draft and for $30 typeset one page. Typeset resumes once were the only choice for the executive because of their polished appearances. But they are difficult to change and are now almost indistinguishable from good quality laser printed word processed resumes. When working for this "perfect" original; do not be rushed to approve a "final," take every bit of time you need to verify spelling and catch errors—then check it again.

... and Reproducing

Once you have a satisfactory original, photocopying is by far the most common reproduction method. Almost every neighborhood in Pittsburgh has a commercial shop that makes high quality copies. But avoid coin-operated machines that turn out streaked, smudged, spotted copies. One recruiter said, "I don't want to meet the person whose resume looks like grey sludge." Even your office's slightly worn copy machine may not be good enough for you. If you can easily tell the difference between the copy and the original, go to a copy shop. For about ten cents you'll have a good copy on high quality resume paper.

You can purchase blank paper and matching envelopes to go with your resume paper. Pick your own out at an office or stationery store. Copy shops sell them, too. Some offer a "resume package": 25 copies of your resume, 25 blank pages and 25 envelopes for about $4.

Attention to details like these has become an expected part of job hunting and is needed to keep you from being eliminated before your resume gets a reading. But the consensus of most employers is that they really go for quality where it counts—in the content. Put your emphasis where the employers do, and you'll do just fine in Pittsburgh.

Resume Writing Books

Catalyst, Inc. *Marketing Yourself: The Catalyst Women's Guide to Successful Resumes and Interviews.* Putnam, 1980.

Dickhut, Harold W. *The Professional Resume and Job Search Guide.* Prentice Hall, 1981.

Jackson, Tom. *The Perfect Resume.* Anchor, 1980.

10

INTERVIEWING WITH A PITTSBURGH ACCENT

Bernie heard from his second cousin, who worked at a small company, that a warehouse job was open. He called up the owner, mentioned his cousin, and asked if he could come in for a talk.

Jerry had a courtesy interview at a foundation in January. In March he heard that there was an opening there. He called, asked for a description of the job and requested an appointment.

Karen replied with a resume and cover letter to an agency's ad for a counselor with a master's degree in social work. A week later she was called to come in for an interview.

An executive recruiter called *Nicholas,* an engineering group leader, at work to ask if he'd like to come over for a chat; he had a client looking for Nick's skills and background.

Paul, a 25-year corporate recruiter, saw an open job posting for a placement director's position while he was interviewing students at a local university. He sent his resume to the head of the search committee.

Steele, a college English professor, launched a highly creative, visibility and credibility campaign for his career change. It lasted nine months and took him to the offices of eleven corporate presidents.

The common denominator in each of these Pittsburgher's job hunts is that the job seeker has to pass through at least one interview before being offered a job.

Because of their importance, interviews spawn fear and trembling in the recesses of the most stalwart job hunter's heart. Some books and practitioners speak of job interviews as warfare or a competitive game to be won. But our philosophy of interviewing, and that of our agency, is that interviewing is a *communication.* It takes place not between opponents but between two human beings both of whom have feelings and are under pressure to make important decisions based on a relatively brief conversation. It is not a social or casual event that should be left to chance. An interview is a spotlight which you use to shine on your best, most employable features. With a communications approach, you need not use a "hard sell" nor do you need the "gift of gab" to interview effectively.

What Works in Pittsburgh?

Can this kind of honesty work in Pittsburgh? From the stories told us by local interviewers, it certainly seems so. Uniformly they expressed, unsolicited, their quick elimination of "someone trying to pull something off," the "slick" ones. They are insulted by attempts at trickery or "answers that parrot back what the 'technique' books advise: like 'my favorite pastime is reading about macroeconomic theory'." One corporate personnel director bluntly talked about the types of people he sees:

> I enjoy interviewing Pittsburghers. The hometown people are natural and open. I can easily judge whether they'll fit with the others in the departments...but people who have been with the corporate structure for a while or who have transferred around (like myself) are a pain. They have almost too much composure. The answers run off their tongues like water off glass. They actually know exactly how long to laugh at my jokes.

That generalization may be unfair, but the message is clear.

At the same time, Pittsburgh is a town with an abundance of qualified candidates. Interviewers may be sympathetic, but they do not hire people who are obviously unpolished or naive. One hiring manager wondered aloud, "How would one of these 'diamonds in the rough' treat our customers and clients?" Says another, "I don't need somebody around who hasn't figured out that he won't get hired by telling me all his faults. He'll probably be off the mark in doing other things, too."

The key is not to put on phony techniques of either sort. Instead, practice and polish your natural style. Even a "good communicator" profits by practice, for job interviews are a specialized kind of interaction in which even the friendliest questions have job-related motives.

The Four Abilities

Look at the interview from the interviewer's side of the desk for a few moments. There are four basic abilities that he or she needs to judge about each candidate. The first is the question of **ability**. Can you do a good job? If you are experienced, the interviewer bases his or her opinions on your past performance. Otherwise, the quality of your training will be the determining factor. Said one interviewer, "The local schools have their reputations. I know who turns out good graphic designers. If you went to the other school, you've got to show me that you are exceptional." Variations on this comment are heard from interviewers throughout the Pittsburgh area—in many fields. If this problem affects you, prepare a proof-filled presentation.

Frequently all finalists' qualifications are about equal. When that is the case, selection will be based on factors such as **compatibility**. Will you fit in? That isn't just a matter of getting along with the interviewer, although that helps; it's more a matter of how you will interact with your future co-workers. One agency director interviewed applicants for several months before filling one staff position, saying "A department takes on a personality of its own, and I am looking for someone whose style will fit ours. I expect competence, of course, but I've seen good programs ruined by in-fighting and dissension."

Compatibility also relates to how well your characteristics match the job's unique requirements as performed in that particular organization. Sometimes, compatibility even goes so far as to mean that you match the image the hirer has about people who fill a particular position. Interviewer attitudes include so many prejudices, judgments, hidden agendas and elements beyond your control as to sometimes seem too whimsical to be a real part of job hunting; but they are. Says one hiring manager, "I don't look for problems, so I avoid anyone who's been involved with controversy or has an ax to grind." Unfair? Perhaps. Another said, "Josephine's been here 17 years and is the mainstay of the billing department. *Anyone* I put in that department has got to be able to get along with her." Since there are no guarantees that your selection or rejection will be based on objective reasons, don't let the inevitable rejections that occur during your job hunt get you down.

A tax accountant in Girard recently refused to hire the most qualified applicant. Why? He could not offer her any opportunity for advancement and he felt she would be dissatisfied before very long. He made a reasoned decision based on the need for workforce **stability.** Because it is so expensive to hire and train people, personnel professionals who consistently misjudge applicants' potential stability are fired. Hiring managers pay for mistakes in lost staff time and decreased productivity. To avoid costly errors they may ask directly, "Are you going to stay?" However, most of the time interviewers try to discern indirectly whether your ambition level and past sources of satisfaction match the rewards and opportunities they have to offer. They ask questions like: "How do you feel about your career progress so far?" and, "What are your long range career goals?" or, "Where would you like to be in three years?"

If you have been able to learn something about the job and its place in the structure of the company ahead of time or early in the interview, you will be in a better position to answer some of these questions. As one sharp job hunter remarked, "I'd rather not be screened out because I answered these questions the wrong way. I'd rather have the option of deciding for myself that I don't want the job because I'd be bored or trapped in a dead-end position."

The final criteria is that of **profitability.** Selling products may be the most obvious measure of profitability, but people who work efficiently, learn quickly, motivate, teach or enhance others' productivity also contribute to employers' profits. If you can show that you have cut costs in the past, you will light up dollar signs in a profit-conscious employer's eyes just as surely as a top-notch salesperson does.

All things considered, when several applicants are qualified for a particular job, an employer may be swayed toward the job hunter who represents himself or herself as a hard-working, reliable, conscientious and enthusiastic individual who wants the job and will do it more accurately, faster, more efficiently and with better cheer than anyone else.

When Is an Interview an Interview?

Every job hunt related communication can be looked on as a kind of interview if it allows others to evaluate you as a prospective employee —for themselves or for someone they know. If you engage a professional associate in conversation or are using a referral method, you may be in a pre-interview situation. In these cases, don't screen yourself out by griping about your current situation.

The impression you make upon receptionists or assistants who accept your application is not always as unimportant as it seems. Their comments can eliminate you from contention. A bad mark can come from the way you are dressed (*But I wasn't going in to see any one, I was just dropping off my resume!*) or a thoughtless comment (*Have all the "big cheeses" taken off early, already?*) or poor grammar (*Are yunz hirin'?*). Also avoid any trace of a condescending attitude or remarks that seem to "pump" people for the inside story.

However, factual information is there for the few job hunters who bother to ask politely. "Do you know when they plan to start interviewing?" "Can I leave a confidential office number with you, to reach me during the day?" or "Is there a fuller job description available?"

Telephone Interviews

The phone is a fast, easy and inexpensive way for an employer to screen an initial group of promising candidates. It may seem casual, but its importance should not be underestimated. Ron Petit, in *The Career Connection,* describes the concerns clearly:

> Applicants who don't pass the telephone screening process, however, are seldom told by the employer that they have failed. Instead, the employer may politely say that no decision about interviewing can be made until other candidates have been screened, but very few employers will make a second telephone call to a job applicant if an invitation for a personal interview is not extended during the initial telephone contact. (p. 66)

Because job *offers* are not made on the basis of a telephone call, your objective is to survive the winnowing and get to a personal interview. When employers contact you by phone, they are usually seriously interested unless you eliminate yourself. Listen carefully, repeat back information. Respond positively since they may use a discouraging aspect of the job to eliminate some applicants: "Will you work overtime?" "How do you feel about time pressures?" Answer briefly; leave a reason for them to see you in person. If there are any doubts, offer to come in and talk about them.

The Screening Interview

The screening interview is another elimination tool for employers. It is carried out in larger companies by the personnel department. In smaller firms a designated assistant gets the task. The focus is on credentials and personal characteristics. The screener is interested primarily in verifying impressions and information received earlier or in a resume and checking to see if the job hunter's background information is consistent. You may be asked at this point to fill out an application form, thus giving the employer three points of reference: resume—application—personal statements. In this situation, consistency among those three points of reference equals truth verification.

To survive such a screening, know your resume thoroughly and be prepared to talk about it. Do not contradict anything in it. Offer brief stories and concrete examples so that you may be more easily remembered. Use the technical language of your field, but not if your screener is unfamiliar with the terms. If, at this point, you think you look like a promising candidate, you can ask what the next stage of the hiring procedure is.

The Selection Interview

A hundred people may apply for an advertised position, but it is the five to ten who are called in for an interview who are really in the running. Selection will be made from these.

While a clear-cut job offer at the end of the first selection interview is possible, it is likely you'll be looked over several times or by several people. They need to reconfirm their impression of you. At large firms, and there are many in Pittsburgh, serious candidates above entry level commonly have a half or full day of interviews, tours, applications or tests and more interviews. Not all are in-depth interviews; some are with potential co-workers who have no hiring authority but whose veto carries weight. Sometimes it is arranged that one person will question you about your work history, another about your personal life and that a third will conduct a stress interview. A good rule is to assume that anyone you speak to is making a judgment about you.

Popular Types of Interviews

Traditional. You can expect that a majority of the interviewers in Pittsburgh who are not personnel interviewers will follow a conservative line. This means that the bulk of the interview time uses your resume as a structural outline. The questions will involve your work history, for the most part. You may be asked:

What did you do best in your job?
What were your supervisor's strengths?
What kind of supervisor gets the best performance out of you?
What are examples of some decisions you were called on to make?
What counseling theory do you use in working with clients?
Your resume says you seek a position in administrative management. What do you mean by that?

Open. The open style of interview gives the interviewer a more subjective impression of the kind of person you are. He or she wants to know not so much whether you have a skill, but how you use it or what your personality style is like. In order to learn enough about you to have a basis to hire you, a skilled professional plans the interview questions carefully. These interviews can be divided into categories such as: focus selection interviews, probe, stress or negative stress interviews. Recognize some of these techniques by the inclusion, along with traditional work-related questions, of questions like:

Who was your favorite teacher? Why?
What were the five happiest events in your life?
What *is* counseling?
What do you think motivates you?
What kind of people rub you the wrong way?

There are no set answers for these questions; that is precisely why they are asked. What you say *and* how you say it counts heavily. The eloquence with which one social worker explained why he did *not* know what counseling was, provided the most convincing point of his interview. Feel comfortable about briefly revealing work and career values which you firmly believe, but be circumspect.

Stress Interviews. These are designed to reveal your weaknesses or to see if your composure stands up. The aggressive question form is obvious: "Tell me why I should hire you!" Likewise, the impossible-bind questions: "How would *you* handle the public statements if our company's product was involved in a 'Tylenol poisoning' type of blackmail?" "Why has it taken you so long to find a job?" If you cannot avoid the situation, then avoid getting sucked up in the fluster. Pause. Reply calmly; be evasive, if you must. Often it is helpful to turn the conversation back toward your interviewer with a question about details. Ask him to redefine the question. This may adequately demonstrate your reaction to stress. Reacting in anger invariably blows your opportunity.

An unexpectedly personable attitude on the part of an interviewer can just as easily uncover unnecessary, and sometimes damaging, information volunteered by the job hunter. Theodore Pettus, in his excellent book on interviewing, remarks:

> Don't ever be tricked into thinking the interviewer is your new best friend. He's busy taking notes on everything you say and in his own quiet way he is looking for reasons why you would not be a good employee. (*One on One,* p. 11)

Group Interviews and Other Mutants. Group interviews involve one applicant facing a group of people who share the responsibility for hiring or a group of applicants artificially engaged in "dialogue" while being observed by the hiring panel. They are passing out of favor unless they closely simulate the work situation. Should you find yourself in the first kind, it is useful to ask questions, directing each question to a particular person, not to the panel as a whole. This turns the spotlight and pressure away from you for short periods and enables you to regain your composure. If you are one of a group of applicants, analyze just what it is that the interviewers want to learn about the candidates. Is it group leadership? Flexibility without passivity? Reaction to stress? Willingness to be different? Verbal fluency?

Good and Bad Interviewers

There are inept and inexperienced interviewers everywhere. Except for those in the personnel department, most of the people who interview you have little or no formal training in the art of interviewing. Even personnel professionals and hiring managers who usually conduct good interviews can ruin one because there are frequent interruptions, work crises or other circumstantial problems during the minutes they have to spend with you. No matter. If it is a poor interview, you are the loser.

John Komar, author of *The Interview Game,* offers this advice:

> When you are interviewed by an uncomfortable interviewer, forget the rule about getting the interviewer to do all the talking...help them by talking as much as need be to keep the discussion flowing. When it appears that they want to say something, stop immediately and listen. Then respond. Look friendly and personable. When the interview is over, say, "Thank you, I enjoyed our meeting." (p. 78)

While you never wrest control of the interview, if the interviewer is interrupted often, pick up the train of thought or summarize after each of those breaks. Ask if perhaps it would be better to return at a more convenient time. Make sure your follow-up thank you letter has a more-detailed-than-usual summary of your personal qualifications. In it, try to match the intent of the questions that the interviewer did succeed in asking. This could salvage your candidacy.

Preparing for an Interview

The tools you have to prepare for successful interviewing include:

1) The attitude that you carry into the interview. The universal admonitions "Be positive! Expect to be offered the job!" are true. If you approach the interview with an attitude of "Gee, I'll never make it," that negativity will penetrate nonverbally through your every spoken word. Getting an interview is a positive event in itself. The worst that can happen is that you will be no further ahead than you are now.

2) Your knowledge of your job skills and characteristics. If you worked on the personal data project, you can talk about your selling points effectively. Also, familiarize yourself with your resume since that is all *they* initially know about you.

3) Your knowledge about the company, its job and the interviewer. Review your basic information on the company. Make sure it is not out of date. Recall and touch base with any acquaintances who do/did work there.

4) Practice. Much depends on your ability to express yourself through your verbal and nonverbal behavior during the interview.

Skillful interviewing is rarely a natural gift and is commonly crafted through repeated practice. In this sense it is much like learning to ride a bike. You do not want to get this practice by wasting away a "prime" interview, although in real life this frequently happens. There are at least four other ways to practice interviewing, including interviewing for jobs that you would refuse if offered, merely to get practice. You can enlist the help of a friend or relative to act as an interviewer. Look into opportunities, for free or for a fee, to get into a group of job hunters who rehearse under the leadership of an employment counselor. You can also use a tape recorder or, even better, a VCR machine and be able to conduct your own critiques. If nothing else, practice answering questions aloud to a chair or a mirror. Think about questions you can answer easily and those that would be difficult for you. Reflect on the meaning behind questions like, "Did you have a hard time getting here?" "Do you like research?" "I see you recently moved to Pittsburgh." Decide how to reply to implied questions. Phrase your statements to fit the needs of employers and present your strongest marketable skills.

Think through all the phases of a real interview and see which parts you need to polish.

A Generic Interview

A standard interview has four main parts:

Preliminaries
The first 5 minutes
The content itself
Follow-up

Careful attention to each phase of the interview will make the best of your opportunities. Here are several techniques that will help you improve your skills in each area.

Preliminaries—Before You Enter the Door

Some guidelines can smooth your way:

1. Know exactly where you will be interviewed. There is a huge difference between being interviewed in Room 425 at Westinghouse, Churchill, and Room 425, Westinghouse Headquarters. Check.

2. Bring the appropriate tools. Your data sheet (for an application form), several copies of your resume, and social security information are standard equipment. You might also need license(s), if appropriate; an inch book for journalists or portfolio for artists and designers. A set of work clothes or boots and hard hat in your car may be a plus if there is any possibility of a job-site tour. Hands-on people should be ready to show they can put their "hands-on."

3. Arrive between five and ten minutes early. Allow plenty of travel time. If you are interviewing directly after work, that is the day to have lunch at your desk so you are not harried up to the last minute. If you have two interviews on one day, schedule them as far apart as possible. Arrive alone, unencumbered by baggage of any type. It is too easy to be remembered for all the faults of the people who accompany you. *(. . . remember the one whose kid popped gum in the waiting room for an entire hour?)*

4. Upon arrival check your physical appearance.

5. Introduce yourself to the receptionist. Wait constructively. An affable conversation with the receptionist may be in order if she is not busy. A quick observance of the message conveyed by the furnishings of the office is possible. Perusal of an in-house newspaper or company brochure will give you something to have in your hands even if you spend most of the time mentally reviewing the items you want to learn or communicate during the interview.

The First 5 Minutes

A study involving job interviews revealed that if the employer formed a negative impression of the applicant during the first five minutes, 90% of the time that person was not hired. Other estimates of first impression length go from an infinitesimal 15 seconds to two minutes.

This first impression depends heavily upon **visual presence** and **nonverbal behavior.** Meet the interviewer as an equal with a firm, dry handshake; look directly at him or her; smile and introduce yourself. Although you should already know your interviewer's name and title, if you don't, get it during the first five minutes. Check with women as to their preference for Miss, Ms., Mrs. or Doctor.

How nervous you feel has only a little to do with the impression you make. One insightful Pittsburgh interviewer remarked, "I like people who are initially a little nervous and then warm up...it says they want the job...and I think they will try hard in the job if they get it, too." A good emotional state is being "up"; or the heightened tension of being "on." Anticipate this interview as a doorway to good things that may result. Maintain a professional attitude that is not aloof.

Visual appearance is one factor you can control, so shift the weight in your favor as much as you can. All qualifications being equal, a manager will hire someone who looks the part. Check out the work place ahead of time so you can dress like the people who have the type of job you want—within reason. The one exception is for blue collar jobs. You still need to wear "interview clothes"—a suit or sports jacket and slacks for men, a suit or tailored dress for women. For an interview, the rule is to be a little more tailored, a bit less casual than you'd be at work.

Although it is a relative term, conservative is the word to describe the clothing most acceptable in Pittsburgh. Even advertising firms and fashion-field hirers feel their expectations are "conservative," compared to what is accepted in other cities.

The parts of your outfit should be compatible with each other. No wrinkled ties, galoshes or furry mittens should be worn with a "dress for success" suit. Reason? If your clothes are to send a message, an odd piece may make the message read that this is just an act. Interviewers skilled in spotting lack of consistency in resumes, application forms and conversations will also be jarred by an out-of-line detail in your physical appearance.

Part of that consistency extends to another important aspect of your appearance—your grooming. William Tranter, the former Placement Director at Community College, urges every job hunter to check things like the cleanliness of your hair, skin and fingernails. Make sure your shoes are polished and there are no threads hanging from your clothing. If you wear glasses, clean them *before* you leave home, etc. Although most people take these things for granted, when you go on an interview, don't.

In the interview itself your nonverbal communication—the way you sit, position your hands, move your eyes—can send favorable silent messages. You can learn to lean slightly forward to indicate interest, when to look in the interviewer's eyes and how to keep your hands from sweating (hold them palm up, exposed to the drying air). While these may be fascinating things to know and to use, don't be overwhelmed by this kind of advice. Absorb whatever you can, but if you begin to feel that you *must* do this and you *shouldn't* do that, you may become so self-conscious that you'll become paralyzed. Instead, tap into the real bases of confidence in yourself; you have proven skills of value and you have prepared for this interview with care and thought.

The Content of the Interview Itself

There is no way to predict the exact direction an interview will take, but there are a number of techniques that will prepare you for whatever happens. The key to successful communication during an interview is your reaction to and assessment of the interviewer's verbal and non-verbal interests. "If there is ever a time to think of the other person, the interview is that time," recommends H. Anthony Medley, author of *Sweaty Palms: The Neglected Art of Being Interviewed* (p. 4).

Listen. Two devastating mistakes made in interviews are answering without preparation and not really hearing what is said. Both can be avoided by *active listening.* Focus on the content of the employer's message. Try to understand why he is saying what he does. Most hirers want to avoid the problems they've had with past employees. Several questions concerning how far away you live from the plant may signal that the interviewer needs reassurance that you will show up in bad weather.

Another tip for being a more effective listener is to keep an open mind. Don't try to decide whether you want the position. Operate as though you want the job (or at least the job offer). Ignore distractions and interruptions; use the time to reflect on what's happening in the interview.

Listen for the skills that the employer needs. If you presumed that the job needed three skills and prepared yourself to talk about your expertise in them, be alert to add a fourth taken from the interviewer's cue. One Oakdale chemist favored working alone but quickly talked about her team experiences when she learned that the job was a group project.

Medley remarks,

> It is important that you get from him *[the interviewer]* some kind of job specification early on in the interview so that you can key what you can accomplish to what he wants accomplished. If you get into a detailed discussion of your skills and experience before you've had a chance to probe what he's looking for, you're adrift in a world of unknowns. (*Ibid, p. 8*)

Spotting a Bummer. When the interviewer begins to describe the job, don't interrupt; listen carefully for specific responsibilities. Also, note *exactly* what is or is not being offered. Most interviewers are well aware of the negatives involved in a job and they may tuck some of them neatly into their descriptions, in a way that is difficult to spot, i.e., ten months travel per year; you're required to turn a profit in three months; overtime four nights a week, etc. Every profession has its own code words and euphemisms for dirty work.

Ask. Intelligent questions can expose needs of the company that you were unable to learn before the interview. You do not ask a question like, "What do you look for in an employee?" However, you can ask, "Which staff members report to the person in this position? What are the most difficult or recurring problems to be solved in this job? How long has the position been open?" If newly created, "Why has this position been created?" If you are told that you are to be interviewed by another person, inquire about his or her title and role in the hiring process. That can help orient you *before* you face more questions.

Your questions affect the employer's perception of you. Think of what you convey if most of your questions are about vacation time or benefits. You probably won't be conveying diligence or enthusiasm for the work.

Talking. Follow the lead of the interviewer and add remarks about your own accomplishments and achievements. You control part of the interview by the way that you answer questions. You can pick up on one topic in detail and drop others.

If the interviewer is looking for a specific answer, give her one. If she asks a general question, turn your answer to your own advantage. You are likely to have that opportunity, so before the interview think out several points that you would like to get across.

Advice books that tell you to present yourself as the solver of the company's problems should caution you not to assume that you can do this before you know what your *particular interviewer* sees as the problems and what solutions have been tried before. It is extremely difficult to learn these facts until the interview itself. Less arrogant and more rooted in evidence is to show yourself as a solver of past problems in a similar vein or in a similar company.

Learning how to describe your job skills without being boring comes with practice. You can use the personal data project you completed earlier to provide the raw materials for interviews, though. There you'll find stories to express your skills in concrete, understandable ways.

How to Improve Your Interviewing Skills

Three Steps to Fluency. One technique for gaining verbal fluency is to describe each point you want to make in three ways. That is how orators make their points and how commercials sell their products. It works like this. First, describe what you actually did on the job in general terms: *I've been an administrator for seven years.* Second, break down all the skills involved into their component parts and/or the step-by-step activities involved in their execution. *I designed and conducted the company's safety training program. What I did was to run six workshops for shop foremen that explained the OSHA safety rules that applied to our operations. I asked them for suggestions on how we could get compliance from the men on specific points, like GFI adaptors, with the least amount of hassle, as well as telling them what we had to do.* Third, summarize the positive results of your actions. You will imply that you are better qualified than some of the other candidates or, at least, that good things happen when you are on the job. *Planning kept safety regulations from becoming an issue. Involving the foremen really aided enforcement and credibility. We run a variation of the program every year now and have never been cited.*

An Avalon man's job title was Assistant Manager of Operations. The three-way approach helped him prepare for interviews by allowing him to avoid repeating over and over that he "manages" things. Some of the key statements that he made in a videotaped practice interview were:

> Managing productivity was an important goal for me (*general*). . . . The flow of paperwork from desk to desk no longer fit with newer equipment so I analyzed the movement . . . with some simple flow charts and diagrams (*step-by-steps*) . . . moving two desks to different locations and giving one person responsibility for three middle stages of the paperwork (*more steps*). . . . This eliminated virtually all of the bottle necks that had plagued our back orders (*results*).

That was just one part of his job. He could also talk about how he "managed" when he set up and supervised vacation schedules or when he was responsible for planning and carrying out a new distribution system.

Remember that general skill words like managing, communicating or educating are shorthand words to describe groups of related skills. It is your responsibility to translate them into their component parts. Use words like designing, planning, executing, problem solving, motivating, supervising, coordinating—whatever terms best describe what you did.

Tell your interviewer about your general skill; relate the stories that show how you used that skill in specific situations, and describe the positive results you achieved. You won't be boring and you *will* be convincing.

General Principles of Interviewing

1. Be enthusiastic! Employers are fed up with employees who log in their hours waiting to live their lives someplace else. Show them that you want to do the work. However, an enthusiastic attitude cannot be faked—(*Wow, your company is the best!*) nor should you merely express joy over finally landing a job. Express the enthusiasm that springs from really loving the work that you do. Although it cannot be taught; it can be tapped. It is an intangible quality that shows through in the animation of your voice when talking about an accomplishment in your field. It is the pleasure that transpires when you meet an interviewer who shares your willingness to talk, literally, for hours about the details of your mutual work. If you have this, you do not have to be a super sales person or pretend to be something that you are not to get a job.

Some jobs require quiet dedication of technical expertise rather than an expansive social personality. Let them see that quality control testing of polymeric coatings turns you on or that you get excited about methods for improving monthly credit collection ratios, or whatever it is that you do.

2. Like the interviewer. No kidding. Why? As one interviewer said, "It is hard to hire someone who you don't like." The easiest short term route to get them to like *you* is to show that you like *them* first. Smile at them. Like something about them. Everyone has a few likable aspects. If you cannot find one, focus on something that you find attractive. Perhaps it is only his suit or the corporate clout represented by her Chippendale office furniture. Concentrate on these and let the positive emotion show. This is not fawning attention, it is the strongest contribution you can make to tipping the delicate chemistry between two people in your favor.

3. Never be negative. Not about anything: your ability, your last job, your former boss or the bad luck that seems to follow you. The easiest trap is to reply to the question "Why are you looking for work?" with an outpouring of gripes about your last job. If it were perfect, you would still be there. Focus, instead, on positive reasons and what it is that you want to do. (*I want to do more selling and less designing*) or (*I want to do more designing and less selling*).

Negative remarks about a past boss are deadly. The reaction they raise in the mind of the hiring manager is, "How long will it take before you say the same things, and maybe worse, about me?" Negative news has a way of traveling around faster and lasting longer than most job hunters imagine. One employee left her job in a Pittsburgh hospital and let it be known that she should have been promoted and that her former boss wasn't such a hot administrator. No jobs were forthcoming in her search. She began to suspect that he had blackballed her in the profession. He did not need to; she had done it to herself.

Having tried and disliked traditional law positions, a savvy career changer worried about the negative image he would project if he replied honestly to the question, "Why, in God's name, do you want to leave that law firm?" Only after he reflected on all the positive aspects of his experience, could he honestly say,

> Being a trial lawyer was really a good experience. It introduced me to mediation. I've done a lot of adversary work, but mediation is really what I like doing. Actually, I became the member of the firm who handled all potential mediation cases. That's what originally led me into this new area of work.

A favorite interview question of one local personnel director is, "Have you ever been fired?" According to him, "The way you handle that question reveals a lot about you." His advice for answering his own trick question:

> Answer in a spirit of objective detachment. Don't pick up on the implicit invitation to argue your case. Speak briefly, without reference to personalities if possible. If that's unavoidable, describe personality conflicts as growth experiences, "I'll know how to handle such a situation better if it ever comes up again."

4. Be honest. The best reason not to lie is because it is not necessary. Leave your skeletons in the closet and let the interviewer ask. Volunteer no negative facts. Omit them from writing and verbally present their positive aspect. (*Yes, my typing speed is lower than I want it to be, but I rarely have to redo a letter because of spelling or grammatical mistakes. I composed about half a dozen letters each week when I worked at Carnegie.*)

Discretion does not mean dishonesty any more than honesty means bluntness. Distinguish between questions calling for factual answers and those which call for your opinions. When you are asked for your opinion, state it honestly, but tactfully. Acknowledge your interviewer's viewpoint first and then state yours, briefly. Your honesty will guarantee the consistency that interviewers look for among all the elements of your presentation.

Closing

If the interview has been moving along, take a moment to get some perspective on it. How much time has passed? Have you had an opportunity to cover the main points you previously decided were important? Is the interviewer relaxed yet, talking and listening, or still asking cut and dried questions? Be alert to signs that he is wrapping up the interview—pushing away from his desk, gathering materials up. You might probe to see if there are any barriers to your desirability. One closing technique is to determine all the objections he has to hiring you. Ask, "Do you see any problems with my application?" Then answer each objection with your strongest positive arguments and proofs.

Leave on as cordial a note as possible and keep the ball in your court. That means unless he indicates a specific date when finalists will be notified, tell him that you'll be in touch within a few days. Then be certain that you are.

Follow-Up

After the interview, there are several things that you need to do.

1. Evaluate the interview. That is what the interviewer is also doing. Reflect on the content. Were important skills covered with factual documentation? Are there any that you can think of now that you omitted? Were there moments of rapport? Include negative points here, too.

2. Record the interview. If you are keeping a job hunting notebook, note the date, correct spelling of the interviewer's name, address and title; names of receptionists, others. Indicate any actions to take later: get back to her in three weeks; send a copy of article, as promised.

3. Write a thank you note, within 72 hours. Don't consider the interview complete without one. Your letter should contain: a sentence that expresses thanks for their consideration; reiteration of some of your assets; a new comment if you need to counter a negative impression or the addition of positive news. Only on the surface is this letter a thank you. It is your opportunity to continue influencing your interviewer. It should be neatly typed, short and custom-tailored for each person to whom you spoke.

Do Pittsburghers really write thank you letters? Yes. Are they expected? No. Local interviewers say that more and more job hunters do send them, as part of the general trend toward better preparation, but you will still stand out if you write one. They were "rare" in the past and are "occasional" now.

Do they leave an impression? We met one hiring manager who said "Yes, I've gotten thank you letters, but not too many . . . here they are." He pulled out a file folder of about twenty letters he'd gotten during the past five years. He hadn't kept the resumes of those people, but he kept their personal thanks.

H. Lee Rust, a former executive recruiter, tells the story of an applicant who spent a full day interviewing at a corporate headquarters in another town. He met individually with nine officers during the day. He wrote each man and woman a note of thanks. Each was short and the wording was varied to avoid embarrassment if they compared notes (which they did). The effect was powerful. He got the job. He was, of course, qualified but so were the other candidates.

Persistence is part of job hunting. You cannot control the number of applicants and their qualifications, but you can use methods where you'll encounter less competition and you can reinforce your candidacy in a variety of ways. Follow-up calls and letters underline the point that you are someone who really wants this job. Send further materials or information on points that arose in conversation. Offer to return for an interview or supply more references. Maintain your visibility in every way you can.

4. Relax. Do something pleasant. Interviewing is hard work and you won't know the results right away. You need a break from the anticipation and tension that frequently builds up.

Negotiating Salary

There is an ideal time to negotiate salary. First get the job offer, then negotiate. Don't accept the job until the salary has been settled.

Don't ask how much the job pays or answer the question of how much you want until you have a positive job offer. If it comes up too early in the interview, use an inoffensive remark like a cheerful "I'm sure we'll be able to agree on something." In discussing figures it is always helpful to leave yourself an out, such as "of course, dollar amounts are not the *only* consideration."

If you are asked directly how much you are making, you might reply that you would consider changing for a salary within the range of X to Y. When asked if salary information is not already available to him on the application form, a company negotiator replied, "Yes, some applicants actually fill that out, so I always check there, too." Another suggestion from a career developer is to total up the value of your entire package—salary plus benefits, vacation pay, holiday pay and profit sharing—to learn the total of what you really draw.

For some jobs all figures are out in the open and negotiating is practically unnecessary. But whenever the initial offer is lower than you expect, there is still some chance for negotiating. Remember that every future raise will be based on your starting salary. Small organizations may need to keep salary figures down, but you can often obtain changes in fringe benefits like hours or duties.

If you are intimidated by the thought of negotiating, a good primer to read is *Winning the Salary Game,* by Sherry Chastain, or check the chapter on negotiating salary in Marge Rossman's book *When the Headhunter Calls.*

Salary negotiating is not a kind of haggling where you are expected to outrageously inflate the initial asking price. You start by knowing a realistic range for your kind of work. In negotiating, you ask for what you want, but not for your minimum. The figure to ask for is a middle one between the range you mentioned of X to Y. Be pleasant but firm in stating that you want a certain amount of money for the position and repeat that you really want to work for the company and hope you can readily reach agreement.

How do the people on the other side feel? Employers are not all trying to get you for the cheapest possible price; on the other hand, they are under pressure not to be overly generous. In addition to the obvious cost, they need to leave leeway for merit raises later and to create a balance with the salaries already being paid.

A personnel representative for a Pittsburgh manufacturer described a hypothetical negotiation with a mid-level assistant manager:

> The manager decides which applicant he wants. I take it back from there because I negotiate salaries daily... Well, we have job classifications and that eliminates a lot of guess-work on my part. His slot is pegged at $23,000 to $27,000. (I don't really volunteer that information.) Once hired, everyone sort of learns quickly where he stands in the salary rankings again, so I have to keep that in mind, too.
>
> But he's making about $22,000 now, I've gathered; and I never want to insult someone with an offer of the lowest entry salary for the job. I like to give every one coming in about a 10% boost in pay... brings them in happy... so, I'd want to start him at $24,200 or so. So when I ask him how about $24,000, if he says $27,000 he is way out of line. Maybe somewhere else there are reasons to do it, but in this company and the other three I've worked at, there is no reason why there should be more than a 10% or so spread between his figures and mine. If there is, I ask myself, "Is this just the beginning of trouble?" Then I'll ask the manager how much he wants the guy. Now if the new guy asks for $25,000, then we're less than a thousand apart. That's O.K. Spread that over a year and it isn't too much. If he's smart he'll go for my come-back offer of $24,500 because that's all the negotiating I plan to do.

Being Turned Down

Surviving one or more selection interviews builds up both your confidence in your desirability and your expectation of getting the job. It should. But when the phone call finally comes, if it has the quiet news that you were not selected, your hopes plummet as the words are spoken.

The most important thing you can do now is to focus on handling the next four minutes of this call with poise. Anger, dejection or tears can come later. You've invested yourself in this opportunity and the company invested time and money to explore your possibilities. This is not the time to be abrupt or tell them you did not "want their old job anyway." Don't try to talk them into changing their minds. (They won't.) An executive recruiter says that the realistic response is to say very simply that you had really wanted the position, knew you could have done well and are sorry you were not selected. You could ask if they would consider you again for other opportunities. Finish with class: within a few days write another thank you note.

They were interested in you once. That is good reason *not* to wipe them off your slate forever. Later after you have gone through all your other possibilities, you can call them again. Ask if there are any new openings anticipated. Polite perseverance can give you another chance when new doors are being opened. Keep them informed that you are still interested. See if you can use them as referrals to other companies in your field. Maintain confidence in your skills, experience and abilities. You do have those or you would never have made it as far as you did.

Turning Down a Job Offer

Do it graciously, gratefully, reluctantly and after thinking carefully. Explain how difficult your decision was and take the time to detail why you cannot accept. If it is true, admit your honest concern that you might be making a mistake. Make an extraordinary effort to ease their rejection. You will never regret it.

Accepting Your Good Job

Whether you get a job offer on your first interview or it takes weeks of persistent effort, the time will come when you will be offered a job. Now is the time to think through questions like these:

Is this job really what you want? Be aware of the compromises you must make between your "ideal job" and this one.

Where will this job lead? Will you enjoy it in one year? Five years? What are the chances for advancement?

What can you learn while you do this job? If you leave in a year or two, what new marketable skills will you have developed?

Can you work well with your potential co-workers?

Is the salary satisfactory? If not, how long are you willing to live at that level?

245

Weigh your answers carefully before you make a decision. Most job hunters find that they make some compromises when they accept a job. Rarely is there a truly perfect job. However, if you've based your decisions on self knowledge and a realistic appraisal of "what's out there" for you, you will know when *you have found your good job in Pittsburgh.*

Once you have decided to accept, be clear about who does what next. Will you receive a positive offer in writing, to be followed by your written acceptance? If the process is less formal, you may want to accept verbally first and then follow up with a letter summarizing job responsibilities and verbal promises that were given to you. It's particularly good to put these facts in writing, especially if you were promised an early salary review or similar benefits.

Now's the time to thank your references and contacts once again. If you wondered earlier what you could ever offer them, rest assured that this is the pay-off. Your appreciation now will provide them with the satisfaction of knowing that they had a share in your success.

As you look back on your job hunt, consider your many accomplishments: the problems mastered, the skills gained, the new relationships begun. They have already worked in your behalf and they will continue to do so as they contribute to the energy, ability and enthusiasm you bring to your new job.

Job Advisory Service
Center for Professional
   Development
Chatham College
Woodland Road
Pittsburgh, PA 15232

☐ Check here for more in-
   formation on JAS programs

☐ Check here for adding
   your name to mailing list

To order more copies of *Find a Good Job in Pittsburgh*

(make check or money order payable to Chatham College)

_____ Copies of *Find a Good Job in Pittsburgh* postpaid @$10.00 $_____

PLEASE *PRINT* SHIPPING INFORMATION BELOW

Name _____

Address _____

City _____ State _____ Zip Code _____

Job Advisory Service
Center for Professional
   Development
Chatham College
Woodland Road
Pittsburgh, PA 15232

☐ Check here for more in-
   formation on JAS programs

☐ Check here for adding
   your name to mailing list

To order more copies of *Find a Good Job in Pittsburgh*

(make check or money order payable to Chatham College)

_____ Copies of *Find a Good Job in Pittsburgh* postpaid @$10.00 $_____

PLEASE *PRINT* SHIPPING INFORMATION BELOW

Name _____

Address _____

City _____ State _____ Zip Code _____